The Hands of History

Parliamentary Sketches 1997–2007

SIMON HOGGART

Atlantic Books
London

First published as a paperback original in 2007 in Great Britain by
Atlantic Books on behalf of Guardian Newspapers Ltd. Atlantic Books
is an imprint of Grove Atlantic Ltd.

Design: www.carrstudio.co.uk

ISBN 978 1 84354 679 5

A CIP catalogue record for this book is available from the British Library.

9 8 7 6 5 4 3 2 1

Printed in Great Britain by
Clays Ltd, St Ives plc

Atlantic Books
An imprint of Grove Atlantic Ltd.
Ormond House
26–27 Boswell Street
London
WC1N 3JZ

Contents

Introduction

When Labour won the 1997 election, kind friends warned me that my job as a parliamentary sketch-writer would become impossible. Instead of the ludicrous, sleaze-ridden, hopelessly riven government led by John Major, I would face ministers and backbenchers who resembled executives in some middle-management consultancy service. Golly, they would be dull. Like Bernard Levin, whose piece on trying to stay awake during a speech by Hugh Gaitskell is one of the finest sketches I've ever read, I would be reduced to jamming the tip of a ballpoint pen under my chin so that the onset of sleep would bring agony.

The kind friends were wrong. This government produced as many weird personalities, as many disasters and as many ridiculous moments as any other. Apart from Blair himself, there were thunderous characters: growling Gordon Brown, John Reid, who, though sober now, remains as aggressive as anyone you might meet in a Glasgow bar. And John Prescott, a gift to sketch-writers for which we must one day sacrifice many head of cattle to the gods. Even the bores – and I suspect the bores are poised to take over the party soon – are boring in a fascinatingly tedious way. And on the Tory side, we have had a new leader every two years or so. Blair left while on his fifth. And there are Ann Widdecombe, Michael Fabricant and Sir Peter Tapsell! Who could fail with such

1

material? All we have to do is write down what they say, and how they say it. The job is done for us. It has been, from our point of view, a wonderful ten years.

I first met Tony Blair himself in 1993. At the time I was a pretty disastrous political editor of the *Observer* (political editors have to know things; making cheap jokes is sadly not enough) and he was a successful home affairs spokesman for the Labour opposition, already known for his slogan: 'Tough on crime, tough on the causes of crime.' I took him out to lunch at the Atrium in Westminster, and he was a good, chatty guest, if in something of a hurry. I soon noticed that he seemed more eager to know what I thought than he was to tell me what he thought. This, of course, was not the reason the *Observer* was picking up the bill. They already knew what I thought and had no need to invest in food to find out more. But every time I raised a topic – crime, immigration or whatever – he would ask earnestly, 'But what do you think we should do, Simon?' Or, 'That's a difficult choice, isn't it? Which would you pick?'

I have sometimes reflected on that lunch. Perhaps it was a way of covering his back. If he didn't tell me anything, there would be no embarrassing headlines later in the week, saying, 'Bang 'em all up, says Blair' or 'Hooligans need hugs, not prison, says Labour'. Possibly he thought I would be flattered, and would tell friends and colleagues, 'Tony Blair really wanted to know my views on dealing with the terrorist threat.' After all, we tend to judge people by how they judge us. This would have meant that at least one political editor was disposed to be kindly to him. The least likely possibility was that he actually cared what my views were, and I discounted that straight away.

But I have seen glimpses of the same approach many times since. The following year the then leader of the Labour

Party, John Smith, died, and soon afterwards there was the famous meeting with Gordon Brown in the Granita restaurant in Islington, now closed, and replaced by an eatery called Desperados. Here, like Spain and Portugal carving up Latin America, the two men split the spoils of the office to come – Blair would be Prime Minister in name, and would cover foreign affairs. Brown would be in charge of all spending departments, which effectively made him Prime Minister (domestic affairs). Blair must have said something to Brown to the effect that he wouldn't be Prime Minister for ever, and he would get his turn. As often happens with Blair, his listener clearly thought he had made a firmer commitment than he actually intended. Blair meant it as a pleasant gesture, one that implied good intentions and avoided a row with his old friend; Brown took it as a promise.

There was another reason why Brown felt aggrieved. Since the two men had met, after Labour's disastrous 1983 election campaign, and had agreed the way that the party could rescue itself from endless future horrors, he had been the senior partner. He was slightly older than Blair. He had spent much longer in the Labour Party, and knew its arcane ways. He was cleverer. Blair was, in Brown's view, a comparative lightweight with a plausible manner – essential for their project of turning Labour back into a party of government, but lacking the intellectual heft required for the highest office. Now it seemed almost certain that he would win it, for after 'Black Wednesday' in September 1992, when the pound crashed out of the European monetary system, few imagined there was more than the remotest chance of the Tories winning another election for quite some time.

I always think of Brown, perhaps grotesquely, as the eldest son of a duke. For all of his life he has assumed that he will succeed to the title. Then his father dies, and the family lawyer arrives to explain that actually his younger brother is going to inherit everything, including the house and land – because he looks better on television. It would be a crushing and humiliating blow. Few people would recover quickly from such an event, and the sight of colleagues he regarded as friends and allies abandoning him for Blair – most notably Peter Mandelson, who has never been forgiven for his apostasy – must have made his bitterness even greater. No wonder he has seemed at times petulant and rebarbative. No wonder that he has behaved towards Blair with an arrogance bordering on impudence – for example, telling him the contents of the Budget just a few hours before delivering it. Take it or leave it has never been Brown's attitude in these matters; take it or take it is the choice you are offered.

Yet of course Brown must have realized that he stood little chance of winning the leadership in a public contest with Blair. If Blair had been a different person, he might have told him to run anyway, and let the devil take the hindmost. This would have placed him in a far stronger position during the thirteen years to come. But Blair is who he is; his instincts are ameliorative rather than combative. Whereas some politicians take pleasure in handing down unwelcome news, Blair is quick to sense what whoever he is talking to wants, and tries to provide it. (Foreign Office officials sometimes despaired when Blair entertained the leader of some small and obscure state. He would be told just how far he could go, offering British aid, or payments for raw materials, for example. Frequently the meeting would end with the visitor leaving Number 10 beaming with pleasure, having got far more than he expected.)

At Granita, Blair realized the depths of Brown's unhappiness and tried to respond. Did he intend to make way earlier than he actually did? I suspect so; what he wasn't to know beforehand was the almost unbearable allure of the job – all those phone calls from world leaders, the murmuring – not of 'yes-men' but facilitators – at your elbow. The way the media imply that everything you do and say is of overwhelming importance. The fact that if you need to fly somewhere a plane is ready right on time, and your armour-plated limo waits outside to take you directly to the jetway. After a while you convince yourself that you have a grand plan, or rather a series of grand plans, whether for education, health, crime or peace in the Middle East, and nobody but you could possibly see them through. Foreign affairs, summit meetings, calls to presidents and prime ministers – these seem important, while the bothersome day-to-day business of ward closures and road-widening schemes can be left to the lesser myrmidons, mere back-benchers. It's a permanent high. You may remember the picture of Margaret Thatcher crying in the back of her car when she left Downing Street for the last time. The only other time we saw her weep was when she thought her son might be dead in the Sahara Desert. I suspect that Blair originally intended to make way for Brown earlier than he did, but when the time came he could not quite bring himself to go, could not push himself into a life where it didn't much matter when he woke up in the morning, or what he did when he got dressed.

Did Blair and Brown hate each other? I think not, though Brown must have been deeply resentful and Blair very wary. People who reach that level employ others to do their hating for them. I remember once walking down the portico that leads from the House of Commons to Westminster tube station. There were Blair and his press secretary David Hill walking towards us. 'Hi, guys!' said Blair, in the affable manner favoured by the cast of *Friends*. Mr Hill merely scowled his dark scowl. (David Hill used to be man-of-affairs for Roy Hattersley, but has not spoken to him for some years. I presume that Hattersley has been deemed insufficiently loyal to the new dispensation.)

What of the public Blair? It has often been remarked that he can affect an estuary accent – 'ah know' – when he thinks it is appropriate. He would never speak like that in the House. Much of his language, especially at times of national stress and strain, can be almost Churchillian. Yet it is delivered in a casual, almost off-the-cuff manner. Blair is a child of the 1970s – or rather the extension of the 1960s into that decade. In the wake of Vietnam, politicians were not popular or admired. Both the Wilson and Heath governments (1964–70, and 1970–74) were deemed failures. People were suspicious of rhetoric. Grandiloquence was seen as a cover for disaster and betrayal. You convinced people more easily if you sounded as if you were asking them in for coffee. Blair is from the generation of politicians that is happier chatting on a sofa than at a podium, when the fine words and phrases seem strained and sometimes incomprehensible: 'my irreducible core'; 'locking horns with modernity'; 'the gates of xenophobia, falling down' – these sometimes sound as if they were generated by a computer.

He also pioneered the verb-free sentence. His conference speeches, which he clearly saw as his message to the British people, sometimes contained more than a hundred of these: 'for every child, opportunity'; 'our streets, free of crime'; 'in old age, tranquillity'. The point about a verb-free sentence is that it doesn't contain what English teachers used to call a 'doing word'. Instead it expresses an aspiration, a longing. Each one should be prefaced by the phrase, 'Wouldn't it be wonderful if we had…' Listening, the audience know that that is what he wants. It's what they want. It's what everybody wants. But will he promise it? No – either because he knows that he might not be able to provide it, or possibly because he knows that no one would believe him. A politician who doesn't make promises is a politician who will not lie to you, merely disappoint you. (As the late Linda Smith used to say, 'When he was elected I had absolutely no hopes whatever of Tony Blair, but even I feel let down.')

In some ways Blair was the victim of an extraordinarily successful campaign against the Tories, between his election as Labour leader in 1994 and his landslide election as Prime Minister three years later. The likes of Alastair Campbell and his minions roamed the press galleries pointing out with contemptuous scorn every Tory failure, every mistake, every scandal, no matter how small and unimportant. Mr Campbell was capable of reducing grown political editors to tears by his abuse, not because they were frightened of being abused, but because they were terrified of being kept outside the loop and so risking their jobs. Saying, 'I didn't get that important story because Alastair Campbell doesn't like me,' would not impress any newspaper executives.

But of course they came to believe their own propaganda. They convinced themselves that the Major government was hopelessly incompetent, wildly right wing and engulfed by sleaze like a man struggling to get out of quicksand. When they got into power they discovered that nothing was quite so simple; there was plenty of corruption on the Labour side (though dismissed rather airily, as if somehow their corruption was less corrupt than Tory corruption, since it was in a good cause – the re-election of the Labour Party). Harold Macmillan never said that a prime minister's greatest problem was 'events, dear boy, events' – what he actually talked about was 'the opposition of events', but every prime minister faces that. New Labour might be sparkling and shiny, but had not been sprinkled with fairy dust, and plenty of things went wrong. It is not surprising that Blair looked weary much of the time. Photographers charted the worry lines on his forehead, and contrasted it with the smooth and eager young idealist who had walked along Downing Street in 1997 to the spontaneous cheers of a carefully selected multitude.

Parliament, which never really engaged him, was a nuisance. Labour MPs were acceptable provided that they were with the programme; Old Labour, the members who stuck to 'traditional values', might for the most part be safely ignored. The House of Commons was principally a forum for Blair to demonstrate his wide command of policy and statistics and outcomes. This could be impressive. Twice a year he faced a body known as the liaison committee, which included the chairmen and chairwomen of every other Commons committee, from foreign affairs to catering. For two and a half hours, without a note and without help from the aides sitting behind him, Blair would hold forth on a great range of topics, from German attempts to reduce carbon emissions, to the exact numbers of people dead in Basra, and the increase in numeracy among primary school children in Leicester. This display was usually enough to win over the massed chairpersons, including the Tories and Liberal Democrats, but it rarely strayed into the philosophical. Indeed, a Labour backbencher once asked him what his political philosophy was, and he had no reply. Instead he mumbled something about getting the famous heart surgeon Yagdi Macoub to chair an NHS committee, which might have been an achievement but hardly amounts to a philosophy. Indeed, asked what his legacy would be, he often said something along the lines of making Labour electable again and defeating the Tories (or 'the forces of conservatism' as he called them contemptuously in a conference speech; to Blair, the past is not just another country, but a sad, backward country with nothing to offer us, any more than we would find valuable lessons for governance in Chad). So, Blair got himself elected in order to leave a legacy. That legacy turns out to be getting himself elected.

All of which might not matter. Denis Healey used to argue that his ideal for Britain was to make the country resemble Austria – prosperous, well-ordered, able to look after its less fortunate citizens, aware of its modest place in the world. He knew that this would not excite Britons who still had folk memories of Empire and military glory, but he felt it was enough. And it's true that if a government can be said to leave a country rather better off than they found it, reasonably content and more or less at peace with itself and other countries, that is not an inconsiderable achievement. Without doubt Britain is richer than it was when Blair took over, and much of the credit must go to Gordon Brown. The gap between rich and poor is wider, but the poorer are nevertheless rather less poor than they were. Education, crime prevention and the health service have improved in some ways, and have got worse in others. Domestically the government has not been a triumph, but it can be counted more or less a success, sort of.

The question that will always hang over Blair's premiership is of course Iraq. Why did we join George W. Bush's invasion? Why were the press and public dragooned into acquiescence if not support through dubious intelligence and reports that had been exaggerated like any tabloid front page? I suspect that it had little to do with Saddam's alleged weapons of mass destruction. Saddam seems to have made a huge miscalculation. He had at some stage disposed of his armoury, but did not wish this to be generally known, since it would be an encouragement for his enemies both at home and abroad. On the other hand, he believed that once the UN realized they were no longer in place, the US would have lost the rationale to invade. But Washington wasn't really interested in the horrors they claimed were there. The neo-cons saw Iraq as the start of their campaign to reshape the Middle East in the interests of 'freedom' – or 'America', since the two words are largely coterminous. The situation was similar to, yet the reverse of, Vietnam. A Vietcong victory would have caused all neighbouring countries to fall to the Communists – this was the domino theory. The imposition of democracy in Iraq would also have a domino effect, but this time a benign one, toppling one despot after another. It was a beguiling idea, but like many theories dreamed up in the abstract by men whose brainpower is greater than their common sense, it was simply wrong.

But what was in it for Tony Blair? This is a mystery which I suspect will fascinate British historians for a long time. He had, of course, had considerable success in the Balkans. Walking through crowds of grateful Albanian refugees, while wearing the Albanian national colours, hearing them shout 'Toe-knee, Toe-knee!' and being told that their babies were to be named after him, clearly had a powerful effect. His determination to persuade Bill Clinton to threaten a ground invasion of Serbia helped bring down Milosevic. Sierra Leone was a little-reported success, as British intervention helped get rid of the vicious gangster militias who were destroying that country. Military might, the deployment of – man-for-man – the finest armed forces in the world, could be used to rid the world of evil tyrannies, bringing hope, freedom and democracy to oppressed peoples. And who better than the people of Iraq? All it required was the means to persuade parliament, and for Blair that was never a difficult task.

But the public was different. Millions of people marched through London to oppose an invasion. Surely he must have noticed them, surely he must have taken into account their rage and frustration? But Blair is a religious man, close to being a devout Roman Catholic, always answerable to a higher command. Unlike Bush, he doesn't 'do' God, though he has said publicly that God will one day be his judge. For him that is not, I suspect, just a turn of phrase. He does expect one day to be facing his Maker, giving an account of himself. He would not want to say, 'Hey, look, I did believe it was the right thing to do, bring down Saddam, right? But, you know, there were just too many people who disagreed, so I couldn't go through with it. Too big a price to pay, polit-ically. Sorry...' No one would want to take part in such a conversation, though of course most of us don't believe it will ever happen.

Every time anyone raised the question of why things had gone so dreadfully wrong in Iraq, and why we had gone to war without evidence of weapons of mass destruction, Blair offered one of two answers and sometimes both. It was right to get rid of Saddam, plain and simple. He was a mass murderer, his people were horribly oppressed, and the world was a better place without him. The other reply was more complicated. Blair's view of the world is Manichean. There is a constant and ongoing struggle between the forces of good and evil, between 'our values' – peace, prosperity, tolerance and democracy – and the forces of fundamentalist Islam. They are our enemies and we must face them wherever they challenge us. To turn our heads away would be to cede victory to them. The implication, though this is never spelled out, is that if we use a policy of appeasement (fear and hatred of that word has been hard-wired into every British prime minister since the Munich agreement), there will come a day that our women will wear burkas and it will be a capital offence to teach girls in schools. This, in Blair's view, is the great struggle of the age, and it is one where we cannot stand on the sidelines. As for the argument that he and Bush have brought about the multitudinous deaths in Iraq, that to Blair is obvious nonsense. Is he sending young men into crowded street markets with bombs strapped round their chests? Is George Bush driving cars full of explosives into queues of police recruits? Far from making the whole enterprise seem like a disaster, to Blair the chaos merely proves his point: the forces ranged against us will stop at nothing whatever, including mass murder of their fellow Muslims. Failure to confront them is simply not an option.

Of course, this misses out the great middle ground where most ideological battles are fought. In Northern Ireland the terrorists on both sides could have been isolated, except that they and the general principles for which they were bombing and shooting had the broad, vague support of great swathes of the population. Likewise in the Middle East. The people who danced in the streets on the evening of 9/11 would probably never set off a bomb themselves, but they felt kinship with those who did. In the Manichean world, there is only good and evil, and you can assume that the vast majority are firmly on the side of good. But they aren't. Blair either didn't understand that, or else didn't factor it into his thinking. As he did with his endlessly pleasing statistics about hospital waiting lists, school exam results and crime reduction, he could cherry-pick helpful facts from Iraq with precision. An opinion poll might suggest that Iraqis felt 'better off' as a result of the invasion. The murder statistics from the south could show a dip. A friendly imam might have an encouraging word. If it proved his point, it was thrown into the sausage mixture, to be blended, packed with bland filler and extruded as a plump and sizzling symbol of success.

It is always tempting at this stage to say that historians will be the judges. The famous hand of history Blair felt on his shoulder after the conclusion of the Good Friday Agreement will either pat him on the back or slap him in the face. But history can't make up its mind about, say, Richard III, after half a millennium. We can't imagine it will reach an agreed verdict on Tony Blair any time soon.

I finish with another occasion that I encountered him. It was a charity dinner in Salisbury Cathedral Close in 2003. I was a friend of the organizers and had been asked to MC, so found myself at a table with them and, to my surprise, Cherie Blair, who had come with her husband. She is patron of the charity, which supports child cancer care. She was in a combative mood. I said that one auction lot was from the local hospital, offering a vasectomy or a mammogram – 'choice of one only'. I said jokily that if I won the prize I wouldn't know which to choose. She said that men got breast cancer too. I replied that I felt my breast in the shower every morning, but only to make sure that I still had a heart.

'Of course you don't, you're a journalist,' she said, adding to the table as a whole, '*Guardian* journalists are the worst, and *Guardian* sketch-writers are the worst of all.'

Once again, one had the feeling that her husband was using other people to communicate the disagreeable. But the meal continued and the conversation turned to teenagers. 'You have children?' she asked incredulously, as if astonished that someone so odious could propagate the species. At which point something inside me snapped, and I said, 'Oh, stop it.'

Which she did. She offered to pull her cracker with me and was charming for the rest of the evening. A friend who knows her moderately well said it was a scouse thing – you test people with aggressive banter and see if they can take it.

Then the meal and the auction were over, and the band, with the Rt. Hon. Tony Blair on guitar, played for the guests to dance. One of them bellowed to me over the wall of noise that he had seen the same pick-up group perform the previous year on a French holiday. 'They played "Summertime Blues", but they won't tonight, because of that line, "Gonna take my problem to the United Nations".' But Blair looked very happy. The rock 'n' roll classics were pounding out, the guitar did exactly what it was told, and he was surrounded by smiling, festive people who hoped he would go on for a very long time.

London, April 2007

Note: A few of the sketches here originally appeared in *Playing to the Gallery* in 2002. They are reprinted to provide a broader picture of the decade.

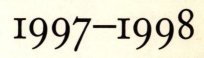

1997–1998

One week after the election, the new House of Commons met for the first time. Just before they started, a confused attendant allowed the hacks in for prayers, which are normally held in private. Astonishingly, the MPs all stand with their faces to the wall and their backs to the Mace, so that the whole Chamber looks like the Gents at half-time in a football match.

Almost the first thing the new government did was to announce that control of the interest rate would pass from the Chancellor to the Bank of England.

The Commons was full of bewildered bunches of people, drifting around, uncertain what to do or where to go, desperately seeking their group leader. Normally these are tourists. Yesterday they were new Labour MPs. When they finally reached the Chamber, it was full to bursting as never before. Those lucky enough to find a seat were stuffed buttock to buttock, so tightly that if anyone had wriggled, half a dozen new members would have popped up like bread from a toaster, described an arc, and landed on the Tories.

At the Speaker's chair they were jammed like a Cup Final crowd. They filled the jury boxes, usually kept for civil servants, and spilled over from the galleries. They actually looked like a landslide. It all resembled a great Frith canvas, perhaps depicting Derby Day. The 120-odd women stood out in this summer's chic shades of orange, fuchsia and lime green. Then, on closer inspection, we could see the fascinating detail. Angela and Maria Eagle, identical twins, both in black costumes with white blouses, both capable of creating massive and pleasing confusion. Anne Begg, the first MP in anyone's memory to be a wheelchair user, tucked up by the Bar of the House, tiny and sparkling with happiness. Dennis Skinner, now promoted to the Edward Heath Memorial Sulking Seat.

The Tories looked furious, with the exception of Alan Clark, who was aiming his heat-seeking eye contact at Virginia Bottomley. Surely not? He has reformed. Probably. The new Prime Minister arrived to cheers and clapping from Labour members, who didn't know that the rules forbid applause. But what do they care? They make up the rules now.

Then it was time for the election of the Speaker. Gwyneth Dunwoody, the first seconder, announced, 'This is a beautiful day. God is in his heaven, and a majority of this House are wearing the right colours.'

Next Tony Benn stood up to make the historic first attack on the new government. It was, he said, the first time he had spoken from the government backbenches since 1 August 1951. 'Then, the British government controlled the lives of millions in Asia and in Africa. Why, we even controlled the Bank of England!'

The Tories were slightly consoled by this and cheered him mightily. (So, inwardly, must a few Labour MPs have felt, on the grounds that they were not swept into office to give more power to bankers.)

Then came the moment when the re-elected Betty Boothroyd had to be dragged ceremonially and as if unwillingly to the chair. No drag queen, she. Never has anyone marched more merrily in that direction. Indeed she almost dragged her seconders along until, on reaching the Despatch Box, they retired, panting and defeated.

08.05.97

In the wake of their terrible election defeat, the Tories held a leadership contest. It was during the night of the long receptions that I first heard an insult to William Hague that somehow stuck.

All five leadership candidates held parties for Tory MPs last night. For an indecisive alcoholic, it must have been four hours of bliss. A lot of effort was being expended in pursuit of a job which will confer on the winner, for five years at least, roughly as much raw power as the Hon. Sec. of a crown green bowling club.

The air crackled with malice. John Redwood started with tea and Pimms in a private room at the Commons. One of his supporters marked our card: 'Michael Howard has been economical with the *actualité*, as usual. He's claiming at least two people who we know are committed to John...Ken Clarke's giving a beer and crisps party. Don't you hate that carapace of affected ordinariness?...Hague? Oh dear, the human embryo...'

The press hung round outside while the members arrived with their wives. People kept reminding us that this was the most sophisticated electorate on the planet. They looked more like Ladies' Night at Hartlepool Freemasons. The wives tend to a fashionable plumpness, like Sophie Dahl only with clothes on. They all had that glossy air of people who know exactly where their next meal is coming from.

Like many other MPs, Peter and Virginia Bottomley went to all five bashes. 'Michael Howard had the best champagne, Peter Lilley had the nicest garden, and John Redwood served some squidgy passion-fruit thing,' observed Mr Bottomley.

Outside the Lilley party three young men, not yet shaving I would guess, appeared with placards marked 'Portillo 4 El Presidente'. They were dressed as Mexican peasants and were swigging from a bottle marked 'tequila' but which looked suspiciously like cold tea. They spoke to the MP for North Essex: 'Meester Jenkin, what about Miguel, 'e is our 'ero. Why you no vote for Miguel? In our country you would be shot.'

They turned out to be Young Conservatives from Streatham, which leaves another mystery: where do you find four Young Conservatives in Streatham?

William Hague arrived at the Carlton Club with his fiancée, Ffion Jenkins. She did not look happy. His expression was relaxed, cool and confident. Her expression seemed to say, 'If you don't leave *now*, I shall call security!'

Ken Clarke had the biggest turnout of former cabinet ministers, including Willie Whitelaw, now very old and frail. There was a surrealist moment when we were briefed by Peter Luff on the food: 'There were those little Indian oniony balls, bhajis is it? And some hammy, cheesy things, and those vol-au-vent thingies, and stuffed cherry tomatoes.' This was the real cutting edge of political reporting. Walter Bagehot, thou shouldst be living...Not soundbites but real nibbles.

10.06.97

Hague, with Margaret Thatcher's support, went on to win the Tory leadership election. That autumn Blair made his first Labour Party conference speech as prime minister.

Mr Blair walked on to the music of Saint-Saëns, specifically the part used as the theme of *Babe*. This is the popular film about a shy talking piglet who learns to round up flocks of docile, disciplined sheep. Just a coincidence, of course. We had just seen a video depicting Five Months of Glorious Progress. Election promises honoured! Blair triumphs in Amsterdam! Ragged cheers greeted these declarations, a reminder that Labour has always had trouble distinguishing between a decision and an achievement.

He walked onto the platform and the audience rose to him in a standing ovation which was, perhaps, slightly more enthusiastic than the one at the end. He kept waving them back down. You half expected him to say that the hall was only booked for half an hour, and if they didn't mind he'd crack on. His whole style is muffled and subdued, even the loud bits. It's not so much a speech as a presentation without slides. The audience is like the congregation in an evangelical church. They want to be writhing on the floor in ecstasy but find they've got a Church of England vicar who hasn't even got a tambourine.

By the end he was talking about the importance of giving. 'Make this the giving age…' He sounded as if he was announcing harvest festival next week. 'But not too many vegetable marrows this year, if you don't mind.' Soon the congregation realized they weren't going to get very much in exchange for their giving. He used the phrase 'hard choices' and even 'harsh choices' eleven times. In the past this has always been Labour-speak for 'No more money'.

And so it is today. But under Mr Blair, harshness is also a virtue in itself. 'Ours must be a compassionate society. But compassion with a hard edge. A strong society cannot be built on soft choices.'

Compassion with a hard edge! The razor blade in the duvet! I wonder what it's like at the Blair breakfast table. 'Which cereal would you like, dear?'

'I want the hard choice, and that means Shreddies. But Shreddies without milk, because otherwise they would become the soft choice, and soft choices are no basis for breakfast for our people.'

As well as being harsh and hard, we must be modern. Being modern is an absolute good in itself, and he used the word twenty-one times. 'We must modernize – and take the hard choices to do it.' Civil servants are to be replaced by computers. Soon a quarter of all dealings with government will be performed electronically. Members of the public can be asked: 'Do you want your choice to be (*click on one*) (a) hard, (b) harsh, or (c) downright pitiless?'

There were curious Blairish phrases: 'The gates of xeno-phobia, falling down', which was almost Blakean. We had anointed him to lead us into the next millennium. 'That was your challenge to me. Proudly, humbly, I accepted it.'

Vainly, modestly, he set to work. Harshly, compassion-ately, he took the tough choices. Loudly, softly, he spoke to conference and, fascinated, bored, they gave him a standing ovation anyway.

01.10.97

In the spring of 1998, Tony Blair went to visit the Assemblée Nationale in Paris. Our Prime Minister walked informally up the path to the assembly building. A military band, clearly unbriefed in the nuances of Cool Britannia, played 'Land of Hope and Glory'. In Mr Blair's new 'real entente' they would be replaced by Blur.

His arrival has been big news in Paris, and scuffles broke out between the local press and British photographers jostling for position. It must be strange, wherever you go in public, to find your route lined by men hitting each other.

'You are in Paris, ici, not in Zimbabwe,' yelled one French reporter. 'Azz'ole, azz'ole!'

We trooped into the Chamber, which is a magnificent confection of gold and tapestries and murals and bas-reliefs and statues and enough marble to denude every quarry in Italy – in short, it would make a perfect *pied-à-terre* for Lord Irvine, our free-spending Lord Chancellor. Watch for it in the April issue of *Better Chancelleries and Gardens*.

M. Fabius, the President of the Assembly, introduced Mr Blair. We wondered whether he would use his famous verbal twiddles, saying, 'Vous savez' and 'I mean, guys, voyez!' but he spoke with a clarity and directness he seems to find hard at home.

He told little jokes. French politicians do not go in for jokes, any more than ours wave pigs' bladders. Jokes are not part of the act. So his jokes were welcome. He invoked Winston Churchill, who famously spoke French like a walrus with a speech impediment, perhaps deliberately. In those days Conservatives thought that having a proper French accent was a sign of moral turpitude, possibly homosexuality.

'Je vais vous parler en français,' said Mr Blair. 'Courage!' They laughed and applauded, because his French is good.

He said that he had worked in a Parisian bar. It was a strict rule that all tips were put into a common pot. After a while, he realized that he was the only waiter who was actually doing this. 'It was my first lesson in applied socialism.'

The Right, who actually do sit on the right of the room, according to revolutionary tradition, and who had turned out in fewer numbers than the Left, suddenly discovered that this was quite possibly the funniest thing they had ever heard in their lives.

From then on it was competitive clapping between the two sides. When he got to the passage attacking dogma and said that what counted was not whether an economy was left or right, but whether it worked, the Right's cheers were aimed at the Left. 'Gauchiste? Huh, he's one of ours!' they were saying.

Then he got on to the Social Exclusion Unit and the Left decided they could join in. Next we were back with the spirit of small business enterprise, and the Right had nudged ahead once more. But hold on! 'We must recognize the unions' – the Left was back in the lead. 'We must be flexible' – code in French for 'We must sack lots of people' and the Right was on track once more. By now they were willing to applaud anything, if only to attract some of that magical popularity for themselves. Even 'Vive la subsidiarité!' possibly the most boring battle-cry ever cried, brought applause.

I think he ought to speak in French all the time. The voters would get used to it, since few of them actually listen to the words, and it sounds so much better.

25.03.98

By the end of June 1998, the opening of the Millennium Dome was getting alarmingly close. The minister in charge at this stage was Peter Mandelson.

Peter Mandelson was attacked yesterday, as usual, over the contents of the Millennium Dome. How, asked Tim Loughton, a Tory from Worthing, could anyone enjoy contemplation in the Spirit Zone, with the roar of the Blackwall Tunnel underneath, a circus nearby, 'and not a crucifix in sight'?

Mr Mandelson said solemnly that there would be, somewhere in the Dome, a place for private prayer. (Though if it's like other theme park attractions, the queues will be endless, with signs saying, 'At this point you are ninety minutes away from the Lost Orison Experience.') Mr Mandelson added, 'Churches are setting up many events, centred on Pentecost 2000.'

Pentecost 2000! It's a perfect New Labour name, being pure PR-babble and also quite inaccurate, since Pentecost happened thirty-odd years after the birth of Christ. (Though of course 'Pentecost 1970' wouldn't work, since it would make everyone think of flared trousers and Sweet records, and the time when Michael Fabricant was one of the top disc jockeys in the Brighton and Hove area, appearing as Mickey Fabb.)

You could rename all the events in the Christian calendar. Christmas would become Nativity Year Zero. Good Friday would be the Hanging on in There '33 Tour, and Casting the Money-Changers from the Temple would be entirely re-themed and launched as In Partnership with the Business Community.

Mr Peter Ainsworth is a man of whom I had not heard before. He has a magnificent head of hair, like a female American TV newsreader, and surprisingly he appears to be the member of the shadow cabinet concerned with culture, media and sport. He complained about the lack of government support for seaside towns. Indeed such places were suffering from tremendous over-regulation. 'Far from receiving a Kiss-Me-Quick hat, any minister visiting the seaside this summer is likely to be told exactly where he can stick his rock!'

I wondered briefly what Harold Macmillan would have made of Mr Ainsworth. I suspect he would have told his gardener to spray him with something.

30.06.98

1998–1999

The Conservatives always end the conference season.

The Tory conference found a new heroine yesterday. She is a replacement for the disgraced Michael Heseltine, whose face has already been airbrushed out of the official histories.

If Heseltine could always find the party's clitoris, Ann Widdecombe gives the party a big stinging smack on its plump red rump. They adored it. But first, we were captivated by the stage set. This includes, to one side of the platform, eight informal Ikea chairs in different colours. In a magnificently snobbish remark, Heseltine was once accused by the chief whip of being 'the kind of man who buys his own furniture'. The Tories have now descended to being the kind of people who assemble their own furniture.

The effect is to make the platform party look very ill at ease, as if an officers' selection board had to meet in a suburban sitting room, or as if they'd all turned up to what they thought was a Tupperware party and the hostess had suddenly offered them split-crotch panties and vibrators.

Behind them is the conference slogan: 'Listening. Learning. Leading'. Speakers repeat this mantra at intervals.

Listening. Learning. Leading. As it went on, the mind began to spin. 'Shaving. Showering. Shampooing.' By mid-morning the conference was getting distinctly torpid. 'Drooping. Dozing. Dying.'

Then suddenly Ann Widdecombe was before them. She was magnificent. It was electrifying. She had learned her speech off by heart, so she needed no autocue and could stalk about the stage, her arms flopping up and down maniacally, like a drowning porpoise, if such a thing could exist. Hattie Jacques had become one flesh with Rosa Klebb.

And what flesh! Like my late great-aunts, Ms Widdecombe does not have breasts, but one single, unicameral bosom, as vast and lavishly upholstered as any Ikea armchair. The hands swerved wildly from side to side. Hectoring. Haranguing. Harassing. The wagging finger waved and, having waved, wagged on. It was superb.

And the voice – the voice ran out of control and peaked alarmingly like feedback from a microphone. 'Just because…' she squeaked, then 'just because…' and her larynx soared into an unwonted falsetto, as if she were about to begin some dreadful Andrew Lloyd Webber song, backed by a hundred dancers, all dressed like William Hague. Now and again she got carried away and said things which made no sense at all: 'And other things have been banned, including varicose veins!' She was cheered dementedly. 'Every time you provide for your own health care, you are freeing up the NHS to provide for someone else's health,' she cried, and the delegates applauded themselves frantically for queue-jumping.

She spoke of the hospital matron. 'She was a dragon and she was a champion. We want her back!' You could feel the sexual frisson charge around the hall, goosing the patients as it ran. Matron! Bed baths! Traction! Catheters! They cheered and shouted and whistled and yelled. With friends like these, who needs enemas?

Finally, spent but happy, the delegates trooped off to the innumerable receptions where they could eat free food and drink free wine, while skulking in the corner and ogling any woman under the age of sixty. Ligging. Lurking. Lusting.

07.10.98

Meanwhile, Britain and the US were engaged in a bombing campaign against Serbia. This was not always successful – at one point bombs hit the Chinese Embassy in Belgrade. The Foreign Secretary, Robin Cook, had a difficult relationship with some of his officials. When a junior minister, Derek Fatchett, died, one mandarin was heard to say at the graveside: 'It's like the Chinese Embassy – right idea, wrong target.'

The Prime Minister was in Brussels, working with Kofi Annan on the plight of the Kosovo refugees. Back on the government front bench another humanitarian disaster was unfolding. His deputy, John Prescott, had taken over Question Time.

It was terrible. It was also ghastly, chaotic, miserable and floor-staringly, mouth-puckeringly, gaze-avertingly awful. In any civilized country a trained SAS squad would have abseiled down the Chamber walls, tossing smoke bombs, grabbing Mr Prescott and hustling him to safety.

As it was, many people felt sorry for him. He is, after all, a working-class lad who has got where he is by dint of hard work, dedication and political flair. Others take a sterner view. He is, nominally at least, the second most powerful man in the land, and at least should be able to patch a sentence together. Or be vaguely aware of government policy on the kind of vital, world-changing issues to which the rest of us devote slightly less thought than whether we want cheese 'n' onion or original salted flavour. Yes, it was hilarious. Yes, but only a boorish oaf would not feel a twinge of pity for the man.

He began by flannelling well enough. Labour's David Chaytor asked him about the role of the Russians in the Balkan war. 'I think that on a number of occasions there has been a concern and it has been a subject of discussion in these discussions,' he said, in what was basically pidgin Prescott. He was reading from a script, and though he skipped several words, the brain, accustomed to the Prescottic dialect, supplied the missing syllables.

Then nemesis arrived in the unlikely shape of the genteel Alan Beith. The Liberal Democrat deputy asked him to confirm that average class sizes are, in spite of Labour's promises, actually increasing.

'I can confirm that we are on target for reducing class sizes,' Mr Prescott said, to Tory jeers.

'But that is not the same question,' said Mr Beith, who rattled off a series of figures which seemed to make his case.

'You asked if we were on target,' said Mr Prescott, changing the subject again. 'And that is the answer you are going to get!' The Tories were chortling, even glistening with pleasure.

Then Michael Spicer demanded a guarantee that the withholding tax would never be introduced in this country.

Mr Prescott scrambled desperately through his notes but couldn't find the page. 'Well, as someone who is now the Secretary of State for the Environment, that disastrous poll tax is one that I am constantly having to deal with. You should bear in mind that what we have now settled with the local authorities is the most generous settlement they have ever received!'

The Tories suddenly realized that he was talking not about withholding tax (which is to prevent people using offshore holdings to dodge tax) but about the council tax. He probably didn't even know what the withholding tax was.

They collapsed in tucks of mirth, some genuine. Ann Widdecombe kept clutching at her own face, as if to hold the hysteria in. 'More, more!' the Tories yelled.

Soon afterwards, Mr Prescott paused for thirty agonizing

seconds, then answered the wrong question. 'There are different ways of doing this at different times,' he said in reply to a query about a new National Forest.

'It's the way I tell 'em,' he said plaintively. 'I have caused some confusion.' (More confusion was caused by Labour's David Taylor, who asked for 'the government cavalry to ride to the rescue of a scheme which is becoming becalmed in a quagmire.' Oh, those poor horses!)

Mr Prescott stalked angrily from the Chamber to further Tory cries of 'More!' Am I just imagining the quiet glee with which this debacle will have been welcomed by Mr Blair and his staff?

15.04.99

1999-2000

The Conservative Party spent much of the decade desperately trying to reinvent themselves, often at the party conference. This year's was held in Blackpool.

The Tories launched their new campaign yesterday under the title 'The Common Sense Revolution'. What an amazing revolution that will be. 'Let's not build any barricades, lads, they'll only make people late for work.' Or, 'Don't burn those buses, they might come in handy later.'

(The common-sense revolutionaries come down from the hills in their trademark Thermawear headbands and Clarks shoes. 'What do we want?' 'Loft insulation!' 'When do we want it?' 'As soon as the builders have finished that job in Sutton!')

Mr Hague started offering us guarantees. There was the Sterling Guarantee, the Parents' Guarantee, the Can Work, Must Work Guarantee. And, what's more, the guarantees were, themselves, guaranteed. 'As anyone who knows me knows, that is guaranteed!' he said.

(Crowds line the streets as the common-sense revolutionaries march through the capital. Their placards declare: 'Regular dental check-ups, now!'; 'Keep eggs in a cool place, not in the fridge!'; and 'You're not wearing that coat in this weather, are you?')

I went into the conference hall. The stage is truly weird. It consists of a series of gigantic blue 'think' bubbles in the shape of William Hague's head.

(The common-sense revolutionaries revere Michael Fish, with his common-sense revolutionary thought and sensible glasses. Their Rosa Luxemburg is Delia Smith.)

A young man of seventeen, Alex Lee from Worcester, spoke in the defence debate. 'Good lord,' you could see people thinking, 'he could be our leader in less than twenty years.' Then he opened his mouth. 'Let us cut our aggressive military commitments,' he said. 'Let us dispense with our outdated military past, and use the money saved to improve people's lives!' The applause at the end was distinctly lukewarm. No doubt he was taken away to be shot, or at least given a friendly ticking-off.

(Meanwhile the mobs have reached the presidential palace. The leader of the Common Sense faction climbs onto the wall. 'Comrades!' he cries. 'The time has come to storm this citadel of privilege and oppression! But be careful not to step on the flowerbeds!')

05.10.99

The jargon that infests New Labour extends everywhere, including the Queen's Speech. Her Majesty opened Parliament, as usual, in November.

What is the point of having all these ushers and courtiers and heralds in Parliament, including Fitzalan Pursuivant Extraordinary, Maltravers Herald Extraordinary, Clarenceaux King of Arms, the Cap of Maintenance (does Queen Beatrix have a Dutch Cap of Maintenance?) and Gold Stick in Waiting, which sounds like a breath freshener you keep for emergencies, but which turns out to be Princess Anne, all of whom seem to have been saved from the tumbrils which carted all but ninety-two hereditary peers off to the guillotine last week – if not one of them can say to the Queen, 'Don't read out this stuff, Your Majesty, it's complete and utter garbage'?

At one time the Queen's Speech at the State Opening

used to be couched in dry, flat, dull language, and contained brief descriptions of coming legislation.

After 1997 it began to be padded out with New Labour jargon about – as it was yesterday – 'a dynamic, knowledge-based economy', 'transparency', 'providing people with the opportunities to liberate their potential' and 'meeting the challenges of the new millennium' – just some of the cringe-making, jaw-sticking, tooth-furring drivel that the poor woman had to read out from the throne yesterday.

I've been going to these occasions on and off for twenty years, and while the Queen has always read out the Speech as if it were slightly less fascinating than the used-tools section of the *Exchange & Mart*, this time she seemed to be infected with a greater ennui than ever. Her voice droned on unhappily like someone who, the moment she has finished, will have to come to terms with some terrible sorrow.

But then this year's speech was worse than ever before. It was without doubt the worst Queen's Speech I have ever heard. It wasn't even a royal speech at all, but a party political broadcast.

'More people are in work in Britain today than ever before, with employment up by 700,000, and long-term unemployment has been halved,' she intoned.

'Education remains my government's number one priority,' she said, like a Dalek with a head cold, and I half expected a video clip to be broadcast on a giant screen, showing bright, attentive children with nice clean hair sitting in a sun-dappled classroom.

'My government are helping people back into work. The New Deal has helped 145,000 young people…inflation is now historically low…raising the income of working families…my government will continue to manage the public finances prudently.'

It was awful, dreadful and horribly embarrassing. The Queen is supposed to be a national symbol, above party politics, not re-created as the latest Blair babe. Next year someone at the Palace should crisply tell Downing Street to spin itself up its own fundament.

18.11.99

I've worked out how to follow a John Prescott speech. You have to think of the speech itself as a chap who is taking his large, bouncy dog – a Great Prescott perhaps – for a walk in the country. Prescott is on a lead, of course, because there are sheep in the fields. But he can't just stroll along. He tugs and pulls at the speech, trying to force it to go the way he wants. Some of these tugs are just small twitches: 'That is something we are particularly, and proud of,' he said. On other occasions, he bounds away, with the speech left running to catch up.

'I think you'll see that the confidence in the public transport as shown by this side of the House in that they think it is an important part of the transport system,' he shouted, and you could hear the poor old speech – no younger than it used to be – panting to catch up without tripping over the lead.

We moved on to the Conservative attitude to local government – 'or their idea of democracy, to "bolish the GLC'. So fast was he charging towards a dozy-looking ewe that he couldn't spare time for mere vowels. On we raced. 'Repeating this' meant 'repealing this'. Tenants were suffering because of 'unscruppolous' landlords, which sounds like a disease sailors catch.

Suddenly he was off the leash and away into the fields. The speech was abandoned, left standing in a cold muddy cart track. 'There are difficult legal complexes – our draft bill this House can take first steps, which is creating a great deal of social injustice in our housing situation.'

The speech tries to whistle him back, but he's still running round in circles. 'The actual people in areas have pointed out that all these things definitely was worse for the taxpayer. I would think they are a body to be actually claimed on our side to welcome best practice.'

'Prescott, back here, boy!' cries the speech across the fields, but the dog hardly notices. 'All have a contributory contribution to congestion,' he barks over his shoulder as he chases the increasingly anxious sheep.

Finally he trotted back to heel and allowed the lead to be clipped back on. But then he was off and running again, tugging the speech frantically to the end of their walk. 'I think there is umanimous support,' he said, pulling onwards. 'It is the issue of our preferred consideration!' Deterioration became 'deteriati'; environment, 'envymen'. 'We are unpacking the damage they have done!'

Mrs Prescott looked on, smiling, from the Strangers' Gallery. Her famous hair was certainly not messed up, but after listening to her husband, I cannot speak for her mind.

19.11.99

It was one of those dreams that make ministers wake up at 3.30 a.m., sweating and perhaps even whimpering with fear. 'Darling, what is the matter?' ask anxious wives and mistresses, as their menfolk wipe the clammy moisture from their brows and crawl downstairs for a cup of tea and twenty restoring minutes of all-night television.

The dream is always the same. There they are in the Commons, confidently beating off Tory attacks, poised, assured, the facts disposed in well-marshalled files, the arguments deployed like a chessmaster's pawns. Their quiet glow of satisfaction sends serotonin, the happy drug secreted by the body, into the correct receptors of the brain.

'The whips are listening,' murmurs the serotonin. 'They'll be telling Number 10 about how brilliantly you laid about the Tories. Margaret Beckett, Jack Straw, Robin Cook – who knows what will happen to them in the next reshuffle? Tony's bound to need someone as intellectually nimble as you to promote to the Cabinet. You only need to keep going.'

John Spellar, the defence minister, dreamed on as peacefully as any child. In his dream, he was being assailed by Robert Key, a Tory spokesman. Mr Key had made rather an ass of himself on the *Today* programme by saying, 'We can't be held responsible for things which happened ten years ago.' In that case, whom can we hold responsible? In any event, this was not a man whose debating skills were going to cause Mr Spellar much difficulty. He could cope with him while fast asleep.

Mr Key was complaining about a cut in the amount of money being provided for service hospitals. 'How is it that when I asked you what had happened to the £1,500,000 allocated for orthopaedic waiting lists, you replied that there were no cuts?'

Mr Spellar grunted gently and rolled over. Outside the first notes of the dawn chorus could be heard, and the soft whine of a milk float wafted from a nearby street. In his dreams he formulated the perfect reply.

'We recognized that these cuts in defence medical services had gone too far,' he said – except that horribly, unimaginably, nightmarishly, he had inserted an extraneous letter N into the word 'cuts'.

The mistaken word was clear and crisply spoken. What made it even worse was that the sentence as it came out made just as much sense as what Mr Spellar was trying to say. There was a short but terrible silence. Mr Spellar must have felt like a man who dreams he is falling out of bed, then realizes that he is, and that his bed is on a clifftop bivouac.

Then the Tories exploded, laughing riotously, slapping their thighs amid a barrage of stage hilarity.

At the end you could say that the government had survived a damaging assault on its credibility. Or you could argue that the opposition had mercilessly exposed its short-comings. Or, as I beg Mr Spellar never to try to say, you could take your pick.

25.01.00

In 2000 we had the first election for Mayor of London. I did an interview with an American TV network who wanted to know why we were electing a Mayor of London when we already had one. I explained that the existing one was the Mayor of the City of London, which was of course quite different from London, the city of that name. They stopped the interview at that point.

Frank Dobson, the Labour candidate, called for a new blitz on London. He was, of course, mistaken. The difference between Ken Livingstone and a doodlebug is that with Ken, the time to duck is when the whining noise begins.

Which it did yesterday afternoon when Ken launched his attempt to become Mayor of London. It should be renamed the Stuff Blair campaign. In the absence of a serious Conservative Party, Ken is standing on behalf of everyone, right and left, black and white, sane and bonkers, who can't stand New Labour.

Meanwhile, Labour MPs, who split roughly into two groups over Ken – those who loathe him and those who detest him – were asking each other, 'What are the two worst things about Ken Livingstone?' Answer: 'His face.'

The launch was at BAFTA, the film and TV association. There were posters on the wall for great British films, such as *The Bridge on the River Kwai* (man commits suicide rather than see his life's work destroyed) and *Brief Encounter* (after months of indecision, man decides to call it a day), so they seemed very appropriate.

The microphones were many and highly sensitive, and Mr Livingstone has a nervous way of grunting while he listens to a question, so the alarming effect was of a bear which has just spotted its lunch hiding up a tree.

But there is no doubt about it: the man is a great performer. From the relaxed opener, 'Is everybody ready? Then I'll begin,' to the line near the end, 'I've almost reached the Buddhist plane where there is no ego,' he was calm and in control. (No ego? Ken without an ego? His ego could survive a frontal assault from the Parachute Regiment.) He faced head-on the charge that he had broken his promise never to stand against an official Labour candidate. 'It is for Londoners to decide what is the greater crime. I'm not looking for a weasel way out. I am not hiding the fact that I am backing out of commitments I have made.' This strategy – 'Trust me, I'm a liar' – may prove hard to break down.

And would he be allowed back into the Labour Party? He flashed us the sweetest of smiles. 'I take heart from seeing all those people in Tony Blair's office who left to join the SDP and were welcomed back. I hope that generosity of spirit can be extended to me.'

It will be hard for poor Dobbo to fight that sweet smile.

07.03.00

Tony Blair gave an important talk to the newspaper conference yesterday. Not for the first time, I was struck by the way
that a Blair speech is closer to a musical composition than to
mere rhetoric. Like a piece of music, its aim isn't to inform
but to create good feelings.

It's no more about facts and policies than the Pastoral
Symphony is an examination of the common agricultural
policy. And, like a piece of music, it has a definite structure,
based on internal rhythm and repetition. A theme is introduced and merged with the earlier ones. The repetition
brings a satisfying familiarity, so that by the end the listener's
brain vibrates with all the interwoven passages.

Nobody ever listened to a Blair speech and came away
saying, 'Well, I learned something there.' Instead they praise
the bravura performance and enjoy the afterglow created by
the mood.

He began, 'My argument today is this.' That was the
equivalent of the conductor tapping his baton. Next he
announced: 'Britain is stronger together than separated
apart.' How we might be separated together he did not
explain.

'True Britishness lies in our value, not unchanging insti-
tutions,' he continued. This was Beethoven's technique:
state the main themes at the start and then refer back to
them at different tempos and in different settings. So
'Britain' or 'British' appeared 49 times in the speech, a rate
of almost five times a minute.

'Values', usually integrated into a longer phrase, such as
'a clear sense of shared values', or 'our core values as a
country', cropped up 17 times. And there were 16 variations
on 'change', or the invariably pejorative 'unchanging'.

In his third sentence he introduced another powerful
theme: 'The constitutional changes we have made...are the

THE HANDS OF HISTORY

means of strengthening Britain for today's world.'

The fourth paragraph bound this theme to the earlier ones: 'Standing up for our country means standing up for what we believe in. It means standing up for our values, and having the strength...to stand up for the core British values.'

As the themes circled round and disappeared up their own treble clefs, the orchestra was in full flight. The violins were soaring, the harps created a loud glissando, and the brass was about to crash in.

'To fail to modernize would be to fail Britain. But we must modernize according to our core values.' So after just two minutes, all the main motifs had reappeared. Then three minutes later, we heard of a 'Britain that is stronger, fairer, modernized...modernization based on values'.

Then a great surge of woodwind, drawing together all the earlier themes: 'Standing up for Britain means fighting for British values.' Next the kettledrums began their climactic pounding.

Except that a Blair speech does not end with a crescendo. Instead we were reaching a diminuendo, a soft, gentle coda in which the main themes were gathered together in verbless sentences, creating mood music, which sends the audience away in a soporific reverie. 'An economy gaining in strength. Pride from a modern constitution which strengthens the nation. We are rediscovering our strength and values. We are uniting those values...to make Britain stronger.'

And so the listeners leave, no wiser or better informed, but with the music echoing round their heads.

29.03.00

After lunch is the most dangerous time of day for Nicholas Soames. What he likes to do is to come to the Commons and shout endearments at the lady members. 'Splendid, absolutely splendid!' he will say, especially when the woman in question has just asked a particularly toadying question.

Yesterday he placed himself at the very back of the backbenches, as if in hiding. He was even behind the lavender-clad figure of Julie Kirkbride, a Tory MP so comely that she causes male Labour members to leave criss-cross trails of drool round the chamber, like snails.

It was culture questions, which are usually dull, being for the most part Tories saying what a failure the Dome is, and other MPs moaning that too little lottery cash has been spent in their constituencies. ('Why was the excellent and costed proposal for Elastoplast 2000, celebrating the history of the plastic-backed bandage, which would have brought scores of jobs to my constituency, turned down?' That's the sort of thing.)

'The government is sitting on £480 million of lottery players' money,' said the Tory spokesman, Peter Ainsworth. Mr Soames began to study his nails, very carefully, one by one.

Janet Anderson, the junior minister, declared that the Dome was the most popular tourist attraction in the country, and she for one was very proud of it.

'The halo effect of investment in the dome is widespread all over the country,' Ms Anderson went on. Mr Soames began to – 'pick' would be an inadequate word – he began to excavate his nose, with all the fastidious care of an archaeologist who has just started work on a hitherto unknown Minoan dig. Possibly this was because, as the current wine writer for the *Spectator*, he needs to get rid of any nasal substances that might interfere with his appreciation of the most subtle bouquets.

Or perhaps, like motorists at traffic lights, he imagines that on the backbenches he is invisible. Nick, old chap: when folk are listening to Geoffrey Howe's resignation speech, all eyes are on the speaker. When Michael Fabricant is discussing the seating arrangements in his local rep, our eyes roll round the chamber in a desperate attempt to find something interesting. That is why they lighted on you.

'Tourism should be at the very heart of government,' said Ms Anderson, and Mr Soames began work on his teeth, one by one, using his fingers to scrape away deadly plaque.

'We have a quality product in our tourist industry,' Ms Anderson went on.

Ian Bruce, a Tory, launched into a dreary whinge about the state of the tourism industry. Mr Soames found an interesting object on the end of his finger – who can say whence it came? – and he flicked it, so that it landed somewhere on his front bench colleagues.

Now, perfectly groomed, all extraneous matter cleared from his system, he was able to join the rest of us. 'Quite right!' he bellowed at the top of his voice, and sank back on his seat, as clean and glowing as if he had just spent the previous week at an expensive health spa.

09.05.00

Fans of A.A. Milne will recall that a heffalump trap is a pit that you dig for a heffalump, and then fall in yourself. Yesterday William Hague dug a beautiful heffalump trap, scooped it out, stuck sharpened stakes in the bottom, covered it with branches, leaves and moss, paused to admire his work, then walked slap dab into it.

Ka-poom! The sound of him crashing down reverberated round the Common for minutes, if not seconds.

It all began with stuff about ministers disagreeing over the euro. 'Will the Prime Minister get a grip on his Cabinet, and stop them fighting like ferrets in a sack?' (Fighting ferrets in a sack might have been a childhood diversion in the Rotherham of his youth. 'Young William Hague took on five ferrets at once before leaving the sack, hurt...' More fun than memorizing parliamentary majorities, which is what he actually did.)

Mr Blair pointed out that the Tories were also divided.

'But I lead my party, and he follows his,' said Mr Hague.

This braggadocio was greeted with wild cheering, at least from the claque seated behind the Tory leader. At a greater distance I noticed expressions on the faces of Tory MPs that were rather more thoughtful, perhaps even mildly embarrassed.

It was then that he started to dig the trap. He decided to quote the private memo from Mr Blair's mentor, Philip Gould, the one in this week's press which said that 'TB' was lacking in conviction, unable to stick to a position and out of touch.

'Does TB himself agree with this, or is it just the rest of us?'

'Well,' said the Prime Minister mildly, 'if he's not careful, I'll start to read what the focus groups say about him.'

This is why Amanda Platell, Mr Hague's personal spin doctor, ought to have radio-controlled cattle prods sewn into his Y-fronts. Sitting in the gallery, she could press a button – left for 'Carry on, you're doing fine,' or right for 'Shut up, for goodness' sake, shut up, *now*!' We would know she had hit the button because the opposition leader would start to twitch madly, which we would all enjoy.

Lacking this high-tech guidance, Mr Hague blundered on towards the trap he had prepared. 'We'd be delighted if he'd read what the focus groups said, because then we could have the whole document placed in the Commons library,' he said, going on to add what was meant to be a mighty peroration: 'He has run out of steam, run out of time and, if he carries on like this, will be run out of office!'

Mr Blair smiled amiably. 'He challenged me to read out the focus groups, so I will. This is what they say about him: "Boring, false, he irritates me greatly, pathetic drip, nonentity, no substance, no personality, complete waste of time, no policies and a very unimpressive team, particularly William Hague".'

Labour MPs, who had been fearful a few moments before, erupted in glee. Tories were deeply, deeply glum. Mr Hague began smiling and laughing, in the strained, half-demented way any of us might, but only if we were sitting impaled on spikes at the bottom of our own heffalump trap.

15.06.00

2000—2001

As the Labour Party gathered for its annual conference two problems seemed to loom over ministers – the fuel protests, which had seen the party fall behind the Tories in the opinion polls for the first time in eight years, and the Ecclestone affair, in which it appeared that in their account of dealings with the millionaire Formula One racing chief, the Prime Minister and the Chancellor had been somewhat economical with the truth. Mr Ecclestone had given a million pounds to Labour Party funds, and we were invited to believe that this had nothing to do with the decision to exempt Formula One from the proposed ban on tobacco advertising.

Gordon Brown sat down to a massive ovation after a dazzlingly successful speech. He had tackled the twin problems of the Ecclestone fib and the petrol crisis head on – by ignoring them. Was he contrite? No, he was not. His speech was as packed with contrition as a frog is full of toothpaste. But the Labour Party has decided it adores him. The stamping and applause and cheering continued for ages, and became even more hysterical when his wife Sarah ran to join him on the platform. As they descended, a vast, heaving mob of cameramen climbed up on top of each other.

The Browns saw the tottering, heaving phalanx advance towards them. They fled backstage, and finally the cheering stopped.

Mr Blair sat on stage clapping and beaming as if his life depended on it, which it possibly does. One imagines him saying sibilantly to Mr Brown afterwards, 'That was jolly, jolly good, Gordon. Now I'm afraid I'm going to have to kill you...'

Earlier we heard from Peter Mandelson, who spoke about Northern Ireland. For most of the delegates this was the equivalent of having a guest speech from Beelzebub on the subject of flower arranging. He did not receive a standing ovation; instead the applause resembled the sound of empty crisp packets blowing across a deserted playground.

By contrast, John Prescott's speech was received with rapture. Under Labour, he said, you'll have noticed – 'no water bans or hosepipe crises'. That's because we've had all that rain, I wanted to shout. It's certainly a first – even this government has never before taken credit for the weather.

'Citizens make cities and cities make citizens,' he raved, adding, 'How true that is!' Yes, how very true, we thought. I wonder what it means? In the exciting world of John Prescott nobody ever makes a mere decision: on trains, 'We shall make a decisive decision!' he told us.

He got huge applause for his attacks on farmers, hauliers and huntspersons. 'Did you see the Countryside Alliance outside, with their contorted faces?' he asked, his face contorted. He did refer to the fuel protests: 'That is no way to make decisions in a democratic country,' he said, adding, 'They should make decisions the British way – by bunging a million quid to the Labour Party!'

No, silly, of course he didn't say the last bit.

26.09.00

One of the important issues at the conference was pensions, and the sense that old people were being denied a fair share in the country's new prosperity.

I sat in the front row for Tony Blair's speech. It was like the monsoon in a Somerset Maugham short story. Hot, steaming sweat flew all over the platform. His shirt was so damp you expected him to rip it off mid-speech and call for horse blankets.

His eyebrows were on fire, blazing with commitment. At times he was excitedly hopping from side to side like a lonely line dancer. The Cabinet (remember them? They used to have a minor constitutional role in government) were herded into a set of seats below the leader and to his left, so that they were obliged to gaze adoringly up at him, with the exception of John Prescott, who took time out from beaming at his leader to glower at the sketch-writers.

The Prime Minister began with a ringing battle-cry. 'We're crap!' he told the delegates. 'Yes, we're crap all right, but we're not so crappy as the other lot!' He didn't quite put it like that, of course, but that was what he meant. It was that rarest of moments, an apology from a politician. The Dome, the fuel crisis, pensions, even Prime Minister's Question Time. But he was sorry, God he was sorry. He would never, ever do it again. Would a bunch of flowers help?

He was feeling our pain. 'There's the mortgage to pay…inflation may be lower, but the kids' trainers don't get any cheaper.' (How true that is. There's the riding trainer, the personal fitness trainer, the ski instructor – do you know what they charge these days?) He set a new record of 163 verb-free sentences, those phrases which, by omitting any doing words, appear to offer a promise without making a commitment.

Once he'd got the grovelling out of the way he was trans-formed. He leapt around as the sweat poured off him like a lawn sprinkler. Would he be the first party leader whose own perspiration made him slither off the stage and crash into the photographers?

Suddenly he left the text of the speech to put in what was meant to be a deeply felt, personal statement. 'If you ask me to put tax cuts before education spending – I can't do it...If you ask me to give two fingers to Europe, I can't do it' – except that he pronounced 'I' as 'ah', which is meant to indicate sincerity, as in 'If you want me to reintroduce slavery, ah can't do it. If you want me to take little Leo's pet hamster and hurl him on the barbecue, ah can't do it.' Oddly enough, he didn't go on to say, 'If you want me to link pensions to the rise in incomes rather than inflation, ah can't do that...'

He has always had a love of clunky phrases, verbal Ladas. He banged on about his 'irreducible core' of beliefs. It sounded like something out of *The China Syndrome*. 'Bweep, bweep! The Prime Minister's irreducible core has gone critical! Put on this lead anorak!'

Moments later he told us that 'Before us lies a path strewn with the challenges of change.' That's the trouble with Blair speeches; they become pastiches of themselves. 'And it is littered with the beer cans of opportunity, knee-deep in the burger boxes and irreducible apple cores of hope,' you expected him to say.

At the end he told us we were on a journey, a journey worth making. But as well as a journey, it was a fight, 'a fight worth fighting'. So the Labour Party were to resemble British football hooligans, who also believe that no journey is complete without a fight. 'We shall hurl the bar stool of opportunity through the plate glass window of privilege,' he didn't say but presumably meant.

It was over. He stayed briefly for his standing ovation, then quickly marched off the platform, no doubt for an urgent swab-down and a bath in a tub full of Lynx.

27.09.00

By spring 2001, Tony Blair felt confident enough to call a general election, though there was a month's delay because foot-and-mouth disease had made much of the country impassable.

Britain's most aggressive candidate stalked across the street in search of new voters to offend. According to the Voter ID sheet, we were visiting someone the computer called 'a firm Tory'. I asked Bob Marshall-Andrews why. 'Because I like to,' he replied grimly.

And he does make a scary sight. With his gimlet eyes, prop forward's build and lawn-strimmer haircut, the Labour candidate for Medway has been compared (by me, admittedly) to a cross between Dennis the Menace and his dog Gnasher.

The voter, a male pensioner, didn't stand a chance. As always, Mr Marshall-Andrews starts gently, to catch them off balance. 'Just came round to say hello,' he began. 'Things going all right here?' With any other politician this would be small talk. With this one, it sounds like a demand for protection money.

'Not really,' said the man. 'Your lot ent done much for me. For a start they took away my mortgage relief.'

'But your mortgage is much lower now. How much is your mortgage? How much? It's not been lower for twenty years.'

The voter didn't recall. 'But they've done bugger all for me. Nah, leave it out.'

Even though it was now clear that he was like Alf Garnett without the ethereal charm, I wanted to shout out, 'Sir! You are tangling with the wrong man.' But he could not be stopped.

'I am definitely not voting Labour. All these bloody asylum seekers coming in, taking all, taking all – all our bits and bobs.'

'You don't want to send them home to be tortured, do you?' asked Mr Marshall-Andrews, his tone by now rather unpleasant.

The man looked as if he could live equably with that prospect, but forced himself to say, 'No', before going on: 'What about the rest of them, then? Coming in by train, under the train, on top of the train.'

'What,' demanded the candidate furiously, 'do you expect me to do? Do you want me to lie on the track, wait for the train, and if I see an asylum seeker, pull him off? Do you?'

The man hurriedly changed the subject. 'They took £5 off on housing, on mortgage relief, put it on the poll tax...'

'The poll tax?' roared the candidate, but as he gathered breath for the next onslaught, the man asked, 'Have you had a pension increase?'

'I. Am. Not. A. Pensioner!' Mr Marshall-Andrews said, as if explaining to a congenital idiot that he wasn't Liza Minelli either.

'Well then,' said the man, with an air of triumph, 'you don't know what you're talking about!'

At some point the door slammed, and I wouldn't be surprised to learn that it was the candidate who did the slamming.

'Of course,' he said, as he stamped away, smiling the smile of one who has just enjoyed the fight he had picked, 'after

Prescott you can't get inside anyone's house. Knock on the door and you hear them shout, "I give in".'

The Labour canvassers spoke with awe of their man's encounter with a send-the-lot-of-them-home voter the previous day. 'The difference between you and me,' said Mr Marshall-Andrews, 'is that you are a racist and I am not.'

'What did they do for us in the war, then?' asked the man, and was told about the Indian and West Indian regiments.

'While we're at it, what did you do?'

'I'm too young.'

'Well, you don't look it. And under no circumstances are you to vote for me. You will not vote for me!'

'I'll vote for who I please,' the man had ended lamely, making him, I suppose, a 'Don't Know'. Mr Marshall-Andrews's majority is 5,326. At the present rate of attrition he should have it down to zero by polling day.

21.05.01

The film Return of the Mummy *had been playing in cinemas around the country during the election campaign. Margaret Thatcher, a woman more keenly aware than most of her own public image, awarded the title to herself shortly before she visited a marginal seat in the Midlands.*

It was *Return of the Mummy II*. Margaret Thatcher's Jaguar pulled up in Northampton market place. She was immediately surrounded by Tories, protesters, television crews, reporters, uniformed policemen, Special Branch officers, a man waving a four-foot cardboard cut-out of her, twin girls performing karaoke versions of Abba hits, a chap with an anti-Kenneth Clarke poster, a Scot with a rasping voice who accused her of hiding bribes from General Pinochet in a secret bank account – in short, a typical cross-section of modern British society.

She clambered out. A woman stepped forward and shyly handed her a banana skin, which she accepted as if it were a bouquet. So when the woman began to harangue her about Tory education policy she swerved smartly away.

'God bless Margaret Thatcher!' Conservatives shouted.

'Boo! Out, out, out!' others yelled.

'But she is out!' one of the Tories raged.

Somehow she made her way to a bald man and stroked his head. (I saw him half an hour later, but he was still bald.) The noise was like Omaha Beach. Mobile phones wheezed classical hits. Booing and jeering was answered by cheers. Photographers shouted, 'Here, Lady Thatcher!' A hundred shutters clacked. The Scotsman screeched, 'In a private account where no one has access!' The karaoke twins, Felicity and Jessica, performed to 'Money, Money, Money' at top volume.

A local TV reporter got close. 'Why are you afraid of the euro, Lady Thatcher?' Foolish fellow.

'Sterling is better!' she barked. 'If you're a broadcaster you should know that. Go on, out you go!' She poked him in the chest, hard, three times. He tried to flee into the crush, but she grabbed his microphone and held it aloft, like the spleen of a vanquished enemy.

'We wish you were still Prime Minister,' someone managed to yell above the din.

'Did you hear that?' she asked rhetorically. That's the merest common sense in her book. But things were getting dangerous. What Americans call a goat-fuck, an unstable, tottering, towering pile of photographers and TV crews, had appeared. Like a tornado, the GF requires the right extreme conditions, but once it has formed, it swirls across the land, menacing all life in its path.

Somehow we pushed along with her into the market. A little girl with panic in her eyes was pushed through to give her carnations. She handed them to someone I can only call a lady-in-waiting. The child fled.

We neared the stalls. 'We must get away,' she said, 'we're *affecting their profits*!' This is the greatest offence in the Thatcher criminal code.

Then it all goes haywire. The face is deathly white these days, and her dark brocade outfit looked as if it had been run up from the curtains in a posh undertakers. The effect is crepuscular, until the eyes blaze like a panther with a coke habit. A bold young woman asked her about Europe. She snorted, majestically. 'What if there were fifteen people who could decide what you did in your own house?' she demanded. The woman came back at her. It was madness. I couldn't hear what she said, but the Thatcher eyes spat fire. 'THAT would never allow any liberty to anyone! What a ROTTEN thing for any British person to say!'

We passed a stand advertising 'Any bag here, £2.99' but who needs any old bag for three quid when we had the greatest old bag in the land for free?

We were swirling now, faster and faster. Stalls were in danger of toppling as the GF heaved from side to side. Someone thrust a copy of her memoirs at her. 'Have you read this? It's a VERY good book,' she said as she signed it. More flowers appeared so that the lady-in-waiting looked like a garden of remembrance. Felicity and Jessica had reached 'Take a Chance on Me'. A brave man in a hat and a quite unnecessary green nylon-knit cardigan said we should join the euro. 'Just because Europe adopts the euro is no reason why we should! We have a *much older history*!'

What on earth did that mean? Who can say? And who cares?

'Are we heading in the right direction? I don't know' – a remark she probably never made while in Downing Street.

The Scotsman kept shouting about Pinochet. 'And she's not even an MP,' he added. 'She's a baroness,' someone else said. 'No, she's a pain in the butt,' said a stallholder. The twins started, aptly enough, on 'Mamma Mia'.

'The NHS is a disgrace,' said an elderly woman, 'they should bring back Matron.'

'Things were run very well when we had Matron,' said the Mummy, before returning to her car. For that, I suppose, was precisely the point the whole visit was intended to make.

30.05.01

The election was won by the Labour Party, which lost a total of one seat to the Tories. I spent election night at the various party HQs.

No election night is boring, but this one came pretty close. At the ITN party, the glossiest bash in Westminster, hardly anyone even looked up from their champagne and nibbles when the conclusive exit polls were announced.

At Tory Central Office there was a mood of miserable, dull acquiescence. It was as if the entire party had been told that its dog had died. The only excitement came when Michael Portillo appeared on television and declared that, whatever happened, he truly hoped that William Hague would remain as leader.

My goodness, we thought, are things as bad as that?

Some took a different view. Over at the ITN bash, someone asked Norman Tebbit if Portillo's remarks meant that he had finally got cold feet. 'I wouldn't know,' Tebbit replied, 'I have never slept with him.'

Last time the Tories had looked stunned as if trampled by a herd of wild horses. Last night it was more as if an old and well-loved relative had finally died after a long and painful illness. Of course you were sad, of course you grieved, but you had had lots of time to adjust yourself.

One Tory official heard the exit poll at twenty seconds past 10 p.m. and said cheerfully that the BBC exit polls had been wrong for the European elections. We munched on little quarters of egg sandwich and decided not to tell him he was a total prat.

Later a more senior official arrived and told us that William Hague remained 'optimistic and upbeat'. Goodness, that man will stay optimistic and upbeat until the day they peg him out in the desert and hungry hyenas arrive to rummage around his intestines.

At Labour headquarters they had decided to exclude the writing press. Suspicious and surly-looking bouncers patrolled the pavements behind metal fencing. A kindly woman official explained there was not enough space; the landlord wouldn't allow more people in, though another official whispered that 1,500 people had already been admitted. The odd soap star arrived.

I was reminded of the end of *Animal Farm*, when the lesser animals watch the pigs dressed as men drinking with the humans in the farmhouse. 'The creatures outside looked from pig to man, and from man to pig…but already it was impossible to say which was which.'

Outside the HQ, we couldn't even do that, since workmen had spent two hours putting up silver sheeting over the windows. Now not even the passers-by could see their once and future rulers toasting their own triumph.

08.06.01

2001—2002

New Labour is a daisy chain of hatred. Start by plucking one flower at random. Jack Straw hates David Blunkett, who he thinks is trashing everything he, Straw, did at the Home Office. Blunkett is disliked and mistrusted by Gordon Brown, because Number 10 has been trying to build up the Home Secretary as Blair's replacement, as and when Blair chooses to go.

Gordon Brown and Robin Cook hate each other for some obscure, distant reason, already lost in the Caledonian mists. Cook also hates Peter Mandelson, but then so does everyone else.

You may wonder where the Chancellor and the Prime Minister come into this. They deeply resent and mistrust each other, but like conjoined twins (they share a heart of stone), who know that one can survive only at the expense of the other's life. In this case, of course, there are no parents around to take the terrible decision, so it's going to be nasty. It already is.

Mr Blunkett, who yesterday introduced a White Paper on immigration, asylum and nationality, must have been delighted to be cheered and applauded by so many MPs. His speech was a huge success. Admittedly, his fans were nearly all Tory MPs, but when you live in a snake-pit, sometimes you have to make friends with the mongoose, an old Parsee proverb which I have just invented.

The Home Secretary came to the Despatch Box without his dog Lucy, but with a vast yellow Braille printout of his statement. You could tell he was sincere; he felt every word. There must be laws, he said, which would mean that new immigrants understood English and had a basic knowledge of our society.

'Hear, hear,' the Tories yelled.

'We will modernize the oath of allegiance, to make clear the fundamental rights and duties of citizenship,' he went on.

'That's very good!' a Tory shouted.

'Secure removal centres will enable us to protect the integrity of the system,' Mr Blunkett continued.

'Excellent!'

'Yah, yah'.

'That's bloody good, well done!'

The opposition was loving every moment. Labour MPs were eerily quiet.

The gist of Mr Blunkett's talk was that he had inherited a terrible mess and was finally doing something about it. Normally you would expect him to have blamed eighteen years of Tory misrule for this situation, but not yesterday. It was left hanging in the air, but we were clearly meant to allow the word 'Straw' to crawl into our consciousness.

Oliver Letwin, the Tory spokesman, seems to agree with Mr Blunkett on almost everything, though he may think that the Home Secretary is even more perfect than the Home Secretary does himself. He has only tiny, tiny little criticisms. He reminds me slightly of those old-fashioned motoring correspondents who would praise a new car wildly, then in a desperate attempt to find something bad to say would add, 'If there is one thing wrong with this magnificent British car, the ashtray is slightly too small.'

Mr Letwin congratulated the Home Secretary on 'tackling the causes of the shambles that he gallantly admitted he had inherited from his predecessor'.

Mr Blunkett, who had admitted no such thing but merely implied it, feebly tried to blame the Tories. But you could tell his heart wasn't in it.

'You will have the backing of the whole House in bringing order to your predecessor's chaos!' Mr Letwin merrily continued.

Dennis Skinner looked ill. He called Mr Letwin 'the Home Secretary's puppet', which provided us with a new daisy chain: Straw v. Blunkett v. Skinner v. Letwin. These are cross-party floral tributes, which garland the whole House.

08.02.02

I went to the Guildhall Art Gallery in the City of London to watch Lady Thatcher unveil a statue of: Lady Thatcher. Iron Lady meets Woman of Marble! The effigy is made of stone, it's around seven feet high, and it's so white and pristine you want to spray it with graffiti. It could not be more perfect for the time or the place.

The sculptor is Neil Simmons. Michelangelo said that he didn't create statues; all he did was chip away the surface stone to discover the image within. Imagine cutting away all those tons of rock and finding…Margaret Thatcher! What a terrifying surprise!

The Guildhall was full of those chaps wearing neck ruffs that resemble antimacassars in a very posh boarding house. The statue itself was covered in a black velvet shroud, so it looked rather like an Afghan woman just before the fall of the Taliban. She and Denis arrived. She was wearing a sort of purple housecoat, as if about to do the vacuuming with a gold-plated Dyson. She had her famous swept-back hair, as if it had just been tested in a wind-tunnel.

Tony Banks, the famously plebby Labour MP, chairman of the Commons art committee, introduced the statue to us. 'She is almost as famous, dare I say it, for her handbag, which we will see when it is unveiled.' There were dark mutterings of 'It's on the wrong arm.'

Mr Banks explained how there were rules that forbid the statue from appearing in the Commons Lobby just yet, since she is insufficiently dead. However, he said, these might be changed before too long. She might even make it while still alive, by 2004. At present there is nowhere to put the statue. But, as he didn't quite say, some day her plinth will come.

She was loving every moment. Adulation, and more of it! That's what makes her come outdoors, even when the moon isn't full.

And Mr Banks, desperate to find things to say that would meet the occasion without enraging what's left of the Labour Party, hadn't finished. 'When policies are forgotten, if I may say so, the fact that you were the first woman prime minister will not be forgotten.'

She looked puzzled. Forgotten? How could she be forgotten? Was he mad? Were we all mad?

Finally she got to whisk the shroud away. 'It's marvellous,' she said, 'but it's a little larger than I expected. Though as the first woman prime minister, I am a little larger than life!'

(Murmurs of approval came at this piece of literal self-aggrandizement.)

'I was fortunate to be there rather longer than some of my colleagues, and so that is the way to portray me!'

(I would have expected some quiet retching at this stage, but heard yet louder grunts of approval from the chaps in the antimacassars.)

'I'm very grateful to the sculptor for portraying me in a way that pleases me very much. Do remember! We had staunch Conservative principles!'

I looked up at the oeuvre. It had no eye sockets. I don't quite know why, but perhaps I could guess.

21.05.02

Later, a protestor hacked the statue's head off. A bronze statue of Lady Thatcher, complete with head, now stands in the Members' Lobby of the House of Commons.

*

One of the great themes of Tony Blair's premiership was reform of the House of Lords. However, not a lot happened. The number of hereditary peers was reduced to 100 or so. They were elected by, I suppose, their peers. A Lord Speaker was also elected to sit on the Woolsack and take over some duties of the Lord Chancellor. In the middle of this there was a futile attempt to appoint a group of people known as 'people's peers'. We had been led to believe that these would be ordinary members of the public who had something to contribute to the legislature. We were mistaken; they turned out to be the usual suspects from the great and the good. Lord Stevenson, who chaired the appointing commission, said their aim had been to select people who would be 'comfortable' in the House of Lords. MPs were furious.

Instead of being hairdressers, bus drivers and teachers, they turned out to be the sort of people who would have made it to ermine anyway. They were the people's panjandrums, and included Elspeth Howe, who became 'Lady' Howe on marrying Sir Geoffrey, a baronet, took the title in more elevated fashion when he became a peer, and now held it in her own right. In the words of Lionel Ritchie, she was 'once, twice, three times a lady'.

Then we heard from Andrew Mackinlay, a man who stands permanently on the brink of rage, like a football fan who has seen the ref award the other side a penalty after a dive. His body language resembles that of the All Blacks' *haka*, designed to intimidate smaller, spindlier rugby players. He stood up and waved his arms dramatically, as if the Angel of the North had come to life.

Sir Herman Ouseley, he said, was on the panel that had chosen the chairman (Lord Stevenson) of the other panel which appointed the people's peers, while at the same time being an applicant himself. 'And by an enormous coincidence he was one of. Three! Thousand! People who applied who became a people's peer!' His arms flapped, soared and swooped, like Batman spotting the Joker from the top of a skyscraper.

'The prime minister should be embarrassed by a wholly irregular, wholly untransparent, corrupt system. So don't come along here with this nonsense suggesting it is a good thing. It is rotten to the core. We must never repeat this rotten scenario again!'

Mr Mackinlay fell back onto his seat, his head crashing back and his feet soaring into the air as if he were on a playground swing.

Next, David Winnick asked about the plan to award a knighthood to Mick Jagger. He felt we should bypass this stage, and send him straight to the Lords, 'if only because of his outstanding performances, which are a great encouragement to those of us of a certain age'. He did not explain whether he meant outstanding performances on stage, or in bed, or both. Either way, Lord Jagger ('Hey, hey, you, you, get offa my woolsack') would get very excited by the signs that go up on the peers' TV monitor during their evening meal break: 'House adjourned during pleasure.' And I hope he doesn't feel that his office is in need of a touch-up: 'Paint it, Black Rod.'

12.06.02

Mr Jagger duly received his knighthood in 2002.

Defence presented, as always, a conundrum for Labour ministers.

Traditionally, defence ministers have been former officers themselves. No longer. Only a few of the present lot of Tories ever served in the forces, and even then they were often in the Territorials, like the present party chairman, David Davis, who served in the TA version of the SAS, so he could strangle the Queen's enemies with piano wire, but only at weekends. Now we have two Scottish defence ministers. Neither was in the military, but both served in the Scottish Labour Party, which offers more lethal hand-to-hand combat than anything in Kosovo or Afghanistan. Men who have served alongside each other in war sometimes say they have forged friendships that last for life. Those who fought with each other in the Scottish Labour Party make enmities that last for life.

It was one of these Scots who answered at defence questions yesterday. Fiona Mactaggart wanted a statement on equal opportunities. She meant that ethnic minorities should be fairly represented in the forces. Adam Ingram, the minister, said he wanted to build on equal opportunities and so create 'an organizational culture that values individuals from diverse backgrounds'.

This is a very worthy aim, to be sure, and it reflects the many changes in British military life over the centuries. 'Once more unto the breach, dear friends, once more, or fill the gap up with a diverse selection of individual stakeholders, within a framework of equal opportunity for personal development, acknowledging at all times the pursuit of best practice.' Or, as the Duke of Wellington might have put it if there had been a Labour government in 1815: 'I don't know what they do to the enemy but by God they strike me as an ethnically mixed group of men and women, reflecting the multicultural reality of the new Britain.'

Mr Ingram was obliged to admit soon afterwards that he had not attended the Trooping of the Colour. The Tories began a long, slow, grumbling rumble, which he cut off with perfect timing. 'I was in the Falkland Islands, representing Her Majesty's Government at Liberation Day.'

In other words, he had been away commemorating Lady Thatcher's finest hour. There was nothing the Tories could do except sit there, fuming. A Labour minister in their place! It was an outrage. They should have been there! Having triumphed so quickly and so completely, Mr Ingram moved on. 'We shall look at our armed forces in a holistic way,' he announced. Or as Churchill nearly said, 'Give us a matrix to structuralize an advanced holistic approach to human resource development, and we will finish the job!'

13.06.02

One of the features of Tony Blair's ten years was the growing influence of select committees, most of which shadow a particular government department. I say 'influence' rather than 'power', because they are largely ignored by the government itself, though they often have some impact on public opinion.

I arrived at the select committee on culture as the chairman, Gerald Kaufman, was chatting to someone nearby. The microphones were live, so I heard him say – presumably of a political trimmer – 'He steers not with a compass but a weather vane.'

How very unlike Gerry K himself, who prefers to steer with a flame-thrower. The committee is presently investigating gambling and the government's lunatic notion that it should be easier for people in this addictive nation to throw their money at sleazy mobsters rather than buy their children shoes and food. Not that I am anything other than open-minded. The roastees were to be senior officials from Camelot, the company that runs the National Lottery.

One of these officials turned out to be Sue Slipman, a name that evokes many memories. Ms Slipman steers with a compass all right, but her magnetic north seems to swivel occasionally through 180 degrees. She used to be a member of the Communist Party, then by some political miracle went directly to the Social Democrats. I vividly remember the speech she didn't quite make at the SDP conference: 'The Communist Party of today is not the Communist Party I joined – a decent party, a party of values, the party of Beria, Molotov and Stalin. It is not I who have left the Communist Party; the Communist Party has left me!' Her present job at Camelot is 'director for social responsibility'. This presumably does not involve standing in newsagents shouting at the customers, 'Don't waste your money on lottery tickets! Buy books for your home and shoes for your children! And in any case the odds at Ladbroke's are much better!'

She had a dark, severe haircut, and a pair of dark, severe glasses on the end of her nose, held on with a thin gold chain. She looked like a particularly fierce female don inspecting a student whose views on the later Wordsworth were unsound.

But nothing scares Gerry K, the terminator. He doesn't change, except his clothes, which become more exotic as he ages. Yesterday he was wearing a suit in a pewter shade, with a vivid garment new to me – the tie-dyed tie. He set his flame-thrower to 'lightly singed' and aimed it at the Camelot team.

Dianne Thompson, the chief executive of Camelot, was trying to explain why she had told her 'players' (their word for customers is never 'gamblers') that they didn't stand much chance of winning anything. Her slogan could be summed up as: 'It probably won't be you.' Had she not done a Ratner on her own business, letting the public know how poor their chances were?

No, she trilled. The important thing was helping good causes. Why, helping good causes was number 1 on the company's list of objectives, whereas getting money for shareholders was only at number 6. Gerry K produced his famous overbite. With eyes bulging, the overbite enquires, 'Why should I believe a single word you say?' He set the flame-thrower to 'crispy'. Camelot, he said, was in business for the profit, not through kindness. Next his fingers moved the dial to 'black and crinkly'. Was not Camelot fabulously well-protected? Her arguments were 'adventitious'. The company was not a charity, but in business to make as much money as it could, and the current law meant that no damage could ever come to it. Ms Thompson smiled bravely but wanly at the Kaufman overbite, hoping he wouldn't turn the switch to 'reduce to constituent molecules'. As I followed her and her team out of the room, I swear they were smoking lightly, but that might just have been a relieved cigarette.

26.06.02

Every month there are questions to ministers for whichever department is now nominally in charge of rural affairs. The secretary of state at the time was Margaret Beckett.

I always go to environment questions, and it always cheers me up. Thank goodness, I find myself thinking, that I live somewhere safe and quiet, like the city. The countryside seems to have changed for ever and for the worse. If Samuel Palmer were painting now, that lovely orange glow would be a pile of old tyres burning. The view of Constable's Flatford Mill would be blocked by abandoned cars. Only the pen of Thomas Hardy could do justice to the feast of misery and squalour presented to our countryfolk. My mind wandered, as it often does on this occasion, and I found myself in the midst of one of his less well-known works, *Tess of the Waste-Disposal Directives*. Every piece of jargon quoted comes from yesterday's Question Time or appeared on the order paper:

A traveller visiting the town of Melchester in the year of our Lord 18— would have observed the merry, bustling scene which denoted the weekly market day. He would have seen a small boy waving a jam jar at his mother. 'Look, Mama, at the tadpoles I have collected from the village pond!'

'Lor, bless the child,' said his mother, 'he knows not enough to call them by their correct name of "bethnic fauna".'

'The traveller's eye might next have lighted on a pillory, in which stood a woman, head locked into place, her hands hanging mournfully down, occasionally suffering the indignity of being struck by a ripe example from the horticultural sector benchmark study. Upon enquiry, he would have been informed that this was Scapegrace Beckett, denounced as a witch, and now subjected to the harsh rigours of the twenty-day standstill rule. And at the edge of the square he could have perceived Demelza MacIntosh, a tall, black-haired beauty, in conversation with the dour Flatfoot Morley, a lumpish youth who was, nonetheless, the most ardent of her many admirers in the town.

'Will you not go walk with me down the church pathway, Demelza?' he asked. 'There is something of which I must speak to you.'

'Flatfoot, I do declare that you will lose your head from your shoulders afore Michaelmas!' she exclaimed. 'Do you not know that the path has been closed as the result of an extinguishment order, permitting local authorities to abolish rights of way as a crime prevention measure?

'And, in any case, it has been blocked this sennight with abandoned fridges and TVs. Also, anyone foolish enough to stroll athwart Farmer Meacher's field would choke up his very lights by cause of it being in a nitrate-vulnerable zone.'

Our traveller, requiring relief after drinking some flagons of ale, asked a passing native for an EU 'wee' directive, but instead of being shown to the town jakes, found himself handed a 2,000-page document in a tongue distantly related to English, but incomprehensible to all. 'Why,' chuckled his guide, after the misunderstanding had been ended, '"wee" stands for "waste electrical equipment", a term incorporating used fridges, microwave ovens and even "electronic greetings cards..."'

At this I was roused from my reverie. Robin Cook, the leader of the Commons, was now outlining next week's business and – this is entirely true – as he spoke a group of two dozen Zulu warriors was filing into the public gallery, their leader naked apart from a loincloth and a headdress. How often life proves to be so much stranger than our dreams!

28.06.02

Now and again the most senior civil servants descend from their Olympian heights to address the mere mortals who constitute the House of Commons, in this case members of the public administration committee. It produced a fascinating insight into the Blairite way of doing things.

I have seen the future, and it smirks. Lincoln Steffens, the American hack who coined the original phrase, did so before he even visited the Soviet Union. I at least went to see Sir Andrew Turnbull before Steffens's phrase sprang to mind. In September he will become Cabinet secretary and head of the civil service, making him our most senior civil servant and a person of quite astonishing power. He will make Sir Humphrey seem like a helpless naïf, stumbling blindly through the corridors of power.

Sir Andrew is a large man, with a large jaw. He wears the rimless spectacles popular among men of power, such as Tony Blair and Sven-Göran Eriksson. His haircut teeters on the brink of being a bog-brush.

And he has a smirk. A great big, jaw-circumnavigating smirk. It's a smirk that says, 'I am in control. I know what I am doing, and what I am saying. I understand everything far better than you do.' Take the document that Sir Andrew sent to the committee and which contains his ambitions for the future. He wants to 'lead and support the reform and delivery programme', a task which he will carry out by, among other methods, 'shared endeavour with ministers', coupled with 'regular stocktake meetings' and 'flexible delivery structures'. There will be people placed in charge of 'consequence management matters', 'cross-cutting issues' and 'single integrated structure units'.

New Labour documents are filled with capital letters, such as this section on 'the e-Government agenda'. 'I want to focus the Office of the e-Envoy (OeE) on work on e-Government. Andrew Pinder will retain his role as e-Envoy…giving greater drive to e-service delivery, focusing government around the customer and Knowledge Management in government.'

Acronyms are sprinkled through the paper like lead shot in a pheasant stew. There are the PIU, the PSAs, the PSX process, the OPSR, the DCP and the OGC. This man has the patter, and in modern government the patter matters.

There was a fine moment when the chairman, the admirable Tony Wright, who speaks entirely in our mother tongue, pointed out that Clement Attlee had brought about a revolution. 'But he didn't have delivery units. He wasn't examining the structure of government every five minutes. Harold Macmillan built half a million houses a year with no delivery units in sight. Why don't you just get on and do things?'

Sir Andrew smirked his mighty smirk. Get on and do things? What kind of talk was that? Didn't these people understand government? Gordon Prentice, a first-rate stirrer, wondered whether Cabinet meetings had become a complete waste of time. Didn't ministers sometimes need to get together and chew the fat?

Sir Andrew said, with some distaste, that they had plenty of opportunities to chew the fat. 'They go off on away-days, and they can *chew the fat* there.'

A vision swam into my head. 'I say, Tony, this meat isn't very lean. It's full of gristle.'

'You'll just have to chew it anyway. There are Cabinet ministers starving in India.'

05.07.02

One of my favourite MPs is Michael Fabricant, who sits in the Conservative interest for South Staffordshire. One time in the summer of 2002 I noticed that he had arrived in the Chamber and promptly grabbed at his own crotch, working at it as if he were making bread. He then received a bleeper message, possibly from the whips, telling him to keep his hands to himself, or at least off himself.

An apology. I have received a courteous letter from Michael Fabricant pointing out that last Saturday he had been climbing in the Lake District, where he suffered a minor groin strain, similar to that suffered by the footballer Michael Owen. 'He was given constant groin massage between matches. Sadly, this facility is not available in the House,' he writes, which is presumably why he has to do the physio's work on himself. Loins led by donkeys, as the German Max Hoffman almost said.

Next we learned that the parents of babies born in nine months' time would pick up an extra £1,300 in maternity pay and the fathers would qualify for two weeks' paternity leave. As the minister for women, Patricia Hewitt, told the Commons with an unfamiliar twinkle in her eye, 'Tomorrow night is the key date for parents who want to take advantage of the new provisions.'

This was the first time I had heard any minister, still less Ms Hewitt, tell the nation to start shagging. Though knowing how nannyish they are, and how Ms Hewitt talks to everyone as if they were members of a remedial class, I'm sure she'd want to be there to make sure they got it right.

'Now I know you're terribly excited, and looking forward to having a super time, but that's no excuse for dropping your clothes on the floor and not folding them neatly. Let the chandelier down very carefully – we don't want any accidents – and take the masala paste in your right hand, just so. Now, can anyone tell me what a clitoris is?'

Ms Hewitt is also industry minister, and she was given a hard time over the Royal Mail, or Consignia, or *PostIt!* or whatever it's called this week. John Whittingdale for the Tories complained that ministers were always devising wheezes which never came to anything. 'All we have had is words. When is the government going to start delivering?'

Aha, the answer to the Royal Mail's problems. Get ministers to start delivering! What a surprise when there's a tap on your door and there is Patricia Hewitt. 'Now this Boden catalogue is much too expensive for your income bracket,' she would tell you. 'And one of the famous plain envelopes. A dirty video, I expect. Look, a postcard from your mother in Polperro. When did you last write to her, I wonder? Has your son finished his thank-you letters yet? I thought not...'

Michael Fabricant complained that there wasn't enough penetration of broadband. 'I'm not talking about lowband, I'm talking about middle- and high-band broadband! The UK is right at the very bottom!' This may have had something to do with his groin strain and the consequent auto-massage.

Phil Hammond joined in. 'Local loop unbundling was to be a significant factor in broadband rollout,' he said. 'But the number of local loops that have been unbundled have been only in the hundreds. Local loop unbundling has failed!'

Once again I found myself in a distant bucolic past. 'Us gets our local loopy fellow, our village idiot, sorr, and us unbundles him, and us throws him in the mill race, sorr, so we do.' Or maybe local unbundling refers to the stern duty Ms Hewitt has enjoined on all of us when we go to bed tonight.

12.07.02

It was in July 2002 that Gordon Brown unleashed public spending.

One of the great misers of British political history broke free from his past yesterday. Perhaps, like Scrooge, Gordon Brown had seen a vision of his own future, hunched over his piggy bank, counting his bawbees, a sad, drawn face reflecting the thin winter sunlight which filters through the windows of the old, empty manse.

Now he was transformed. 'Prudence' got a single lonely mention at the beginning of his speech, like a devout Catholic reciting a Hail Mary before going off to an orgy. Suddenly the Chancellor became a manic Santa, dashing frantically from rooftop to pediment and onto gable end, hurling presents down chimneys, into porches, flinging them through windows, lashing his reindeer to new, more ferocious efforts. Dasher and Dancer, Donner and Blitzen – all we lacked was Lord Irvine as the red-nosed reindeer. Cheering soldiers heard news of the extra £3.5 billion for defence. The sleigh raced on to Bush House, where BBC workers were ready with huzzas for the extra £38 million they're going to get. Aid workers, scientists, farmers and the people who build flood defences were almost knocked unconscious when a bag containing £2.9 billion smashed directly at them.

No one was safe from the Chancellor's bounty. Regional development agencies got an extra £400 million a year, 'as local people make more of the decisions about meeting local needs', which I translate as: 'Unelected local bureaucrats generate heaps of jargon and action plans that will achieve nothing at all.'

So many roofs, so little time!

On he raced. There was 12 per cent more for transport, plus an additional £38 million for 'sustainable energy initiatives'. What an amazing bargain – less than two quid a household to save the planet!

Michael Howard, the shadow chancellor, made an effective and scornful speech in reply. It enraged Father Christmas. As Mr Howard spoke, he scrawled frantically on a piece of paper, in huge letters, underscored, circles, scribbling with rage as if his pen were a machete. When he rose to reply, he waved page after page of this stuff, which had come to look like the letters we journalists often receive from people who have failed to take their medication. He flapped it furiously at Mr Howard, then at the Speaker. Iain Duncan Smith, the Tory leader, tried and failed to calm him down by repeatedly holding up his hand, palm outward. If this had been the Greek parliament, it could have led to a brawl, since in that country the gesture means: 'Your mother was no better than she ought to be.'

16.07.02

The sketch-writers always loved John Prescott, Deputy Prime Minister for the whole Blair government. His extraordinary tussles with the English language – he could fight it for hours without either winning – were a gift to all of us. He was deeply resentful, and blamed it on the fact that we were all public school snobs, though I myself was educated at the public's expense in Mr Prescott's own city of Hull.

Facing the Deputy Prime Minister was Eric Pickles, a Tory. He is not an inconsiderable character. Like Mr Prescott, he is a northern grandee. He is a large man and aptly shaped like a great big gherkin. In an earlier age, before adverts became so smart-alecky that you can't work out what they're for, he would have worn a green gherkin costume and marched round Giggleswick with a placard reading: 'Pipe up for Pickles' Pickles, the pickles picky people pick.'

On this occasion he had, perhaps, over-prepared. Mr Prescott had said that he would intervene with local authorities and indeed with anyone who did not meet his own exacting standards. Mr Pickles felt this was a form of centralism.

'The Deputy Prime Minister is a deeply sentimental man, much given to romantic gestures,' he began. 'We rapidly approach the fiftieth anniversary of the death of Josef Stalin, and just as the generalissimo felt frustration with the figures about tractor production in the Urals…' And so he went on, far too long.

But then Mr Prescott replied at too great length. He doesn't so much talk as download. It is as if he is trying to send an email to a Third World country with bad phone lines. There are strange jerks, bleeps and inexplicable breaks in the transmission.

'I would like to engage in an issue of long term,' he said. 'Also on behalf of looking at the education,' followed by, 'and when I look at the urban cities.'

'I am very keen on the built environment,' he added, which is true, since he has access to so much of it: his flat in Admiralty Arch, the big rent-controlled union flat in South London, the Dorney Wood mansion, and of course his own castellated home in Hull.

As always with Mr Prescott you can work out what he is saying between the squawks and the elisions. Or almost always. Here he is on the topic of affordable housing which turns out to be worth more than the buyers pay for it: 'On the other hand, when I look at the urban cities and I look at how we use our money, there are issues where the need to buy issues, quite frankly, and it's bought at a price and a very discounted price, which we all agreed to be doing, but then it's sold at a very high price back to the state when they want to do something about improvements, well, that's costing us literally millions of pounds.'

Or try picking the bones out of this: 'I think that we are prepared to tolerate that, because it's not a policy different only, it's all those peoples [sic] who haven't got homes, the doctors and nurses, the people who are in [sic] homeless, they're the ones who've been carrying the pain for that.'

19.07.02

2002–2003

Politicians take August off, then in mid-September the party conferences begin. The Liberal Democrats start, as if the anti-climax had been shifted to the beginning of the season.

Someone from the chair announced, 'The first vote will be on amendment number 1, which you will find at the bottom of page 34 of your agenda document. The second vote will be on lines 84 and 85, and the next vote will be on amendment 2, which is, in effect, to insert the word "future" in line 86, then we will have a vote on the whole of lines 86–88, however that may have been amended, after which we are going to have a vote on amendment 3, and finally…' – here there was a reversion to plain English – '…we are going to vote on whether to throw the whole lot out.'

Miraculously, everyone there understands every word! Yesterday we had a vote. 'Your vote will not be counted unless you are sitting down!' the chairwoman told them. 'Sit down and be counted!' – the Lib Dems' new battle-cry. Solemn men and women took the precious figures to a counting table, like votaries bringing sacrifices to the altar of some ancient, pagan church. And there is a hushed, religious air throughout. As the vote proceeds nobody speaks, as you would not during the gaps in a royal wedding.

In the debate on 'freedom' one man seemed to be arguing that we shouldn't go to war in Iraq because it would delay our entry into the euro. Another man, sitting behind me, uttered a noise you rarely hear – a whispered 'Hear, hear'. 'That is why public service issues are freedom issues!' said another man, and the very faintest applause could be detected, the sound of one hand clapping.

'Why did you want to enter politics in the first place?' he asked, his words falling into the limpid stillness, like a leaf descending on a pond in a deep forest. 'I want you to revisit your ideas!' he added, and I had a vision of Lib Dems revisiting their ideas, like elderly relatives in a nursing home.

In the Gents someone had put up a sticker. 'I hate chain store skate shops,' it read. I reflected that that is the special charm of the Liberal Democrats – they can fret simultaneously about the great issues, such as freedom and the environment, and about lesser matters, such as retail outlets for leisure equipment.

24.09.02

I like to collect Liberal Democrat moments at these conferences, such as the chairman saying, 'First of all, we shall take the second vote!' And the chap who shouted despairingly, 'Whatever we do, the press will still say, "Lib Dems call for hypothecation"!' Yeah, right, I thought, next to 'Bombs rain on Baghdad' and 'David Beckham's toenail – latest'.

*

By this time the invasion of Iraq was looming. At a special session, Tony Blair spoke to the House of Commons.

You don't realize at first that he is doing his Winston Churchill because the voice is light and skittery; sometimes he throws whole lines away, and says dorky things like, 'That'd be really, really serious,' which you can't imagine Churchill ever getting his throat round. But for the most part the language is straight out of the *Bumper Boy's Book of Wartime Speeches*. All he needs is a cigar, a watch chain and a homburg.

Try reading this, not in Tony Blair's normal voice, but in a low, aggressive growl: 'If people say, why should Britain care? I answer: because there is no way that this man, in this region above all regions, could begin a conflict using such weapons, and that conflict not engulf the whole world!'

Or this: 'At any time he could have invited the inspectors in, and put the world to proof.' Put the world to proof! What on earth does that mean? It doesn't matter. When you are Winston Churchill you can make up the language as you go along.

If we didn't like his famous dossier, that didn't matter either. Our intelligence people might not have got it right, but – who do you believe? Them or the Iraqis? This missed the point – the fact that we don't trust Saddam doesn't mean that the dossier was right, but it skates neatly round the point. He was skating masterfully now: double axels and dazzling twirls.

Then he shivered our goose pimples and made our teeth chatter: 'The biological agents we believe Iraq can produce include anthrax, botulinum, toxin, aflatoxin and ricin. All eventually result in an excruciatingly painful death,' he said with something approaching relish. By that time we realized that the excruciatingly painful political death he might have faced has, for the moment at least, been postponed.

He ended: 'This House, as it has in our history so many times before, will not shrink from doing what is necessary or right,' and you could almost hear the squeaks, the popping, the grunts of the old man in his heyday, or at least how he might have put it if those great wartime broadcasts had been in Blairspeak: 'Hey, you know, never before in the field of human conflict have we owed you guys such a lot, and, well, we're really, really, grateful, you know. Right?'

25.09.02

The party conference season resumed. Labour always holds theirs after the Liberal Democrats. In 2002, at Blackpool, the party experimented with subtitles for the hard of hearing. The words were flashed up on the screen mere seconds after they had been spoken.

There are only occasional mistakes. 'Seductive' appeared as 'Se Duck Div'. We learned that Nato plays its part in 'der twending Britain'. But these were small glitches. On the whole the apparatus worked well, right up to the point that the junior minister Ian McCartney stood up. Mr McCartney is a short, round man, who looks as if, were you to flick him over, he would roll right back up again. He has a Glaswegian accent so thick you feel it could be cut into slices and served with bacon for breakfast.

At first he was merely alarming. 'The devolution train is leaving the station, and thank goodness, it's John Prescott driving it.' Then he began to speak faster and faster and the words on the screen grew more and more haphazard. The word '{inaudible}' began to appear in curly brackets. 'Would you like to pe my jockey?' he enquired. 'That joke became jalt government!' He went on: 'We are tamule a party of government!' At one point, the screen read: 'Msssss' as if the stenographer's head had slumped onto the keyboard. 'A policy of Nssssge!' and a system known to us all as 'Mockr twockr democracy!'

'Iain Duncan Smith has been snupt!' he said, to cheers and applause, and we reflected that if John Major had been snupt a few years back, it might have saved his party a lot of trouble.

Next day the on-screen transliterations had gone, which must have been quite a relief to John Prescott. 'I was going to have my own subtitles so you weren't couldn't not [sic] understand what I was saying. But now they've given up and gone home.' Sitting wrapped in blankets, with a mug of hot milk and a bottle of Prozac, no doubt.

Then he got angry. Golly, he was cross. Apoplectic is what John Prescott does. Until 1997 he used to be furious about the iniquities of the Tories. Now he appears to be enraged by the successes of the Labour government, which, for some reason, drive him into the same uncontrolled frenzy.

'Conference!' he yelled. 'We've worked hard! We've earned the people's trust in two elections!' – a point he illustrated by holding up six fingers. 'This is the longest serving Labour government in history!' he barked, as if the thought cried to the heavens for vengeance.

It soon became clear why he was in such a froth. He had been given the job of defending the private finance initiative, which is deeply unpopular with Labour's rank and file. So he made himself enraged about all the pensioners who are not now waiting for operations thanks to Labour's embrace of the private sector. 'Do you really want a freeze on that? Is that what this party wants? All the children sitting in their leaky classrooms!'

It was a superb sleight of voice. As the conference pondered, not a dodgy investment deal, but their own piteous offspring trying to study as a cascade of freezing water soaked their tiny bodies, he stalked back to his seat like a volcano suffering from eruptus interruptus.

If Mr Prescott was cross, Gordon Brown was beside himself with barely containable fury. His face was black as he almost promised 'a world free from poverty, and a world free from fear!' But he was just stoking his own internal boiler. Next he moved on to the government's multitudinous achievements. They did not improve his mood. 'A new long-term policy for stability and prudence!' he raved. 'High and stable levels of growth and employment!' His hand made a claw shape and crashed onto the podium. He looked like a caveman eviscerating a dead mammoth before the sabre-toothed tigers arrived to steal it.

'Unemployment is lower in this country than it is in America!' he yelled. 'This is a country of low debt and low unemployment!' He seemed to be choking with rage, his hand thrashing wildly at the air, adding its fury to the horror of what he had just told us.

I suppose the reason for all this anger is that these people created their rhetorical style during eighteen years of Tory government and they haven't yet adapted. They'd do the same at a friend's wedding. 'We wish the bride and groom every possible happiness!' they would scream, before the fist crashes down and breaks half a dozen champagne glasses and the little model couple on top of the cake.

1.10.02

Weirdly, the Labour leader's speech always comes on the Tuesday afternoon, making the rest of the conference something of a let-down. This dates back a century, to the days when the speech was entitled The Parliamentary Report, and MPs were only a very minor part of the movement. Much as they are today. It is one of Labour's few time-encrusted traditions that Tony Blair never sought to change, possibly because it enabled him to do what he pleased for the rest of the week.

As ever, Tony Blair appeared as several people. For a large part of his speech he appeared as a mystic, squatting in only a loincloth, a bowl of rice in his hands, the Bentley hidden in a garage round the back. 'Caution is retreat, and retreat is dangerous,' he informed us in that light, high-pitched voice, faintly reminiscent of the Maharishi. 'Influence is power is prosperity,' he said, and we all wished we'd thought of that.

At times he seemed to be in a colloquy with inaudible disciples. His replies, however, were in the speech. 'What is the antidote to unilateralism, oh master?' they must have asked, and he replied, 'Partnership is the answer to unilateralism.'

'Is that all there is to partnership?' they presumably enquired. Apparently not. 'Partnership is statesmanship for the twenty-first century,' he replied. The disciples must privately wonder what on earth he is on about, though they also know that the path to wisdom is a steep and rocky one.

'Teach us, oh master, what comes from hope!'

'From hope comes change, my children!' (I regret to say that I made the last two words up.)

'Enlighten us, oh caretaker in the mansion of truth, with what must we not drench progress?'

'We must not drench progress with cynicism!' he replies.

'Oh guru, to whom all is known, what is happening?'

'From progress here to life and death, change abroad, it is happening.'

The followers have a spot of bother with that one, but they plough ahead. 'Tell us, what is the time?'

'About 3.25. Sorry, scrub that, NOW is the time. So if you'd like to leave your contributions to promote the spread of wisdom to all peoples of the world in the bucket provided, I'll get on. I've got a boy band wants to know the meaning of life at half-past.'

Then, suddenly the loincloth disappears and is replaced by a tweed jacket. He has become the retired major in the lounge bar. He complained about police officers being hamstrung by civil liberties legislation. 'It's not civil liberties, it's lunacy!'

'You know the problem isn't just crime. Yes, another gin and tonic if you would be so kind, no I'll tell you what the problem is – it's disrespect!'

At this point – the only bit I made up was about the g&t – the audience cheered wildly. Then, just as suddenly, the yogi was back with us. He talked about how Christopher Reeve, the actor, might be able to walk again because of British scientific research, helped by £2 billion of funding. 'I made that choice for Britain,' he said. Tony Blair – not only walking on water, but making Superman fly again.

Next we were whisked off to Mozambique where, he said, a doctor in an AIDS hospital had told him, 'Thanks to you, the docks in Maputo are being rebuilt!' So, when they are out canvassing, and grow tired of knocking on doors, they should remember that doctor and feel proud of what they did.

Labour's next battle-cry: 'Rebuild Maputo docks!' We could picture the scene. 'Excuse me, I'm canvassing on behalf of the Labour Party. Can we count on your support?'

'Your lot have done nowt for me, nowt!'

'Yes, but sir, the docks at Maputo are undergoing a rolling programme of containerization. Think on't!'

The end approached, and the guru was back with us.

'When are we at our best, oh swami who is all-wise?'

'At our best when we are boldest!' he concluded, before nipping off to welcome Bill Clinton.

02.10.02

…Who had just arrived in Blackpool with the film star Kevin Spacey. He ate at one of the many parties which take place every night of the conference, then, deciding he was still hungry, took steps to fortify himself at a branch of McDonald's on the front.

Bill Clinton took to the stage the next day, to deliver a speech in favour of Tony Blair's government.

The former president was brilliant, dazzling, charismatic, seductive and completely shameless. The Labour Party loved nearly all of it. I bumped into a minister straight after the speech. 'I've just been for a fag,' he said, 'I always like a smoke when I've been made love to.'

And that is how it felt. He wooed them all the time. He didn't stop. He cast his eyes down coyly. Then he raised his head, smiled, and looked slowly round the audience, gazing deep into their eyes. He is the Princess Di of the political world. It was thrilling.

They adored him when he warned about an unelected despot with access to weapons of mass destruction, who was dragging his own country to the brink of ruin, and was now threatening the whole world. He also had harsh words for Saddam Hussein. But there was no doubt that the real enemy, the man in his cross-hairs, was George W. Bush.

Thank God, there was still one man who could save the planet! Yes, it was the superman on his right, Tony Blair! 'As an American, and as a citizen of the world, I am glad Tony Blair will be central to weighing the risks, and making that call,' he said, somehow implying that our Prime Minister alone could halt that demented freak now occupying the White House. Sadly, most Labour delegates do not share his admiration for their leader. But no matter.

They decided to forgive him anyway, right up to the point, during the standing ovation, he gave Peter Mandelson a hug – a big, full-on, force the breath out of your body and send your lunch flying, whopping great bear hug. You could hear his credibility draining away.

He had been introduced by Tony Blair, who got a foot-stomping standing ovation, far louder than the one he had received the previous day. But this time he was telling them something they wanted to hear: that Bill Clinton was on next.

'Conference, Clinton, Bill. Arkansas CLP,' Bill said. It was the perfect little in-joke, offering grace combined with the delegates' own self-obsession. Then he started the speech, low and husky, intimate and caressing. The little, secret smiles darted around the audience, as if directed only at you – yes, you, the lady on the fifth row!

There were several shameless passages in the speech, including one in which he praised the McDonald's where he had eaten the previous night. This sounded absurd, unless you recognize that, by Blackpool standards, McDonald's offers Michelin-starred gourmet dining. He also told us that he loved this country, which had given him the best two years of his life. Really? How would he have felt about us if he had inhaled? He loved the Third Way. They managed to love him for loving it, even though they themselves can't stand it. He flattered them. He flattered Tony Blair. He flattered them for loving Tony Blair, and they didn't even care that they don't. He ended to great gusts and gales of applause, and cheering, and general all-encompassing ecstasy. If I were working for a tabloid newspaper, I would write: 'He was a love machine! He scored 10 out of 10 in the sack!

03.10.02

One of the more popular characters in British politics is Ann Widdecombe, the Tory MP for Maidstone and a former Home Office minister. Through the miracle of television – and her own obvious honesty – she has moved from being the scary 'Doris Karloff' figure to being everyone's favourite maiden aunt. She is also a novelist.

'Strike a blow for the clean novel! Buy my clean novel!' Ann Widdecombe was doing a signing session at the Tory conference for her new, clean novel. 'Two hundred copies!' she whispered at me as I walked past, before resuming her cry, possibly reminiscent of an eighteenth-century herring seller.

I said I thought I might have to write some filthy bits in, just to perk it up. But that did not prove necessary. By the afternoon she had been joined by my colleague Matthew Parris, whose newly published autobiography includes accounts of cruising and gay sex. I suggested he should start shouting, 'Strike a blow for filthy memoirs!' He declined. But nothing was going to stop her, even if delegates walked past the book stall with bleeding ears.

I trailed Ms Widdecombe to a fringe meeting, which is where she has been banished now that she is no longer a member of the shadow cabinet. How can the present-day Tories, a bunch of lacklustre nonentities, get by without her? I have in the past compared her to Britney Spears, in that she is more a role model to her own sex than an object of lust to the other, while both make much of their chastity and have terrific stage acts. The main difference is that at a Britney Spears concert it is the audience that is doing the screaming. Now Ann Widdecombe has lost several stone in weight and has gone blonde, the comparison seems less fanciful.

She got up to speak and began to pop. Pop! she went, as she inhaled great lungfuls of air. Pop! she went, as she pondered Labour's views on criminal justice. All this popping conceals the fact that her views are essentially liberal and reformist. The poor suffer most from crime, she says, and prisoners should be given useful work to prepare them for life outside.

A barrister stood up and called for the return of capital punishment. 'We should hang people in a caring way,' he said, adding that the party could demonstrate its inclusivity by hanging members of ethnic minorities too – 'provided they are guilty,' he added as an afterthought.

09.10.02

The Tory conference united against the real enemy yesterday. It turned out to be the BBC. In a wonderful, demented moment, the conference rose to its feet stamping, cheering and applauding a woman who had ferociously attacked the Corporation. Forget Labour, the Lib Dems and Saddam Hussein – it was dear old Auntie they wanted to see destroyed.

At one point I feared they might rise and march on the glass-fronted BBC cubicle, smashing the equipment, hanging the crew from their own microphone leads, disemboweling the interviewers and waving aloft their still beating hearts. But at the very moment the woman was in mid-rant, and the audience was being whipped into a lather of rage and hatred, the lights inside the cubicle went on, revealing those two famous – and startled – old lefties, Ann Widdecombe and Andrew Neil.

It had all been so dull up till then. There was no mention of capital punishment. Camila Batmanghelidjh talked about rehabilitating vulnerable young people instead of thrashing them to within an inch of their lives, and was warmly applauded. A delegate warned that there were 'no quick and easy answers', a view which would have been booed off the stage a few years ago. Of course there were quick and easy answers. They were known as hanging and flogging.

One woman was even allowed to talk about young miscreants 'with huge self-esteem problems', without anyone suggesting that there was nothing wrong with their self-esteem that a few days in the stocks wouldn't cure. Though it must be said that the same woman lost them when she said that young tearaways should be taken on dog-sledding trips to the Arctic, without adding that they should be left there as snacks for hungry polar bears.

Then Lydia Rivlin arrived at the rostrum. Quivering in red, pulsating with a sort of satisfied fury, she announced that it was little wonder youths were badly behaved when you saw their television programmes. She had seen one Saturday morning show on the BBC in which, if contestants failed in a game, they had to watch a cherished possession taken to bits by a circular saw. 'It's a great image, isn't it, a child's teddy hacked by a circular saw!'

The conference sighed happily. This was the stuff, not all this nonsense about rehabilitation that they were expected to clap these days. And what better object of their hatred than the body called by Denis Thatcher 'the Bolshevik Broadcasting Corporation'. Or the Blair Broadcasting Corporation, as some of them call it.

'Look at that box,' shouted Ms Rivlin, pointing at the cubicle. 'How much reasoned debate will there be in twenty years' time? It'll just be some bloke with a circular saw.'

Ms Rivlin received much the most enthusiastic standing ovation of the week, far more excited than the one offered later to Oliver Letwin, the shadow home secretary, who was perhaps a little too thoughtful for their tastes, and whose speech ran in the second half of the *Six O'clock News*, way down the bulletin, proving once again the BBC's ineradicable left-wing bias.

10.10.02

In the autumn of 2002, firefighters threatened a national strike. John Prescott was the minister in charge of the negotiations.

Heaven knows what will happen if the people who staff Hansard, the official parliamentary report, ever go on strike. Day after day, with no thought for themselves, these brave men and women go into action, grabbing the words of politicians, cutting them out of the wreckage, rescuing whole speeches in danger of collapse.

Yesterday they were faced by a four-alarm statement by John Prescott about the firefighters' strike. We can imagine the scene in the Hansard office. 'This is it, lads, the big one,' says the station commander (or 'editor' as he is known in their professional slang). Card games are abruptly halted, phone calls ended, cups of tea pushed aside. They scramble for pens, notebooks and stenography machines. MPs, ministers, civil servants and clerks squeeze themselves to the walls as the crack team hurtles down to the gallery, ready to do their duty unquestioningly, without any thought of their own safety.

As they arrive, the situation is becoming desperate. The Prescott has caught hold. It is already smouldering, the temperature is rising, and very soon structural damage will threaten the perilous stability of the whole speech.

'Can I say to him that his last statement about the circumstances of events is totally untrue and he wasn't even in the

102

country at the time, so let me deal with that point to begin with, as to the statement of the wage, most public authority negotiations have all been at least twice the level of inflation, that's the gain they had under this government, and not under the previous administration, so it would be most unusual for me to be opposing it with regard to the Fire Brigade Union, if I was actively involved in it...'

It was already too late to have the chamber evacuated. MPs were going to have to find breathing apparatus, or run from the Chamber with wet handkerchiefs over their mouths.

'It is true that we have been asked for, but the circumstances are such that we put it back to the employers that it's your judgement to make about the age negotiations that were going on at the same time and were in a different situation.'

Sinister cracking noises could be heard. A fountain of sparks erupted from the roof as one of the speech's central beams crashed to the ground. Now and again there was a roar as air rushed in to fuel the conflagration. The Fire Brigades' Union became the FBU, then the FBO, and on one memorable occasion the FBI. Their general secretary, Mr Andy Gilchrist, alarmingly turned into 'Andy Christ'.

'I made it very clear to him, to be fair to him, he accepted that I hadn't interfered with those negotiations, and has gone on record since to make that precise point, and now he makes a different point at this present in time!'

At this present in time! The Hansard team exchange grim glances. They know what needs to be done. It has to be put into English, and only they can do it.

But there is worse to come. As smoke billows from the statement, they hear the sounds that tell a trained ear that the blaze is out of control. 'We believe an independent body should make consideration of that,' he says. 'Let me say quite clear', 'the safety of the citizens are served' and 'denied them in the name that it wasn't a fire service'.

The government has pledged that if the Hansard writers ever do go on strike, they will be replaced by soldiers equipped with crayons, many of them up to fifty years old.

23.10.02

Later that month the education secretary, Estelle Morris, resigned, saying that she felt she was not up to the job. It was thought to have been a unique moment in British political life – a minister actually saying they could not fill the post because they were not competent. If everyone took that attitude, we probably wouldn't have a government at all.

Estelle Morris had resigned on Wednesday evening. At 11.25 yesterday, Thursday, it was announced that she was being replaced by Charles Clarke. At 11.30 he was in place for the monthly session of education questions. This is the British system: one can be a total ignoramus on a topic, then five minutes later be transformed, by the magic of prime ministerial patronage, into a wise and all-seeing polymath.

Not that Mr Clarke chanced his luck. He spent the entire fifty-minute period in silence, making the odd note, for the most part merely glowering. He was well advised to keep schtum, because it turned out that he was replacing the greatest figure in British public life since Churchill died and Florence Nightingale hung up her lamp. The Chamber, or at least the Labour side of it, looked stunned. If a block of frozen urine had fallen from an airplane toilet and killed Tony Blair himself they could not have been more stricken.

First up was the junior minister, David Miliband, who provided an extract from the *Lives of the Saints*. He talked about 'the deep shock and sadness felt through the whole education world'. In the new Elysium ushered in through her stewardship, 'pupils are taught better, by better-paid, better-trained teachers and better-supported teachers. But she did more. She acted at all times with complete integrity and total dedication.'

What had been her goal? Had it been to make herself rich and impose her jackboot on the necks of the nation's children? Indeed it had not. 'Her one goal was not her own advancement, but the advancement and achievement of her pupils.'

How would those working in the field of education react to her departure? With indifference, or even vindictive pleasure? Certainly not. 'Anyone who has any interest in education will deeply regret her departure. And the world of politics is a lesser place with her absence from the top table.'

Drained, he sat down. But this was only the first of many encomia. Thanet's Stephen Ladyman was close to tears. Would Mr Miliband please pass on his love and his best best wishes to, to – here he managed to hold back a great racking sob – to her?

Love? I wondered what Macmillan or Attlee would have had to say if members had used the Chamber to pass on 'love' to their fellow MPs. What next? Mwah! mwah! air kisses to the culture secretary? A pile of bouquets at the despatch box, where the beloved Estelle fell, leaving a void in the nation's hearts that can never be filled?

So shattered and appalled were Labour MPs that some of them completely forgot to pass on a grovelling welcome and congratulations to Ms Morris's successor, who sat throughout glaring in silence, but no doubt taking names.

25.10.06

After the 2001 election, Robin Cook was demoted from Foreign Secretary to Leader of the House of Commons. But, as ever, he hurled himself into his new job.

Robin Cook launched his plan for a reformed and modernized House yesterday. Mr Cook had a lot to say, but not much time in which to say it. He solved the problem as he always does: by swallowing the words and eliding the consonants.

He spoke of the need for 'scroony of gummt bills'. To improve these bills, they should undergo something called 'pre-legs scroony', which sounds like a Chicago gangster, but may well mean pre-legislative scrutiny. Tories became the 'fissial oppo'. Rather than wasting time by asking, 'May I say to my honourable friend?' he enquired: 'Mess ate mon fren?' Most disconcertingly of all, he kept talking about 'karaoke'. We in the House of Commons, he said, could introduce karaoke. But the House of Lords might well decide against it.

Other MPs leapt up to point out that the peers' rejection of karaoke might allow them to continue to destroy bills from the Commons, such as the one designed to ban fox-hunting. Quite. Who would want to have Sir Nicholas Winterton, somewhat the worse for wear on eight Bacardi Breezers, desperately trying to keep up with the backing track on 'My Way'? Or Gwyneth Dunwoody belting out 'I Will Survive' only half a tone flat? Most MPs would kill any bill – indeed any minister – rather than listen to that.

A kind colleague has pointed out that what Mr Cook was talking about, in his Scotsman-trying-to-finish-his-chips-before-the-pubs-shut haste, was not karaoke, but 'carry-over'. This is the wheeze that would mean that bills didn't fall at the end of the parliamentary year, but could be pushed through the next year. That would deprive the Lords of one of the reasons for their existence, so I should imagine they would prefer karaoke to carry-over.

In his peroration, Mr Cook said that he loved the House of Commons. It derived its authority from the trust and respect of the public. It was 'the crucible in which governments are forged and broken'. His voice hushed, as he continued movingly, 'I do not want it to jentle dwindly into a museum.'

It was a lovely image, this fine old crucible, forged in the heat of 800 years of democracy and debate, dwindly jentling into irrelevance and obscurity, relieved only by Mr Cook grabbing the mike and giving us a burst of 'Donald, Where's Yer Troosers?'

30.10.02

By November 2002 it was clear that Iain Duncan Smith's leadership of the Conservative Party was drawing to a close. To call Tory MPs 'vultures' would be unfair, since vultures never kill their prey. Hyenas, on the other hand, quite often do.

Yesterday morning Michael Portillo appeared on *Start the Week* on Radio 4. He said that he would never stand as leader of the Tory Party, would never be chosen leader if he did, and – to paraphrase him very slightly – he would rather have a vasectomy performed by Ainsley Harriott with a set of steak knives than ever accept the leadership of the Conservative Party. Ah ha, I thought, he really is desperate to get the job.

And I was right. A few hours later he was in the Chamber shafting Iain Duncan Smith. It is a measure of the pickle the present incumbent finds himself in that his colleagues have now stopped knifing him in the back and are knifing him in the front.

For some unfathomable reason, IDS had decided on a three-line whip against the possibility of unmarried and gay couples adopting children. Mr Portillo, who has taken recently to sitting at the back of the Chamber, rather like Edgar Allan Poe's raven, only less talkative, uncoiled from his perch and silkily inquired whether his hon. friend – the shadow minister, Tim Loughton – recalled a speech that had been made on the last day of the Conservative conference. The orator, whom we all knew to be IDS himself, had said, 'We must understand the way life in Britain is lived today and not the way it was lived twenty years ago.'

'Given that sentiment…can we return to the question of why this is a three-line whip, please?'

It may not sound like much, but believe me, in Tory terms this is the equivalent of the rapier of chased Toledo steel turning the lower intestines into a kebab. They say that when you are knifed, at first you don't feel pain; it is only when the blood gushes that you realize how badly hurt you are.

Some strange things were said in the debate. The Tory David Hinchcliffe said that there were same-sex couples 'living together in long-term relationships who would be offended by being called homosexuals and lesbians'.

The only ones who came to mind were Holmes and Watson, and I wondered how Conan Doyle would have approached *The Adventure of the Adopted Baby*.

'What is that infernal noise, Watson? I am grappling with a three-pipe problem.'

'It is our baby, Holmes. I think that she must be hungry, or cold, or needs her nappy changing, or else she is teething.'

'You know my methods, Watson. The evidence, please.'

'Well, she has just had a feed, I've put an extra blanket on her cot, and her nappy is dry.'

'Then how many times must I tell you? When you have

eliminated the impossible, what remains, however improbable, must be the tooth.'

05.11.02

The debate on adoption led to a revolt by backbench Conservatives, of whom many ignored Mr Duncan Smith's three-line whip. Realizing how desperate his situation had become, he held a gathering at Central Office where he made a brief 'back me or sack me' statement, then disappeared without answering questions. It was thought to have made his position even more perilous.

'D'you think we've peaked too soon?' asked a Tory peer I bumped into just after Iain Duncan Smith's plaintive announcement. Graveyard humour is the only kind they have left. You can't underestimate the terrible *Heart of Darkness* horror that has gripped the Conservative Party. 'Who persuaded IDS to make that crass, that catastrophic statement?' asked one front-bencher. 'He holds a press conference to say, "I lead a party that is out of control, and there is nothing I can do."' Many Tories recalled with something less than fondness the forty-six times IDS voted against the John Major government, or was it forty-seven? Nobody seems sure. The red mist has come down, and they stagger about the place blinded by fury and despair.

'He was a fifth columnist, a saboteur,' said a backbencher. 'Now he asks for loyalty. Him! Loyalty!' Others were less elliptical. 'That bastard was the most disloyal bastard of all the disloyal bastards John Major had to cope with. And do you know why? Because he's a bastard!'

I had a cup of tea with a Labour MP who knows a lot of Tories. 'Whatever IDS thinks, it's not a cabal gathered against him. It's just a lot of individuals who think he's no good. And it's going to get worse. After the battle of Austerlitz Napoleon turned his cannon on the river ice, so that thousands of Russian and Austrian soldiers drowned while they fled. That's what Labour are going to do to them. There'll be plenty of screaming, but no mercy.'

The statement was indeed a curious and painful affair. IDS was flanked by loyalists who are, for the moment, still loyal, though Oliver Letwin gazed up at him with what was meant to be earnest interest, but actually seemed to be saying, 'I know I've seen this bloke somewhere. Was it on TV? Or at that awful dinner party?' The statement – it lasted all of 2 minutes and 47 seconds – was meant to sound tough and resolute. Instead it was plucking and pleading. His words were abrasive and authoritative, but his body language was soft, shrinking and defensive. He begged for our good opinion. He had never underestimated the task ahead. He had never flinched. He had sought to do every-thing 'with courtesy, decency and honesty'. This was getting embarrassing. Napoleon was wheeling his cannon towards the ice, and the Russians' commanding officer was asking us to praise his good manners and tact.

He concluded: 'My message is simple and stark: unite or die!' And with those three words, he became the first leader of the Conservative Party to turn himself into a suicide bomber.

06.11.02

This year's Tory conference offered us the best-known, perhaps the only known, phrase ever coined by Iain Duncan Smith. He had just over a year left as Tory leader.

The high spot of Mr Duncan Smith's speech came when he described himself as: 'the quiet man'. By this time he had, in any case, become almost inaudible. 'When I set myself a task, I do it,' he said, as if talking about someone else in the room to whom he didn't want to give offence. (I was able to consult the copy of the speech helpfully given to us beforehand by Conservative staff.)

'Do not underestimate the determination of a quiet man,' he concluded, his voice now so hushed that delegates had to strain to hear it. Some of them looked baffled. Was he telling them to buy a flan? Or promising to hire a van? He seemed to be on the brink of dropping off. His voice drifted away like your grandpa towards the end of Christmas dinner.

'Wake up, Mr Duncan Smith!' I wanted to shout. 'You're addressing the Conservative Party conference. It's not some terrible dream!'

But the delegates, once they had worked out what he was saying, adored it. He was telling them that he knew he was boring, that nobody would ever be excited or moved or inspired by anything he said, but it didn't matter. He was a quiet man, and therefore determined. The quieter he got, the more determined he would be. That's his strategy now: a visionary gaze, a jutting jaw, and total silence. Tory election broadcasts would be ten minutes of nothing. John Cage's executors will sue for copyright.

All this hush helped conceal the fact that this was a speech Tony Blair could have made. He began by saying how awful the Conservative Party had been and how everyone hated them. 'The challenges changed, but we did not change to meet the challenges,' he told them – and try saying that after a good lunch. They were crap! But at least they knew they were crap, and they would be whispering that to anyone who could make out what they were saying.

10.11.02

Tony McWalter is the Labour backbencher who, a year or so ago, asked the Prime Minister what his political philosophy was. This completely stumped Mr Blair, who lacks a political philosophy in the way that I lack a giraffe. He has no use for it, and it would only get in the way. At the time he stumbled around a bit, then said something about how he had persuaded Sir Magdi Yacoub to help out with the NHS.

This might be a good idea, but it doesn't amount to a philosophy. You will search the *Critique of Pure Reason* a long time without finding a reference to heart surgeons, however eminent. But no wonder Mr Blair was flustered. MPs are supposed to ask about hospital waiting times, and spending lottery money, not about the meaning of life.

Yesterday the same MP struck again. When the Prime Minister exercised 'his considerable powers of appointment, which many people believe are quasi-medieval,' started Mr McWalter – quasi-name, quasi-guy – 'what emphasis does he attach, what weight does he give, to a capacity for displaying independence of mind?'

Now, we all knew the answer to that, which is 'none'. Those few Tories who weren't rolling around in laughter shouted it out for him. This is New Labour we are talking about. You don't need independence of mind, any more than a Jesuit priest does, or a squaddie taking orders from the sergeant-major. Mr McWalter might as well have asked what capacity the peers had for dropping their trousers in public, or painting their hair pink – it would not only be entirely irrelevant to the job description, but would make it harder for them to be appointed.

Now and again, by accident, some people make it onto the Labour benches in the Lords who do demonstrate inde- pendence of mind. The names of Lord Winston and Lord Peston come to mind. These people are not consequently thrown into gaol as they might be in some countries. Instead they find that they are surplus to requirements. They make speeches in the Lords, but nobody pays any heed. Quangos are set up but their names are not put forward. Important meetings are held on topics of which they have specialist knowledge, but they are not invited.

This time the Prime Minister was ready for Mr McWalter. He said crisply that he had precisely the same attachment to independence of mind as any prime minister before him. (We also took this to mean 'none'.)

'I have not yet had the chance to demonstrate this to my hon. friend, but he never knows.' The cunning suggestion here was that Mr McWalter was only angling for a job himself and not, as I suspect, desperately trying to find what is going on in the Blair mind, like an Egyptologist who is convinced that somewhere in the tomb is a secret chamber stuffed with treasures. But most of us think it unlikely.

21.11.02

The firefighters' dispute continued. Mr Blair took over control from his deputy and was asked what he was doing at a press conference in Downing Street.

Now and again he lapses into weird speech patterns, just like his deputy. 'Well, I mean, I totally understand, you know, when you get into a dispute like this…and it's how you put it all together, and I totally understand how people, if they're following it in great detail…' Doctors have warned for years about the dangers of Secondary Prescott. You can pick it up by being in close proximity to Prescott, over time, in smoke-filled negotiating rooms. Tragically there is no known cure, not even a patch to wean people off it.

26.11.02

For some strange reason, the following day Mr Prescott was back in charge of handling the Fire Brigade's Union strike. He was watched from the public gallery by the general secretary, Andy Gilchrist, or 'Andy Gilcrust' as the Deputy Prime Minister insisted on calling him.

'Let me be clear!' Mr Prescott said to the House. Tories set up a barrage of mock cheering. But the DPM did put the government's case in some detail, so I thought it would be helpful if we had him reply to your questions about the fire dispute. All answers are verbatim from John Prescott's remarks in yesterday's debate:

Should statutory law be invoked, to end the strike on grounds of public safety?

'The agreement is taking place. I tell him properly that if his judgement to make a judgement on the public interest and the safety of the community. That is not my judgement, it is the judgement given to the Attorney General.'

Should the TUC deploy their own agreement, by which unions do nothing that might jeopardize public safety?

'As for the question about whether the TUC have agreement if the members of the 1978 agreement, that is a matter for the TUC and their agreement, but it is a matter for me to an agreement, as I informed the House, I did seek to find an agreement which I failed on the first occasion, dealing with this really exceptional in conflict.'

What should be done about pay differences between full- and part-time firefighters?

'When I asked for – can't we have the figures? That seems simple to calculate what the money is but then you have to renegotiate the whole allowances that you then find out, that's not easy to do it immediately – I put forward perhaps one understanding.'

Will the government use the law to stop London tube drivers from taking secondary action?

'I've already mentioned quite frankly there may be a 100, previously, then it was down to one yesterday, now it's no. Not. And I think we should welcome that as a fact.'

Why won't the government get all sides into one room and feed them beer and sandwiches until they agree?

'I think it's more wine and canapés at the moment.'

How can MPs complain about the firefighters asking for 40 per cent when they recently voted themselves a 40 per cent rise?

'The 40 per cent increase was given to the Prime Minister and only the Prime Minister. It was done by independent inquiry and not by this House.'

Why can't ministers make sure the army can use the 400 fire engines that are available but standing idle?

'There are 400 engines, some without an engine, some without wheels, I mean, I don't know what you mean by that.'

Might the firefighters be more willing to adopt new working procedures?

'I personally have always had that to my mind, and in particular for the consequences of fire service. I visited my fire stations. They posed the question of what is the work of the firefighter, and that precisely what we have to dress ourselves to this. This should be in front of every one of us. It's certainly to the front in my intentions, and I intend to see we can achieve it.'

27.11.02

It is surprising how body language can betray MPs, even under the television cameras.

I need to bring you up to date with the romantic soap opera that continues in the Tory Party. Dashing, lip-curling shadow Deputy Prime Minister David Davis, who twice broke his nose defending a lady's honour, or possibly attempting to remove it, is enamoured of the lovely Theresa May, the party chairwoman who wears leopardskin shoes. It is Mr Davis's practice on Wednesday afternoons to sit next to her and place his arm along the back of the bench. This causes him to turn his magnificently manly torso in the direction of his leader, Iain Duncan Smith, while bringing him closer to the object of his affections. He does not let his arm fall upon her shoulder, for he is always the gentleman. Well, quite often the gentleman. But in the excitement of Prime Minister's Question Time, it is inevitable that sometimes her back arches and wriggles – oh so softly! – and brushes against his arm. He lives for these brief, but magical moments.

Yesterday, however, she was not present. He looked distraught, his eyes flicking from side to side, desperate to catch a glimpse of her returning form. Labour MPs, who have been following this story for months now, as if it were a lavish BBC costume drama, noted that in her absence Mr Davis did not place his arm round Jacqui Lait, the MP who occupied Theresa's position, but not the place in his heart. Miss Lait's breast was not to swell with passion, and her heart lay still within its cage.

Then suddenly, a whiff of perfume, and She was there. But where could she sit? The bench was jammed. A Labour MP who was watching all this provided me with a plan over tea. The chief whip was at the end, represented by a milk jug. Next to him was Mr Davis, in the shape of the sugar bowl, and hard against him Ms Lait, the extra hot water.

Theresa paused for a brief and, for Mr Davis, anguished moment. Then very carefully and deliberately she placed herself between the sugar bowl and the milk jug – that is, between the two men. She was next to Mr Davis, but on the wrong side! For him to arrange his arm like tinsel on a tree, he would have had to turn away from IDS, an act of treachery which could not be ignored or speedily forgiven. And so, for a man sad and bowed, yet still proud and strong, he managed to survive the thirty minutes, consoled only by the proximity of the lovely Theresan thigh.

05.12.02

Some readers may recall the strange affair of the Blairs and a conman called Peter Foster, and his one-time girlfriend, Carole Caplin, who became Cherie Blair's 'personal lifestyle adviser'. This affair was rumbling on at the time of the annual publication of the Register of Members' Interests. In response to pressure from MPs, journalists also have to send information to a register.

It was Sleazy Thursday at Westminster. The press corps were descending upon the Prime Minister's spokesman in the building where his briefings are now held. This used to be William Gladstone's house. I wonder how he would have survived in today's hostile, irreverent media world.

'The Prime Minister spent the day felling trees,' his spokesman might have said. 'Are you telling us he got his chopper out?' they would have replied.

The hacks were furious with Tom Kelly, the Number 10 spokesman who had told them earlier this week that Peter Foster had not been a financial adviser to Cherie Blair. It turned out that she had, however, taken financial advice from him – clearly a quite different thing, or so we were invited to suppose. Mr Kelly maintained a dry, civil servant's calm, refusing to be drawn or riled. The reporters demanded to know if he had lied, or been lied to. It seemed rather pointless. Under this administration, 'truth' has no objective meaning, and instead is defined as 'what you can get away with'.

Meanwhile, the new Register of Members' Interests has been published. This is supposed to reveal all MPs' income, gifts and perks. Being politicians, they understandably use it to demonstrate how wonderful they are.

Ann Widdecombe, for example, declares: 'Cheque for £721.48 from Women in Business, donated to ZOCS, a charity in Zambia. The money was raised from an auction of tea with me at the House of Commons.' All that money for a cuppa with Ann! Imagine the scene: 'Shall I be mother?' 'Only unless there's something you haven't told us.'

Each year I like to work my way through the register and make mental notes of the awards I would give to MPs.

Most misleading self-description goes to Gerry Adams, who calls himself a 'writer', no doubt because 'political director of terrorist gang' would not look so impressive.

Most appropriate gift received (third place): Sir Patrick Cormack for 'bronze maquette of the sculpture of Margaret Thatcher, presented by the sculptor, Neil Simmons'. Useful for private worship, or else for slicing the miniature head off.

Most appropriate gift (second place): Theresa May, Tory chairwoman, for a 'gift of three pairs of Hot2Trot shoes from Russell and Bromley'.

Most appropriate gift (first place) goes to Alan Duncan: 'gift of a ceremonial tribal dagger from the government of Yemen'. This was followed by another in September, which means he can stab two colleagues in the back at once.

Most boring gift (fourth place): Lembit Opik, 'trip to Estonia to attend Eurovision Song Contest, overnight accommodation provided by Tallinn City Council'.

Most boring gift (third): Russell Brown for 'two season tickets for Queen of the South football club, provided by club'.

Most boring gift (second): Douglas Alexander for 'visit to Sweden to attend a policy seminar, travel and accommodation paid for by Social Democratic Party of Sweden'.

But the winner of *Most boring gift* goes to Alan Johnson, the MP for Hull West: 'framed painting of Hull fishing docks'.

And the winner of *Most politically incorrect entry* goes to Edward Garnier: 'a day's shooting in Bedfordshire, as the guest of the Tobacco Manufacturers' Association'.

So we have learned almost nothing from the directory. Well done, everyone!

06.12.02

MPs were debating human rights for transsexuals, a matter, said the Liberal Democrat Vince Cable, 'of real urgency'. But first they had a chance to take a pop at Lord Irvine, the Lord Chancellor, who said the other day that he didn't think people would mind if convicted burglars stayed out of prison. He didn't believe that the public would be 'disturbed'. I know quite a few lawyers. Many live in the real world. Others, however, inhabit a fictional planet, similar to Narnia, or Oz. Lord Irvine belongs to this latter group. You may recall that a few years ago he was challenged about the £650,000 spent on refurbishing his apartment. He felt that the public would rejoice at this news, crying – and I quote him – 'Three cheers that this work has been done! Three cheers for the committee that chose to make the decision!'

In the same fantasy world, people get back home from holiday to find their front door bashed in, their drawers emptied all over the house and the wife's jewellery gone, and they say, 'Right! I just hope they catch the bastard who did this and make him spend fifty hours repainting an old folks' home!'

Lord Irvine also believes that the night courts experiment was a success worth building on, even though it cost £4,000 to try every yob caught peeing in the streets. Of course, to most lawyers, four grand isn't a great deal of money.

The Commons moved on to the topic of transsexual people, who, at the moment, are unable to register their new sex in official papers. This can cause embarrassment at passport control. Or – to pluck a name at random – if John Prescott were to become Joanne Prescott, he would have to wait until he was sixty-five to claim his full pension, even though he would technically be a woman and might thump the post office clerk if he (or she, or both) didn't agree.

08.01.03

Shortly after this topic cropped up in the Commons, I found myself having breakfast with Frost, a treat enjoyed by people who had just appeared on Breakfast with Frost. *It turned out, to Sir David's surprise, that fully one-third of sex change operations are on women who want to become men. He asked if a man who had once been a woman could ever have an erection, and the look on Sir John Major's face at this query is one I shall cherish a long time.*

*

Meanwhile, the Iraq war loomed.

Tony Blair is a lucky man – lucky in his opposition, lucky in his friends, lucky in the news of the day. Yesterday he was supposed to face the harshest parliamentary test of his premiership. Labour MPs are increasingly angry that he seems to be toadying to a rightwing American president who looks like a chimpanzee that hasn't quite got the hang of bubblegum. But yesterday he walked away with the cheers of his party echoing round the Chamber. It must be an extraordinary sensation – to arrive facing thirty minutes of complaint and to leave hearing huzzas, bellows of applause and the demented waving of order papers. It was a little like one of those documentaries about the last war, in which Winston Churchill thrills the House with his defiant oratory. The actor with his cheeks stuffed with cotton wool says something like, 'I shay to zish House that I shall never – nevair! – shell the birthright of the Brish people for this mesh of pottage!' The bravos and the hip, hip hoorays are a little too loud, over-enthusiastic, too actory.

My own surmise is that Alastair Campbell has had a silicone chip installed in Mr Blair's Y-fronts. In his Downing Street office, Mr Campbell has one of those revolving switches, like in the cab of old railway trains. Usually he leaves it in the 'moderate' position. Every now and again, however, he likes to swivel it round to 'full speed', if only to see what happens.

It was the Plaid Cymru leader, Elfyn Llwyd, who inspired Mr Blair's triumph. Mr Llwyd is a charming and a witty man, but his mien, lugubrious and slow, reminds one of a morose sheep on a damp Welsh hillside. How, he asked, could Mr Blair justify war in Iraq if it were backed neither by international law nor by British public opinion?

That is the moment that Alastair Campbell hit the switch. The current coursed through the Prime Minister's private parts. His body tensed. His face went red. He began to thump the Despatch Box. As it happened, he didn't say anything he hadn't said a few days ago, but this time he sounded as if he meant it. If we didn't act now, terrorists would have access to weapons of mass destruction. If, in August 2001, he had warned of the menace of al-Qaida and called for an invasion of Afghanistan, nobody would have believed him.

'Sometimes the job of prime minister is to say the things that people don't want them to say...the threat is real, and if we don't deal with it, our weakness will haunt future generations!'

Passion, commitment, real belief! The PM's pants were on fire. The House erupted, Mr Campbell moved the switch back to 'idling' and for the first time Mr Blair had spoken about Iraq as if he meant what he said, rather than regarding it as just another tedious problem cluttering up his in-tray.

16.01.03

Of course, we all know now what he didn't know then, which was that the weapons of mass destruction had vanished some time before all this happened. Their absence was to haunt Blair's remaining four years in office.

*

The government made periodic attempts to reform the House of Lords. At one point in 2003 Robin Cook brought several alternative systems to be voted on by the Commons; every one was defeated. My own view was that peers should be chosen by lot from the electoral register, rather like juries. This would bring a cross-section of the public in to help with legislation. None of them would be beholden to the party whips. But I recognize that this plan is unlikely to be adopted, since it would provide no patronage for senior politicians to dish out. This would make it, in their view, pointless.

Tam Dalyell, the father of the House, managed to get himself thrown out of the Chamber yesterday. This is one of the oldest rituals in our constitution, like the Changing of the Ravens, or the Trooping of the Apes in Gibraltar. It took longer than usual. At one point it seemed as if the Speaker had forgotten his own role in this ancient ceremony. For quite some time he failed to throw Mr Dalyell out. Tam stood there, anticipating the word of dismissal. It was as if Charles III were waiting to feel the crown hit the top of his head, only to discover that the Archbishop had accidentally left it at home.

In the end, he decided for himself that he had been banished and traipsed towards the door in accordance with time-honoured practice. It was rather moving. Say what you like about this country – we can still do pageantry like this better than anyone else.

I had arrived in the Commons after spending time in the Lords. I was there to see the Lord Chancellor in action. The House sits for around 150 days a year, so even on his emaciated salary of £180,000, Lord Irvine still gets £1,200 per sitting day. At 2.28 p.m. he arrived in the lobby, accompanied by men in tights and his trainbearer, Nora Dobinson, who for some reason wasn't bearing a train but holding a cushion.

He then went into the Chamber for what turned out to be a total of thirty-seven minutes, including the time taken for his arrival. He had already made £64.86. We watched him as he sat on the Woolsack, hoping to work out how he earns such a substantial daily crust. At 2.35, after prayers, he smiled at everyone. Then he pulled a big red hanky out of his pocket and blew his nose.

At 2.37 another lord came over and whispered in his ear. This is difficult if your addressee is wearing a full-bottomed wig and consequently looks like one of the Flopsy Bunnies. The Lord Chancellor lifted one flap of the wig, absorbed the message and resumed smiling. At 2.39 he took a moment to pick his teeth. Then he pulled out the hanky again and used it to mop his forehead. He was already £357 to the good.

At 2.41 he began to write what appeared to be a letter. At 2.42 he heaved a sigh. At 2.43 he put his pen down on the Woolsack. At 2.50 he picked the nail of his middle finger with the nail of his thumb. £713 and counting!

At 2.57 Lord Campbell of Croy expressed outrage about the bill which will allow pubs to stay open all day. 'Is this the only known case of a government legislating to condone inebriation?' he asked. Lord Irvine, his face as red as the Woolsack, or his own hanky, seemed untroubled by this prospect. Indeed, his smile returned.

At 3.05 questions were over and he swept out, having completed thirty-seven minutes' work and clocked up the full £1,200. (I am told he has other duties as well – chiefly making sure that other lawyers get even more money.)

Back in the Commons, Tam was demanding a statement about the government's Iraq dossier, the one which was apparently written by a graduate student twelve years ago, with additional material from the *Boys' Bumper Book of Botulism*. The Speaker, having deemed this to be out of order, told him to sit down. He refused. The Speaker asked again. He refused again. The Speaker appeared lost. Finally he asked him to withdraw. Did he mean withdraw his remarks, or withdraw from the Chamber? We didn't know. It was like watching two old men in a home trying to have a pillow fight from their wheelchairs.

So Tam, who at least remembered his part in the centuries-old rite, shuffled out of the Chamber, leaving behind, rather poignantly, the cushion he uses to ease his discomfort while sitting on the bench. It remained in place, symbolizing eloquently the impotent rage and fury of its absent owner.

11.02.03

The debates on Iraq continued.

Cometh the hour, cometh the man. Or at least cometh Adam Ingram, one of the junior defence ministers. For days now MPs have been demanding an account from the government about why its alleged dossier of defence secrets on Iraq seems to have been drawn from, among other sources, the *Big Chief I-Spy Annual* and back numbers of *Eagle* comic. Finally the Speaker had agreed to a statement. This should have been made by the defence secretary, Geoff Hoon, but he was in Washington, and what is thought there is deemed considerably more important than what is thought in the House of Commons.

(The two people who have the greatest influence on the Prime Minister's policies are George Bush and Alastair Campbell, both of them dry drunks. What is it about reformed alcoholics that so entrances Tony Blair? Does he believe they have access to some deeper wisdom and insight? On the basis of recent events this does not appear to be the case.)

The importance of Mr Hoon's mission did not entirely satisfy the Tory spokesman, Bernard Jenkin, who bizarrely accused him of 'scuttling out of the country, albeit on the most legitimate business, in order to avoid being cross-examined by this House'.

What on earth did he mean? It's like accusing someone of committing a 'foul and despicable crime, albeit entirely justified'.

In the meantime, as we face this terrible war, I make a plea for MPs to adopt some new clichés. Yesterday in health questions there was a discussion about a ghastly form of cancer called mesothelioma, which the minister, Jacqui Smith, pronounced as if she had confused it with the old name for Iraq. Tony Lloyd, the MP who had asked the question, didn't even try to pronounce it. 'Messer,' he said, 'is the Cinderella of the world of cancer.'

What a strange thing to say! Presumably the poor, put-upon girl has now become a dead metaphor, like Alice in Wonderland, whose spirit presides over most other government mistakes. But if they must use children's stories to pep up their speeches, can't they find some new ones? 'The government must kiss the frog of underfunding and turn it into the handsome prince of a properly resourced health service!' perhaps. Or, 'Home Office ministers must learn that criminals are like Goldilocks – they need more porridge.' It would be more entertaining if backbenchers, instead of accusing Gordon Brown of 'Peter Pan economics', were to say, 'The Chancellor, like Toad of Toad Hall, is clothed in the washerwoman's rags of misleading statistics, which will soon be stripped away to reveal the escaped convict of financial meltdown!'

There was a small consolation. I love it when both David Kidney and Bob Blizzard speak at the same session, for then we can truly say that MPs are all piss and wind.

12.02.02

Tony Blair adopted a new public image in the hopes of persuading the Commons to his way of thinking on Iraq. It was, of course, something of a sham.

'The moral choice in relation to this is a moral choice that has to weigh up the moral consequences of war,' the Prime Minister told us yesterday. It was a new Tony Blair we were seeing. Mild, gentle, discursive, both religious and religiose.

In the past, he has been more of a medieval princeling. Tributes, real and metaphorical, would be laid at his door. Petitioners queued for the chance to pluck his sleeve and bestow their humble offerings upon him. 'Is my right honourable friend aware that my constituents are overjoyed that, thanks to his lavish funding of the health service, in Mudchester we now have more hospital beds than inhabitants?' Or, 'Does my Rt. Hon. friend know that, thanks to his street crime initiative, armed gangs are jettisoning their guns and devoting their lives to bring-and-buy sales to raise money to buy mah-jong sets for old folks' homes?'

There were none of those yesterday. There haven't been for a while. But then he does not expect them. He has become an itinerant, penitent monk, bowed under a brown cowl, his brown gown tied at the waist like a dressing gown, walking from town to town, dousing us all with a moral dressing-down. Tim Boswell, a Tory, wanted to know how the Prime Minister could expect to be trusted when his dossier on Iraq turned out to be based on a GCSE crib, downloaded from the internet, plus a strip in *Viz* comic called 'Mustapha Phagg – He's a Spy in Drag!' (I exaggerate, but only slightly.)

In the past Mr Blair might have been riled by this attack on his probity. Instead, he replied with courtesy and calm and, as it happened, in complete gibberish: 'The part of the document that dealt with intelligence was indeed from intelligence sources as the document stated, and I think that's important that that is underlined, and of course particularly at the moment it is important that we give accurate information to people and indeed the information was accurate.' We realized that he must be more rattled than we had thought – he had begun to sound like John Prescott.

13.02.03

The war came ever closer.

It's easy to talk against a barrage of noise. It can excite and inspire, it can provide a heightened sense of being, an affirmation of you own importance. Or to misquote the Acts of the Apostles, lots of pricks to kick against. Prime ministers relish the noise at Question Time, the sheer volume of the row acting on them like the lightning through the electrodes of Frankenstein's monster.

But how can you speak to a silence? Particularly the kind of suffocating silence that comes from a Chamber that is packed, with MPs perched on the steps, listening from the gallery and standing at the Bar, all combining to create a massive and oppressive, total absence of noise.

You get no input. It's like talking to someone wearing sunglasses who won't reply to your questions. You have only body language to go on. You have nothing to hear, nothing to react against.

Only when Tony Blair finished his statement yesterday did the terrible silence break, like a thunderstorm at the end of a long, hot midsummer day. He had the disconcerting experience of being cheered by the Tories and hearing still the dark, rumbling quiet from the Labour benches behind him.

Since the war began to loom, the Tories have split Blair into two. There is the evil, scheming, duplicitous, inadequate, incompetent, evasive bossyboots who stands complacently by as old ladies are mugged by the thousand, educational standards fall to below those in Rwanda, and the health service kills more people than it cures.

On the other hand there is the rock-jawed statesman, a man whose vision and courage speak for and inspire a whole nation (or roughly one-third of it, as the polls suggest).

26.02.03

Then in March came the crucial vote.

At 10.11 the chief whip, Hilary Armstrong, reached across the front bench and gave Tony Blair a note. He leaned back, folded his arms in relief and could be seen to mouth, 'So that's all right, then.' John Reid and Jack Straw, the cabinet ministers nearby, smiled like cats let loose in a dairy. John Prescott scowled, but then he usually does. He probably managed a scowl for his wedding day photos. It was not a great result, but from their point of view it was a perfectly adequate one.

At times in the debate that preceded it, the House resembled a bus which has just plunged off a cliff. Some passengers were insisting that we were headed in the right direction, some that there was still time to turn back, while the rest were shrieking in terror.

The Prime Minister could take much of the credit – or blame – for the result. He seemed to have summoned up unknown reserves of energy. Recently he has looked tired, drawn and drained. His face is still grey, and his hair seems to be shrinking back into his scalp, but yesterday he was alive, roaring, quivering with tension, like a young lieutenant about to lead a platoon into battle. He blazed with conviction and the certainty of his own rightness.

His opponents may be just as sincere, but yesterday their attacks pinged off him like air gun pellets off a suit of armour. By the end he heard a noise which has become unfamiliar of late – the sound of Labour MPs cheering him. At one point he said that Saddam's claim that he had destroyed his weapons was 'patently absurd'. At this point he heard loud Tory applause, but this time even louder Labour silence. Then there was his attack on France, for we always find it easier to forgive our enemies than excuse our friends.

Again, the Churchillian phrases were wheeled out, for every British prime minister has a template for the oratory of war. 'For twelve years, we have been a victim of our own desire to placate the implacable.' At the end he kicked into full Henry V at Harfleur mode: were we to 'tell our allies that at the very moment they needed our determination, that Britain faltered?' Finally the vote: the Labour Party more split than ever, but the Commons almost 2–1 in favour of a war.

19.03.03

Of course they did not know that Saddam's claim that he had destroyed his weapons was, far from being patently absurd, absolutely true.

*

Militarily, of course, the onslaught was a huge success.

Since the attack ended, the government has become very militaristic. It's not surprising. The armed forces did as promised. They were given a job and they carried it out. Very few government departments can make this claim. So they all want to rub some of the magic dust in their scalps.

Take health questions yesterday. Of course, they have always believed in 'hitting targets'. Now we are repeatedly told that 'new funding is getting through to the front line'. Alan Milburn, the health secretary, said yesterday that 'now was not the time to take our foot off the accelerator'. He made reform of the NHS sound like the infantry's dash to Baghdad.

Next we moved on to mental health problems. There are lots of people with mental health problems living among us, and some are causing trouble. The government's answer, we learned, is to recruit 'assertive outreach teams'. Apparently throughout the UK there are 191 assertive outreach teams, or 'the SAS' as we used to call them. They are helped by sixty-two 'crisis resolution teams' and 'early intervention teams'.

It must be awful. There you are in the park, a can of strong cider in your hand, waving it round and screaming harmlessly to yourself, when suddenly a bunch of people in camouflage, with blacked-up faces, run up and shove you into the back of a van.

David Lammy is currently in charge of dentistry, which makes him a minister of the crown. He talked yesterday about a 'personal dental service pilot', presumably a sort of flying doctor who crosses enemy lines looking for evidence of caries and impacted wisdom teeth. Then they start parade ground drilling. He talked about 'dental support teams' who are ready to fly anywhere in the country where dentistry is urgently needed. 'All right, men, here is tonight's mission. You see this strategic root canal? I want you to seize the bridge. Gentlemen, to your choppers.'

All this came amid yet more jargon, which under New Labour proliferates like ground elder. A minister was banging on about 'finished consultant episodes', which does not refer to doctors who have been struck off for groping female patients. It means people who not only get an appointment, but actually see the consultant – not always the same thing. Hazel Blears, another junior minister, spoke of 'the patient journey'. We assumed this meant the journey to France for an eye operation, or to India for a new hip. Apparently not. 'We shall bear down just as hard on the patient journey as on the treatment part of the patient journey.' Does this mean anything at all?

30.04.03

Hazel Blears went on in time to become chair of the Labour Party. I couldn't help but wonder if she had been appointed by Tony Blair's subconscious – his late mother was called Hazel Blair. Perhaps it assuaged some deep guilt he felt about not having been a loving enough son. Or perhaps not.

*

Meanwhile, I had come to look forward greatly to the interventions – usually disappointingly brief, but always thunderously grand – of Sir Peter Tapsell, the MP for Louth and Horncastle. He always seemed to me to be one of the very few surviving specimens of the mighty beasts that once dominated the Conservative Party, the knights of the shires.

Yesterday we had the first Prime Minister's Questions since the sort-of victory in Iraq, yet the subject did not crop up until the end of the session. MPs have already pushed it to the back of their minds. They are concentrating on the local elections, which are to be held very soon. Why bother about Baghdad, when there are votes to be picked up in Bagshot?

Luckily the MP who finally raised the topic was Sir Peter Tapsell. Sir Peter is no mere person; he is a personage. When he rises to his feet, the editor of Hansard sends an urgent message to the foundry, for his words are not merely recorded on paper, or in the evanescent signals of the electronic media, but are cast in bronze, so that in a century – nay, in a new millennium – generations unborn will be able to read them and ponder their eternal wisdom. Teams of scholars will debate their meaning endlessly, as they do with the Rosetta Stone.

Sadly, some Labour MPs do not take Sir Peter with the seriousness that he does himself, or indeed that I do. He rose to a sarcastic chorus of cheers and applause. He faced down this tidal wave of scorn, gazing at his tormentors with mingled distaste and contempt. He puffed out his chest, like a pigeon doing gymnastics. Then he let loose the single word, '*If!*' He paused briefly to let the jeering die away.

Rarely has one single syllable resounded round the Chamber quite like this one. He invested the two letters with a solemn portentousness we had rarely heard before. Even Churchill's 'if' in 'If the British Empire lasts for a thousand years…' was, by comparison, a throwaway remark. Kipling's 'If' was mere doggerel.

'If,' he continued, gathering strength as the great wall of words pressed forward, 'it eventually twanspires [Sir Peter has a slight speech impediment] at the time of our invasion, Iwaq no longer produced weapons of mass destwuction capable of thweatening this country, and the Prime Minister led this country into war – UNDER FALSE PRETENCES – will he *WESIGN*?'

Mr Blair tried to flip him aside, which is trying to flip aside a boulder while wearing flip-flops. He was convinced the weapons would be found. 'And when we do, you and others will be eating some of your words!'

'Will *you* resign?' the feisty Andrew Mackinlay bellowed at Sir Peter. I found myself pondering the thought of him being obliged to eat his words, smothered in a rich Madeira and onion gravy, accompanied by a great mound of roast potatoes.

01.05.03

Unaccountably, Mr Blair did not heed Sir Peter's advice. Which cannot have pleased his Chancellor, who was already counting the days until he moved next door. Sadly for Mr Brown, unlike a prisoner chalking each day on the wall of his cell, he had no idea how long his sentence might be.

Treasury questions yesterday, and Gordon Brown seemed cross. The impression he likes to give is that he is taking time out from his incredibly busy life to answer footling questions from Tory backbenchers whose understanding of economics is roughly the same as his knowledge of ancient Armenian palimpsests. To this end, he and his team sit with huge piles of notes and files on their laps. They work furiously on these while Question Time goes on around them, as if only half-aware of the exchanges. They scribble notes in the margins, circling important statistics, under-lining passages and stabbing at them with pens, like soldiers on bayonet practice.

The Chancellor in particular waves sheaves of random documents in the air, like a man trying to read a newspaper on a windy beach. The implication is that he could be working on these documents if he didn't have to answer questions from some fool who hasn't yet got it into his head that everything the Treasury has done under Gordon Brown's stewardship has been absolutely correct and is working perfectly, you idiot!

He was pressed on whether we would enter the euro. He replied that this depended on his famous five tests, though since – as one Tory pointed out – the five tests are cunningly designed so that they can never be passed, this was the equivalent of saying, 'We shall join as soon as science finds a way of turning tap water into petrol.'

Towards the end of the session, Tam Dalyell asked what had been the total cost of the war in Iraq. The Chief Secretary to the Treasury, Paul Boateng, told him it was too early to say, but that £3 billion had been put aside in the reserve fund, announced in the Budget last week. Mr Dalyell rose with one of his celebrated short questions. 'Is £4 billion wide of the mark?' and sat down in a plonking kind of way, like a darts player who knows he has scored a treble twenty without looking at the board.

I was reminded of the old joke about the age of the dinosaur in the Natural History museum. A custodian says, 'I know it's 75 million years and six months old, because it was 75 million years when I arrived here, and that was six months ago.'

What did Tam expect? Mr Boateng to say, 'It has now risen to £3 billion and 95 pence, since after the Budget Lance Corporal Boddis lost his cap badge'?

09.05.03

Guardian *readers tend to get cross with me if I go too long without mentioning Michael Fabricant, the luxuriantly coiffed MP for Lichfield. Latterly he has become – or tried to become – something of an elder statesman. But the occasional opportunity to mention him still presents itself.*

Forget Iraq and the euro. A single topic dominated the Commons yesterday – what had happened to Michael Fabricant's wig? It used to be roughly normal length, finishing around the level of his ear lobes. But yesterday the thing had reached his shoulders, a great lustrous cascade of tresses curling over and even caressing the collar of his jacket.

MPs on both sides of the Chamber were transfixed. How could a wig not only grow, but grow so fast, and to such a length? In the press gallery one of my colleagues sat gazing at the sight, murmuring 'gorgeous, gorgeous' to himself, for these were locks that would not have disgraced Michael Heseltine, or even the original Tarzan, Johnny Weissmuller. How many My Little Ponies, we asked, had died to make such a creation?

Theories were being urgently whispered by MPs and hacks. For example, it is said by some that Mickey has several wigs and tries to fool us by using the short one, then a slightly longer one, and finally the longest of the lot, before he pretends to have had a haircut and goes back to the shortie. But this was no such subtle change. This was as sudden and startling as it would have been if he had grown a second head.

There are three principal theories, and argument will persist until Hans Blix is sent in. First, it could be his winter wig and he picked it up by accident when he got dressed yesterday morning. But this could not be true, since even in cold weather the wig does not reach this length. Possibly the regular wig had met with a terrible accident. It could have melted in the unseasonably warm April weather we have been having. Or a bird of prey might have swooped and seized it from the top of Mickey's head – you could raise a family of kestrels in there.

Or – and this is my own belief – the wig is actually growing. Just as Pinocchio was carved out of wood but became a living boy, the wig has embedded itself in the Fabricant skull and, thanks to some terrifying genetic mutation, has started to draw nourishment from his scalp.

Mickey had a question yesterday for John Prescott. He wanted to know why an out-of-town shopping centre near Lichfield had been demanded by his voters, approved by the inspectors, given the nod by the relevant councils, yet refused by Mr Prescott's office. The DPM said grumpily that he could not comment where an appeal against his decision was outstanding.

Our parliamentary system is a wonderful thing! The Deputy Prime Minister makes a decision which is so unpopular that he is taken to court. And the very fact that he has been taken to court means that he does not have to be accountable for his actions. Among the advanced democracies, only we in Britain can make this claim.

Michael Fabricant meanwhile had casually rested his feet on the bench in front, revealing a pair of black and pink hooped socks. Gorgeous at both ends! But a word of warning, Mickey: don't go near any open flames or power lines in your new superwig!

15.05.03

I once wrote that Peter Mandelson was the only man I knew who could skulk in broad daylight. At least I must have done; I have no memory of coining the phrase, yet it appeared in a book of political quotations. Then in another, then another and another, since all of them simply copied from the rest. My colleague Michael White may or may not have said of another journalist: 'If he was twice as good as he is, he'd be half as good as he thinks he is.' This appeared in Private Eye, *and when he was bearded by the victim, Mike replied, 'I don't recall saying it, but it sounds like me, doesn't it?' I feel the same about Mandy's skulking.*

For years Mr Mandelson has been described as the dark genius behind New Labour, a man whose dazzling knowledge of the arcane political arts and flair for mist-shrouded secrecy have made him irreplaceable to Tony Blair. MPs can beg the Prime Minister to take one decision or another. Cabinet ministers can, rather pathetically, try to promote their own views. World leaders may plead. But all this is naught compared to a single bleeper message from Mandelson. He is Thomas Cromwell, Cardinal Richelieu and Svengali, all rolled into one, but more powerful than any of them.

And yet his record has been of endless, sometimes hilarious, disaster. Yes, he was involved with two election victories. But these were interspersed with events which would be ludicrous if they weren't so catastrophic. The Sheffield rally, which helped destroy Neil Kinnock in 1992. The Saddleworth by-election, at which an unpleasant negative campaign handed the Liberal Democrats a seat Labour should never have lost. And of course the Dome, which some of us might have forgiven if he hadn't made such ludicrous claims for it. ('Surfball – the game for a new generation!' Surfball never existed, except in Peter Mandelson's head.)

And on top of all that, not one but two resignations from the Cabinet, a whiff of corruption clinging to him like stale smoke on a cigar lover's jacket. Evil genius? He is to politics what Mr Bean is to art restoration, or Laurel and Hardy to piano moving.

Two days ago he surpassed even himself, shoving himself into the agonizingly constructed peace accord over our entry into the euro, accusing Blair of being manipulated by Brown, and generally acting, in the words of Raymond Chandler, 'like a tarantula on a slice of angel food cake'.

And afterwards, having unburdened himself in front of eighteen political journalists, he complained about his privacy being breached! There are recluses in the deserts of Namibia, anchorites in the caves of Kashmir, who have a better working knowledge of the world than him.

Yesterday Iain Duncan Smith, still miraculously leader of the opposition, took advantage. 'The words of your close personal friend show how vicious and personal this feud has become,' said IDS, offering Mr Blair the chance to spring to Mandelson's support, an opportunity he conspicuously failed to seize. Poor Mandy. He seems to be without any admirers on either side of the Commons. Still, he always has himself.

22.05.03

Over the years I lost count of the number of 'worst days of his premiership' that Tony Blair suffered. The following day's papers would be packed with predictions of his imminent fall, then he would pick himself up, dust himself off and start all over again as if nothing had happened. This time the crisis came when it emerged that there were no weapons of mass destruction in Iraq.

It was the toughest Prime Minister's Questions Tony Blair had ever faced. Or so we were told. Some of us did wonder, just faintly, if he would still be in office at the end of the day.

Silly us. He was brilliant. He was evasive. He ducked and weaved. He was Billy Bunter explaining the jam tarts in his study. He was Bill Clinton saying that he had not had sex with those weapons, so to speak. He dodged every question like Jonah Lomu heading for a try. If Saddam had been half so clever, he would still be in power.

Of course Mr Blair was helped. Iain Duncan Smith was pretty well hopeless, and you could see the look of sad, crumpled despair on his backbenchers' faces. Freddie the Frog, who creates the nervous 'creagh, creagh' noise in his throat, was back. He plugged on regardless. Memo to the Tory leader: when you're in a hole, stop coughing!

Then there was the sheer, deafening weight of noise from the Labour side. Record producer Phil Spector might be facing a murder charge, but his wall of sound lives on. Ike and Tina Turner, the Ronettes, the Crystals – none of them could have made themselves heard against this barrage. They used to say of Harold Wilson, 'How do you know he is lying? When his lips move.' In Tony Blair's case, it's when the backbenchers scream.

But did he actually convince anyone? I doubt it. Did MPs conclude that neither he nor his goons in Downing Street had tweaked the intelligence? No. But he did have a good day. A brutal dictator had been ousted. 'The British army and the British people should be proud of the role this country played in removing him!' There was a thunderous cascade of applause behind him.

This is what I think of as the *Any Questions* defence. It doesn't matter what you say, provided you finish with a terrific patriotic tag-line. 'Yes, I stole from the orphans' fund. But I say this – the British workman is still the finest in the world!' Or, 'I freely admit to having had sex with goats. But I am proud to point out that this is still the greatest country in the world!'

Soon Mr Blair, no doubt buoyed by the mega-decibels around him, started gloating. We haven't had much of that, but yesterday we got a long, serious gloat. 'They said there would be thousands dead. They said it was my Vietnam. They said that the Middle East would be in flames!'

05.06.03

But of course he was wrong. Iraq at least soon was in flames. Meanwhile, Iain Duncan Smith's failure to make much headway against Tony Blair worsened his position, if that were possible.

Yesterday's main political event came at around 8.20, on the *Today* programme, when Jim Naughtie was interviewing the shadow leader of the House, Eric Forth. Mr Forth is known for his showy ties. One I found particularly striking shows a tropical beach resort, complete with palm trees and lurid cocktails. His neckwear is like David Beckham's hairdos – you might not care for his taste, but you do admire his courage.

He was asked about Iain Duncan Smith's feeble performance against the Prime Minister on Wednesday. 'Given the potency of this issue,' asked Mr Naughtie, 'why didn't your leader knock Mr Blair to a pulp?'

You have to know that British politics has language as formal as Japanese court etiquette, or French correspondence. It's like ending a letter: 'Please agree, dear sir, to the expression of my most distinguished sentiments'. You may not mean it, but its absence would be offensive. And it is the bounden duty of every front-bencher to support his boss totally, right up to the moment that he stabs him in the back.

So the correct answer to Naughtie's question would be along these lines: 'What do you mean, he didn't knock him to a pulp? The Prime Minister was evasive and dishonest. He dodged every question he was asked. The fact that the Labour lot kept up such a racket that Iain couldn't be heard doesn't mean that he wasn't asking the right questions. And will go on asking them, until we get some answers!

'And if you're quoting the views of the sketch-writers at me, you might as well canvass the mice behind the skirting board in the Members' Dining Room – at least they don't make it all up!'

That would have been the answer that propriety demanded. Instead Mr Forth said, 'Well, [pause] that is a fascinating parliamentary question, and as I come up to celebrating my twentieth anniversary in the House, it's a great privilege and honour...'

Eh? This was burbling. But he went on. 'It was put to me by a Labour member in a private conversation. He said, "You know, you've got the most open goals you'll ever have..."' In other words, Mr Forth was telling us, 'Our useless leader couldn't even score in an open goal. Pathetic!'

06.06.03

The issue of the euro was, along with Iraq, once a topic of frequent discussion in British politics. How dated that seems now! Iraq, of course, is still with us.

Gordon Brown made a statement on the euro yesterday. It was painful. He doesn't like the euro. The thought of it makes his skin crawl. I was reminded of a middle-aged man asked by the neighbours if he and his good lady would like to try wife-swapping. His every instinct screams against it, but he doesn't like to give offence. 'Well, um, that sounds like a fascinating idea, but, er, I'm not sure that the timing is absolutely right. I find that my stamp collection absorbs most of my leisure now…'

The Tories had heard it all before. They laughed at him. At him, the Iron Chancellor, with his cast-iron piggy bank soldered to his bedroom floor! His old girlfriend, Prudence, had gone, to be replaced by stability. There were thirty-four mentions of 'stability' and 'stable', and almost as many of 'flexible'.

The weather was warm, the message was old, and as someone who finds it easy to snooze in the Chamber I was delighted to see so many in the arms of Morpheus. Former shadow chancellor Francis Maude for one; Douglas Hogg for another. Now and again you would see one of them wake with a start, then they would become vaguely aware of a line like this: 'The issue at the present time is, however, being sure that there is structural convergence that is sustainable for the long term, and we also have to be sure that if real interest rates or business cycles do diverge, Britain will have the necessary flexibility to sustain growth, stability and employment.' It was more Secondary Prescott! You would see their lids close again.

Sir Peter Tapsell rose in his pomp. Hansard writers scrabbled round for their parchment and quill pens.

Following the disaster of our entry into the ERM long ago, did the Chancellor recall, he asked mysteriously, a French play in which the inmates of a lunatic asylum tried to slit their throats, and spent the rest of the play debating whether to commit suicide again? Should the British people have to slash their throats a second time?

'I thought,' Mr Brown said drily, 'he was describing events at a Conservative Party conference.'

10.06.03

In June, Tony Blair had what became known as the 'botched reshuffle'. He tried to abolish the post of Lord Chancellor. Alan Milburn, the health secretary, said that he had resigned to 'spend more time with his family'. One Labour MP asked, 'What makes him so sure that his family want to spend more time with him?'

It was another sultry day. In the House of Lords they were hot and bothered because Tony Blair had tried to abolish the office of Lord Chancellor without consulting them. Or consulting anybody. The new Lord Chancellor, the man who is committed to abolishing the office while simultaneously holding it, was Charlie Falconer, who is an old flatmate of Tony Blair. I suspect that this is all the result of an old bet between the two men. It's late. There has just been a terrific party in their flat and the last guest has gone.

'Tell yer wha', mate, when we're in charge you're going to be lor' chanzzler, rye?'

'Nah, mate, I gorra berra idea. I'll be pry minster. You can be lor' chanzzler.'

'Awight, lissen, tell yer wha', you can be pry minster. I'll be lor' chanzzler an' you can 'bolish me.'

'You lost me there pal. Anyfing lef' in tha' Party Seven?'

And so, nearly thirty years later, Charlie is wearing the great long-bottomed wig, as part of an undergraduate prank that went wrong.

Back in the Commons, the only ceremonial wig on display was worn by Michael Fabricant. Like the rest of us, he was listening to John Prescott talk about his plans for new regional assemblies. David Davis predicted that people invited to vote for these would 'give the government the same hand gesture we have come to expect from the Deputy Prime Minister'. Here is Mr Prescott's reply, or at least a part of it:

'They want to have a referendum, but nevertheless there's a county council here, he starts reeling through some of these people who are opposed to it, can I tell him I have some of those polls and by the way Mori poll, for example in March '99, that's less than 2,000, and many people actually accept the authority of these polls when they come out with their results, the Mori poll said 62 per cent want a referendum, BBC poll in 2002 said 72 per cent want it, and indeed council council network the very council councils who are opposing this, set up a review in their own area and...' [We could hear the sound of birds falling off trees all over Westminster.] '...70 per cent of the people said they needed a review, they want a referendum and the county council themselves, they paid for that review and 70 per cent said they wanted a referendum and so I'm a, a little cautious when I hear the Right Honourable Member talking about it, and when you bear in mind that in all these referendums, basically, they were part of the county council network [Tory jeers] well, I know you don't like insults, but that is what happened in all these areas we have shown whether trade unions, whether the business, whether organizations or individuals, they have called for a referendum…to hold that referendum and properly so, and therefore I think that there is considerable evident [sic] to be taken alongside that which I have laid before the House today, and as to the abolishment of county council reforms that he made in his contribution…'

And still it wasn't over then. It was a bravura performance, and we should all be very proud of him.

17.06.03

The Tories kept returning to the confused and confusing reshuffle.

When the Prime Minister is pinned down by an unanswerable question, he does something quite simple: he answers an entirely different question. Yesterday Iain Duncan Smith attacked him over the 'botched, bungled reshuffle', which, among other things, will lead to the abolition of the ancient office of Lord Chancellor, either quite soon, or in a few years, or round about the time that Alpha Centauri becomes a black hole. IDS's point was that nobody knew what was happening, the official version kept changing, and the whole thing had been sketched on the back of a beer mat in the Red Lion, the pub almost opposite Downing Street. I exaggerate, but you get the general idea.

Mr Blair floored him with a simple riposte. He accused him of wanting to be a cross-dresser. Not in so many words, but that's what he meant. Was IDS, he enquired, going to fight to the death to keep the man in charge of the court system 'in a full-bottomed wig, eighteenth-century breeches and women's tights? That says a lot more about the Conservative Party than it does about us!'

The implication was clear. Tories get an oooh-so-thrilling frisson from even thinking about a man dressed in women's tights! And frilly silk nether garments, or figure-hugging Lycra!

The slur was nonsense of course, and John Redwood asked whether it would not save a lot of money if they were to buy the Lord Chancellor a pair of trousers. Mr Duncan Smith, who appeared to be wearing a suit, shirt and tie, though I can't be entirely certain what was underneath, seems to think that if he talks for long enough, the Prime Minister will suddenly snap and say, 'My God, you are right! I have been blind! Thank heavens you are here to strip the scales from my eyes!' Instead he just wades through more mud for the Prime Minister to throw back.

And it's not only IDS who gets the wet pie in the face. Take Bob Marshall-Andrews, the Labour MP for Medway, who has embraced the removal of his own leader as his life's mission. Mr Marshall-Andrews, who is a QC, has been compared – by me, at least – to a cross between Dennis the Menace and his dog, Gnasher, except that he has just had a new haircut, so he looks as if Gnasher had been in a fight with a hedge-trimmer.

He said that he and many of his friends had campaigned for years to get the executive functions of the Lord Chancellor transferred from 'an unelected, patronage-appointed official, to an elected minister answerable to this House. Now we have instead an unelected, patronage-appointed official in the Lords, answerable to the unelected House of Lords!'

This intervention may have sounded churlish, but it was, of course, entirely accurate. So it had to be quashed. 'Having campaigned for something for many years,' said Mr Blair, 'when we do it, he opposes it!'

A great 'Whoooo!' arose from the Tories. It was meant to indicate their pleasure at seeing a Labour MP put down by a Labour prime minister. Instead, it sounded totally camp. You wondered what they might all be wearing under that grey worsted.

19.06.03

Another of my favourite parliamentary characters is Desmond Swayne, the Tory member for New Forest West. He was almost unique among legislators – having voted to send men and women off to war, he swiftly followed them.

The house was stunned to learn yesterday that Desmond Swayne was a member of the Territorial Army and has been posted to Iraq. Swayne! A man whose very name causes Labour MPs to emit howls, like trainee werewolves spotting the full moon. I have always had my own suspicions about Mr Swayne. His air is of a man who should be driving through France in an ancient Bentley some time between the wars, the car's bonnet held down by leather straps, roaring through sleepy villages at 80 mph, knocking over rural gendarmes, stopping only to seduce the daughters of simple innkeepers.

His hair is just a little too bouffant, his manner a shade too swaggering. One catches a whiff of unpaid gambling debts, of angry fathers paid not to report him to the colonel, or a half-heard whisper about who should really have won that DSO...

All this is entirely unfair. Mr Swayne is a blameless family man, a father of three, who spent most of a quiet career as a systems manager somewhere in the banking sector. Admittedly, he has a collection of right-wing views which, if you heard them, might strip away your epidermis. But there is something admirable about his posting to the sharp end. MPs are occasionally willing to send young men off to die. It is not often that they are prepared to put themselves in harm's way.

Whatever next? Will they have to accept the same dodgy pensions as the rest of us? Or even wait their turn in the taxi queue?

24.06.03

My Swayne returned safely after his tour of duty, and was indeed promoted to glory – or at least was appointed parliamentary private secretary to David Cameron when he became Tory leader.

*

In June 2003, a prankster, dressed as an Arab, infiltrated a party being given at Windsor Castle for Prince William. The Home Secretary was called to the Commons to account for this.

Few among the MPs gathered to hear his sombre words knew that the minister, Sir David Blunkett, had sought assistance from my old friend, Father Brown, whose many baffling cases have been chronicled by Mr G.K. Chesterton. None noticed in the Strangers' Gallery the figure of a short, plump Roman Catholic priest, dressed in black, a shovel hat on his head, his nondescript appearance emphasized by the tall figure seated next to him, an imposing Frenchman and former jewel thief named Flambeau, whom Father Brown had once rescued from a life of depravity – saving with it his immortal soul.

Flambeau seemed to be in a state of some agitation, since it seemed to him that MPs were not taking the matter as seriously as he did himself. The Home Secretary was describing the events of that terrible night. 'As Aaron Barschak advanced along the terrace, he was challenged by a contractor. By this time he had changed into fancy dress...'

'It must have been the Lord Chancellor!' exclaimed one from the Conservative ranks.

'I am not aware that he was wearing a wig at the time,' replied the blind statesman.

'He was! He was, and ladies' tights too!'

'*Sacré bleu, mon ami!*' exclaimed Flambeau. 'They make a *blague* of this outrage!'

'And he kissed him!' shouted another Conservative lout. Flambeau, goaded beyond endurance, tried to clamber over the rail into the Chamber, being restrained only by his friend's insistent arm.

The minister continued with his grim tale. 'Mr Barschak's actions have exposed an appalling failure in security at Windsor Castle which should simply not have happened.'

'It is a mystery, a confounded mystery,' said Flambeau. A liveried attendant signalled them to remain silent.

'The mystery,' said Father Brown in a low voice, 'is that there is no mystery.'

'I do not know what you mean, my friend! In the name of all that is holy, let us get out of this infernal place!'

Moments later the two men emerged, the priest blinking owlishly in the summer sunlight, his friend striding out towards St James's Park, where his upraised stick sent a flock of ducks into the air.

'At least,' said Flambeau, 'the wretched constable who caught the blackguard then sent him on into the party will be dismissed, and I hope sentenced to a generous term in prison!'

'On the contrary,' replied his friend. 'I hope that he will be spared, for he is the only man in this sad sequence of events to emerge with any credit.'

'What the devil can you mean by that?' demanded Flambeau.

'How would an Arab terrorist arrive at a fancy dress party?' asked Father Brown. Would he come as an Arab terrorist? Of course not. He would be dressed as a comical lion, or as David Beckham. Or even as the Queen herself.

'What he would not do would be to come in a beard and a keffiyeh. The constable who saw him realized this – realized that the only man who would not conceivably harm the Prince was a man dressed as someone who might wish to harm the Prince.

'And he was right. I hope he is promoted in short order.'

25.06.03

My old chum Michael Fabricant was, at around this time, promoted to the Conservative front bench. It was a moving moment for us both.

Mickey has been made a shadow trade and industry minister, and what a great responsibility he bears! I have seen a list of the topics on which he is supposed to speak for his party. He is in charge of all our international trade policy, the post office, export credits, enlargement of the EU, the single market, the euro and British preparations for entry, all e-commerce, the communication and information industries, radio, science and technology including nanotechnology, the British space programme, research councils, weights and measures, chemicals, and the manufacture and maintenance of hairpieces.

No, he isn't! I made the last one up. Though it could be covered by the nanotechnology brief. 'Dr Oostner of Dresden has discovered that a single pubic hair from a

Barbie doll can spontaneously turn into a wig the size of the Albert Hall! He must be stopped, and you, Fabricant, are the only man who can do it!'

Hercules himself would have regarded those portfolios as a heavy workload. Tomorrow Mickey will be asking questions of Patricia Hewitt. Sadly, a prior engagement means that I shall miss the event.

No matter. Yesterday they held a debate on small businesses, and for the first time Mickey was able to sit on the front bench. The front bench! The Mecca, the Elysium, the Utopia for all politicians. Oh, the green leather may look the same as elsewhere in the Chamber, but it feels so much softer; it caresses the backside so lovingly; the view is so much more inspiring.

I had to go and see him. I felt like a divorced dad, banned from visiting his children, standing outside the school gates, desperate for a glimpse. He looked terribly happy. Now and again he glanced in my direction. Was it to say a silent 'thank you' for all the help I have given to him in his career? I like to think so.

03.07.03

The controversy over whether the government had exaggerated the threat from Saddam Hussein grew in volume.

The impressionist show *Dead Ringers* always does Tony Blair with a voiceover of him instructing himself on how to look and sound in public. 'Deep, furrowed brow,' you hear him mutter. 'Sincere smile, warm chuckle.' Since most politicians end up looking like their caricatures and sounding like their impressionists, it is hardly surprising that we have come to hear the same voices.

Yesterday, for example, he appeared before the Liaison Committee, an occasional session at which he answers questions from MPs who are chairmen of other committees. He keeps them for two and a half hours, until some are beginning to whimper for mercy. Yesterday, before they were overcome by both the heat and the sheer pointlessness of human existence, they tried to nail him on the missing weapons of mass destruction and the dodgy dossier. They failed, as they always do, since he simply denies everything and implies that even to ask such questions is to remove yourself from the comity of decent society.

He was asked right away if he had misled the Commons over the dodgy dossier. ('Eyes blazing with righteous anger!' we heard.) 'I refute that entirely!' his real voice said, out loud. 'We put our case before the House of Commons and the country, and I stand by that case totally. It was the right case, and we did the right thing!' ('Stick out jaw and raise lower lip to give impression of unchallengeable determination' drifted across in our direction.)

'The central allegation that I myself, or anyone else, inserted information into that dossier, that central allegation, is completely and totally false. Indeed, I don't know anyone who believes it to be true!' ('Turn face away as if you can't bear to risk making eye contact with someone who might have allowed such a vicious and malevolent thought to creep into their mind.')

The problem is that he looks as if he has a drama coach prompting him in the wings. He mimes anger, but doesn't seem to feel it. He does outrage without looking outraged.

Donald Anderson, who chairs the Foreign Affairs Committee, declared that the jury was still out on the weapons. ('Flashing eyes, hands chopping in disbelief.')

'Donald, for me, the jury is not out...I have no doubt at

all that the evidence of those weapons will be found, no doubt at all!' ('Look of mild exasperation that anyone could think otherwise.')

08.07.03

A few people noticed a subtle verbal shift here. While protesting angrily that he had not misled the House or the country, his certainty that 'the weapons' would be found had been replaced by 'the evidence of the weapons'.

*

Meanwhile the country was exercised by remarks made by Mr Andrew Gilligan, a reporter on the Today *programme. In an early morning bulletin he said that experts in the field believed that some of the evidence in the so-called 'dodgy dossier' had been 'sexed up'. The remarks caused a furore, and the government went to some trouble to find Mr Gilligan's source. His name, Dr David Kelly, soon became public knowledge, and he was asked to give evidence to the Commons foreign affairs committee.*

Throughout his session, Dr Kelly spoke in a voice barely above a whisper. Air-conditioning roared and it was hard to make out what he said.

Dr Kelly spread confusion and despair among the committee. Was he one of theirs, or one of ours? Was it a single bluff, a double bluff, or a Möbius strip-style interconnected, self-referential triple bluff? It was lucky that Dr Kelly was not Deep Throat in the Watergate scandal, or else the parking garage would have resounded to Bob Woodward's cries of 'How's that? Come again?' Time and again, the chairman asked him to raise his voice. Though it was a hot and muggy day, they had to switch off the air-conditioning.

Dr Kelly admitted having met Andrew Gilligan in May, in

a London hotel. When he read and heard his reports, at least some of the material seemed familiar. That is why he had contacted his bosses, admitting that he might have been one source. But he had not been the main source. That must have been someone else.

One MP asked him about Gilligan's interviewing style. Had he used the C-word? Dr Kelly looked like someone who did not know what the C-word might possibly be, in any context. It turned out to mean 'Campbell', as in Alastair. Yes, the name had cropped up. But, he said, he had not breathed the word in a significant way, as Gilligan had reported his source as doing.

Dr Kelly was asked if he had met any other journalists and spoken in the same way to them. He was evasive. Labour's Andrew Mackinlay was infuriated. 'This is the high court of Parliament and you are under an obligation to reply!' The recipient of this magnificent, hand-stitched threat raised his voice to a whisper and gave a couple of names.

Mr Mackinlay returned to the attack. It was clear to him that Dr Kelly was 'chaff' put up by the government to fool the committee's radar. 'You're the fall guy!' he said, loudly. 'You've been set up!'

Dr Kelly looked mildly pained at this, but only very mildly.

My guess is that it was all a mistake. Clearly Gilligan couldn't hear Dr Kelly's hushed voice above all the noise in the Charing Cross hotel.

'We should have a drink. I'll get the barmaid to set 'em up.'

'Aha, sexed up, was it? I guessed as much.'

'We could have some wine. The house white is a bit of a gamble.'

'Campbell, eh! I thought we'd be hearing that name!'

'I've just had a word with the maitre d'. Apparently we can have lunch in four to five minutes.'

'Launched in forty-five minutes! Thank you, David, I think that's all I need!'

16.07.03

The session described above was an exceedingly useful lesson in how little we see beneath the surface. At the end I thought that David Kelly looked relieved that the questioning was over, but not particularly anxious. Mr Mackinlay's questioning had sounded far more aggressive than it really was, though some foolish people even blamed him for Dr Kelly's suicide a few days later. The real damage seems to have been done by the questioning of David Chidgey, a Liberal Democrat. He had received from Andrew Gilligan – who in turn was anxious to protect his own reputation against charges of exaggerating what he knew – an account of what David Kelly had told a reporter from Newsnight. *When this was read out to him, Dr Kelly seems to have realized that his own story – that he had given only partial information to Mr Gilligan – was coming apart. He feared being exposed as a liar, and losing his job and the pension that went with it.*

The sad thing is that he clearly did not realize that if he had exposed then and there the misleading elements of the dossier, and the duplicity of at least some people in government, he would have become a national hero and would have lacked neither work nor plaudits.

I am not one of those who suspect that he might have been murdered. Cui bono? Was it conceivable that the authorities might have wanted to attract the outcry, the scandal and the subsequent inquiry? No one was to know just how naive the conclusions of Lord Hutton's inquiry would subsequently appear.

*

Meanwhile, it was the end of July and the political year was drawing to its close. Mr Blair had heard the news of Dr Kelly's death as he flew from the United States, where he had received a standing ovation from the US Congress.

The Prime Minister arrived for his first press conference in Britain since the Kelly affair broke. It must have been one of the toughest he had ever attended, and could have broken his premiership.

We knew he was nervous because he walked in, barked 'Right!' and favoured us with his Jack Nicholson grin, the one that looks as if the corners of his mouth will meet at the back. 'Welcome to this evening's press conference!' he said. Since it was 10 a.m. at the time, this might have been more evidence of mental turmoil.

But with the next sentence, his strategy became clear. He was going to bore us into submission. 'Michael will talk to you about the delivery of public services,' he said, with an air of promise, as if Michael were the conjuror at a children's party. He did not, however, tell us who Michael was. Foot? Portillo? Fabricant? Schumacher? Vaughan? Mouse? None of them seemed likely.

Michael turned out to be Michael Barber of the Number 10 Delivery Unit – not a posh name for the post room, but for the people in charge of trying to make sure stuff gets done. Michael spoke largely in New Labour jargon, no doubt having been programmed that way. We learned about trajectories, targets, milestones and stocktakes. We were told to wait for 'real-world outcomes', step changes and 'key outcome indicators'. He talked about 'bottom-up pressure for change', which may refer to liposuction, and 'top-down initiatives', which may mean breast enlargement.

The Prime Minister resumed. Every now and again someone would try to raise the topic of Dr Kelly, and who had given his name to the press. He told us we should wait for the Hutton Inquiry to report. 'I think the public wants us to get on top of the economy, crime, the health service and schools.' Was he still trusted by the electorate? 'I think the public will judge us on the economy, the health service, on schools and on crime.'

(Nobody ever does this one the other way round. No one ever says, 'Yer know, down at the Dog and Duck, I don't think they're too worried about public services. They want to know how Dr Kelly was shopped to the media.')

By this time he was motoring. He knew nobody was going to get past his guard. Someone asked about Nasser Hussein, the England cricket captain, who had spoken about the burden of leading his country, about running out of ideas.

'No,' he said, 'I think captaining the England cricket team is probably a rather harder job!'

Then he flipped into the camp mode he adopts when he knows his troubles are temporarily over, the assault course has been successfully negotiated, and a decent lunch awaits. A German reporter, a handsome young woman, was confused about whether he had called her.

'Do you want me now?' she asked. He gazed at her, paused for a brief moment, then said, 'I want you any time.'

It was an electric moment. She became totally flustered and said, 'That's quite something!' and he replied, 'Er, I mean that in an, er, "non-whatever it is" way.' I assumed that he just could not bring himself to use the word 'sexual'.

Either way, he may be morphing into Hugh Grant.

31.07.03

The Hutton Inquiry began to hold its hearings at the Law Courts in the Strand. Almost every day brought a new and exciting witness. Tony Blair's evidence was, perhaps, the most eagerly awaited.

He arrived promptly at the inquiry and gave Lord Hutton a little smile, as if to put him at his ease. He kept calling him 'my lord', which was faintly creepy since there is only one person who creates lords in this country, and it's him.

The atmosphere in court 73 was oddly muted. We might have been witnesses to a great historic event, but for most of the dozen or so lawyers and the press it was just another day at the office – the same faces, the joshing, the same forest of computer screens, the same Caffè Nero run, the same endless box files. Even Lord Hutton and the inquiry's fleshily handsome barrister, James Dingemans, looked firmly unimpressed. When you're a top judge or QC, it's cool to look unimpressed.

What did the rest of us expect? That he would break down and cry, 'Yes, I killed Dr Kelly as surely as if it had been my own hand on the knife!' But Tony Blair doesn't do sobbing, or rueful contrition. What he does do is calm, factual, look guys, let's be reasonable about this. This week we learned that Dr Kelly had been greatly stressed by the oral exam for his PhD. Tony Blair would have turned up with a ring binder, a Caffè Nero and a welcoming smile for the examiners.

He began well. Where had he been when he first heard about Andrew Gilligan's allegations on the *Today* programme? 'I was in Basra, with British troops.' ('Thanking our brave lads for their sacrifice, while the wretched Gilligan was peddling his lies through the sewers of the metropolis,' we were supposed to think.)

The gist of his defence was, 'Look, I'm a pretty straight sort of guy. If I'd lied, I'd resign, but I didn't lie. I'm also very busy, so I had plenty on my mind. I agreed to release Dr Kelly's name because I thought it would have been wrong to keep it from MPs. That's because I'm a pretty straight sort of guy. As I may have mentioned.'

He didn't seem nervous, except when questions reached the period after Dr Kelly had admitted talking to the BBC. At this point – how did he decide to name Dr Kelly? – his language began to go haywire – literally like the thin wire used to bind hay, in that it flew all over the place, tangled up then sprang apart again and was liable to poke out its user's eye. 'The quandary was this. We didn't want the foreign affairs committee to look into this, at the last minute, forward comes someone who might be the source of the allegation – did you inform the FAC immediately, which is one possibility and which I have no doubt afterwards people would have said to us, we should have done? Did you try to get greater clarity of whether this was indeed the source or not? So how did you handle this? And the reason why I thought it was very important to involve the senior officials is that he made the whole allegation...'

At this point he started to wave his hands in strange shapes and patterns. Us old-time Blair-watchers know that this indicates a 'Why don't you believe me?' kind of agitation, as if somehow the gestures will make the point where words alone cannot succeed.

He seemed happiest when he led us through all the work he, as Prime Minister, has to do on our behalf. On Monday, 7 July, one of the most important dates in the Kelly story, he had 'breakfast with information technology consultants, a series of meetings on school funding, a big speech at the Queen Elizabeth Conference Centre on the criminal justice system, a meeting with the head of the Olympic committee, a government reception in the evening, I had to prepare for the liaison committee on Tuesday and for Prime Minister's Questions on Wednesday…'

Enough already! I wanted to shout. Those aren't tasks, they're make-work. Much of it doesn't matter at all! And it must be so dull that you would sometimes rather tear your ears off than listen to another speech, let alone one of your own!

We went through a memo Alastair Campbell had written, asking for changes to the September dossier. Mr Campbell had been picking holes in it: '"Might" reads very weakly. "Could" is weak – "capable of being used" is better. Doesn't need "probable".'

It all seemed somehow familiar, and I sensed we were back in Mr Campbell's past, as a *Daily Mirror* trainee in the West Country, working on the *Tavistock Times*. 'Oi, you, Campbell,' says the chief sub-editor. 'This agency stuff is crap. You've got five minutes to knock it into shape. What's this "probable" crap? Blimey, put a bit of life into it. It's crap, this is.'

I don't think the dossier was 'sexed-up'; it was put into tabloidese, which is a slightly different thing. It must have shocked all those spooks, who write in measured, balanced, weighted prose, designed to protect their own backsides. But there is a ferocious chief sub somewhere, perhaps retired, possibly dead, whose voice was ringing in Alastair's ears as he wrote. 'Oi, Campbell, that's crap, that is.' I hope he is giving a small satisfied grunt right now.

29.08.03

The inquiry continued for several weeks.

In an unprecedented move, the chief of MI6 appeared in public before the Hutton Inquiry yesterday. In fact, 'C', as he is known to his friends, did nothing so compromising of his personal security as to actually appear. Instead he manifested himself through his voice. Even the link to the computer screens in the court seemed to have been covered by sacking just in case they inadvertently gave a clue to what he might look like.

We weren't told where he was, though a technician said he was not in the MI6 building, but 'somewhere north of the river', which may be intelligence slang of some kind. My private fantasy was that a cupboard door in the corner of the court would fall open and a very embarrassed spymaster would drop out.

Wherever he was, it was rather noisy. At one point we seemed to hear a toilet flush. Then there were other mysterious clangings and bangings, as if 'C' were using a traction engine rally as a cover for his briefing. At one point, he even had to be asked to speak closer to the microphone. Perhaps he was at home and didn't want his wife to learn what his job is.

The world depicted by 'C' – or 'Sir Richard Billing Dearlove', which is his code name – seems a long way from the glamorous life of James Bond. There was no mention of Aston Martins fitted with rocket launchers, or pistols disguised as pens. Nor did we glimpse the more workaday world of George Smiley, gazing at the Berlin Wall.

'I hear Rczski has gone north of the river.'

'Yes, that was a regrettable lapse in security.'

Instead, the day-to-day life of the average spook seems to consist, as it does for most civil servants, of meetings and paperwork. We learned that intelligence reports are known as 'CX' in the business, and that he had been 'shocked' to discover Dr Kelly had been discussing a CX report with the press. 'It was a serious breach of discipline,' he said, in the same appalled voice as the chief of police who discovers there is gambling at Rick's Bar in *Casablanca* – that is, not shocked at all.

We also learned that the people who get to read these CX reports are known as 'customers', as in: 'The reference to forty-five minutes did not evoke any comment from customers at all.'

This may be another clue. After all, customers sometimes make demands, as in: 'Haven't you got anything stronger?'

'All right, hang on, I'll have a look in the back. Can do you thirty-five minutes, if that's any use…?'

We had a long discussion about what constitutes a reliable report, and it turns out that a single source can be quite enough. 'Much high-quality intelligence comes from single sources.' This is, of course, the point that Andrew Gilligan and the BBC have been trying to make, without much success. Apparently it's OK when the single source is talking to secret men with no faces; an outrage if it's talking to a reporter.

At the end, the inquiry's counsel, James Dingemans, asks, as he always does, if there is any other light the witness can throw on the death of Dr Kelly. They always say no.

I yearn for someone to shout, 'Yes, it was me! Me, I tell you! But you'll never catch me alive.' (Plunges out of window, last seen heading for north of the river.)

But 'C' simply said there was nothing he could add, and doubtless went for a much-needed cup of tea with two sugars, stirred not shaken.

16.09.03

Two days later, Andrew Gilligan gave evidence.

Mr Gilligan was cross-questioned by Jonathan Sumption, a barrister who, we are told, earns roughly £2 million a year. He turned out to be the Iain Duncan Smith of the legal world. Like the Tory leader, he has the right ideas. He can put a sentence together. He knew what he was talking about. He is plainly a decent man. What he cannot do is land a fist on an opponent.

He was good at that dancing thing boxers do. As he asked his questions, he pranced in a most surprising fashion, his feet describing the sort of diagram you used to see in old 'how to dance' books – the waltz, the foxtrot, the samba. You half expected to hear Harry Smith-Hampshire, the old BBC dance commentator, describe it all: 'What a simply marvellous display here at the Tower Ballroom in Blackpool. Jonathan Sumption, dazzling us all with his partner, the lovely Jonathan Sumption.'

It would be wrong to say that Mr Gilligan escaped altogether, though it was other counsel who elicited the damaging stuff, such as the email he sent to members of the foreign affairs committee [the one that probably let Dr Kelly know that it was known his version of events stopped short of the full truth]. For this he was obliged to apologize.

Oh, and the fact that the notes of his meeting with Dr Kelly got entirely lost at some time unknown. Now there is no record of what exactly happened between the two men. I hope that Mr Gilligan looks after the title deeds to his house with more care.

But Mr Sumption drew very little out of him. In fact, what he did was drag a nit comb over his evidence and consequently came up with a handful of nits. He seemed quite appalled that Mr Gilligan had implied the government might be guilty of dishonesty. A maiden aunt would have been less shocked at finding her nephew in bed with the chambermaid. 'Was that not an accusation of bad faith?' he asked, about Downing Street's role in the dossier. Bad faith? Downing Street? Where on earth has Mr Sumption been living?

At this point Gilligan was still nervous, his head bobbing up and down as he gulped down water. But it didn't last long. Mr Sumption accused him of running his story on 'an anonymous allegation'. But it wasn't anonymous to him: he knew Dr Kelly very well, and knew that he was one of the world's greatest experts in the field. He tried to trip Gilligan up over calling Dr Kelly 'a member of the intelligence services', which he wasn't. Gilligan pointed out that he had made that mistake once in nineteen broadcasts and had corrected it later.

Finally, there was an angels-dancing-on-the-head-of-a-pin argument about whether Dr Kelly worked 'in' or 'for' the Ministry of Defence. It was all gloriously silly and proved little beyond the fact that Gilligan had, in the torrent of words at the time, made a few slips of the tongue. Maybe he has been making it all up. But Mr Sumption did not come remotely close to showing that.

Maybe they could save a bit of money by giving the job to Carole Caplin. Or IDS.

18.09.03

There was a splendid face-off at the Hutton Inquiry yesterday. Richard Hatfield, the personnel director at the Ministry of Defence, became one of the first people to fight back against the majestic briefs who are doing the cross-examinations. He faced Jeremy Gompertz QC who is appearing for the Kelly family. I don't think I have ever seen two people simultaneously patronize each other – both with some success. The QC had all the top barrister's bag of tricks: ersatz incredulity, sarcasm and long meaningful pauses. Mr Hatfield for his part stared over his gold-rimmed glasses as if wondering who this little man might be, asking him all these impertinent questions. Mr Gompertz had to use all his cunning devices, since Mr Hatfield was determined not to give anything away. It must have been like trying to open an oyster with a plastic spoon. In fact, the man from the ministry could conduct a master class in how to hold your own against a highly paid barrister. Civil servants, fraudsters, even car radio thieves would pay good money. All quotes are from the hearing.

1. Condescend. Say in a plonking voice, 'Quite obviously that is the case,' or, 'As I think I made plain earlier...'

2. Stand your ground. Asked, 'Would you adhere to that?' say firmly, 'I would.' When the brief asks in exaggerated astonishment, 'You would?' reply, '*Yes*, I would!'

3. Stare a lot. If you don't like the question, take time out to peer at your interlocutor as if you can't quite believe anyone would say anything so silly.

4. Repeat phrases back. Mr Hatfield suggested that the MoD had offered Dr Kelly 'outstanding' support. Faced with the suggestion that this was nonsense, describe everything you did for him, adding the word 'outstanding' at each point.

5. If you don't like the question, decline to answer. Or, like politicians, answer another one of your own devising.

6. Flip the charges back. If someone accuses you of behaving 'harshly' say that, on the contrary, you didn't act harshly enough. Asked if you would like to be treated like that, bark, 'I *have* been treated like that.'

19.09.03

Four days later we got a glimpse of the core documents in the investigation – Alastair Campbell's diaries. You need to recall that ministers agreed that they would not actually name Dr Kelly as Gilligan's source. But if journalists were to guess his name, they would confirm it. Several reporters working in the field knew there could only be a handful of people under suspicion, so two at least got the name very speedily.

The Campbell diaries exploded on top of the Hutton Inquiry like a shellburst over the chateau where the officers are billeted. They were sensational! Right in the very first paragraph he wrote 'G[eoff] H[oon] and I agreed that it would fuck Gilligan if that was his source.'

We gasped. We reeled. The thought that a senior official in the British government would use the word only once in the pages of his diaries was unimaginable! This is a man who probably reads his children stories like *Now We Are Fucking Six* and *The Wind in the Fucking Willows*. Were the diaries a forgery? It seemed a real possibility. None of us wanted to be caught out and made to look foolish, like Hugh Trevor-Roper with the Hitler diaries.

But if they were, why was he there to launch them? For a launch was what it was. There was everything except the warm white wine and cheesy nibbles. The inquiry clerk began by describing them. 'They were written not for publication, or indeed for anyone except Mr Campbell to see,' he claimed, to cynical laughter. Where do they find these legal types who believe that kind of stuff? In caves? Anyhow, they could use that quote on the jacket.

Authors these day present publishers with a 'proposal', which is a summary of the book plus a few teasing extracts, designed to whet the appetite. But few writers get to offer their proposal to umpteen barristers and the world's press. I suspect that in the space of one short hour he may have doubled his advance. Ka-ching!

Clearly some work will have to be done at the editing stage. For example, Mr Campbell tried hard to persuade the inquiry that he hadn't wanted Dr Kelly's name to be published. But according to the diaries, he wanted to get it out through the newspapers. What could that mean?

'This is diary writing – it doesn't actually express what is going on,' he said. Rather a good example of the Blair spin machine, expressing nothing of what is actually going on.

Mr Campbell persisted. He hadn't wanted 'it' to happen. Lord Hutton asked in a baffled sort of way what 'it' was. 'It is me, at the end of the day, scribbling whatever comes into my head,' Mr Campbell replied. So that's how the dodgy dossier was compiled. I think we'd already guessed.

Earlier, Geoff Hoon, the defence secretary, another lawyer, produced some fine obfuscation. Asked if thought the government had done anything wrong, he eschewed both 'yes' and 'no'. Instead he replied, 'Having followed your cross-examination carefully, I can see that there may be judgements about the precise timing of particular decisions, the precise point at which those decisions had an effect which are within what I would describe as the reasonable range of judgement people can make when confronted with this situation.' So that's all right, then!

He even insisted that his ministry had not released Dr Kelly's name, which took some tortuous reasoning. In short, he was both ingenious and ingenuous. For Dr Kelly's outing was not, as one QC claimed, like *Twenty Questions*. It was more like *Give Us a Clue*, in which each player is desperate for the others to get it right. 'Fingers in his ears? Is it "quiet"? No, he's tapping his chest, it's a stethoscope. He's a doctor! Now he's cupping his ear, means "sounds like". He's rubbing his stomach. Is it "Dr Tummy"? No, I know, it's a belly! Gilligan's source was George Melly!'

23.09.03

2003–2004

The Hutton inquiry was still rumbling on when the Lib Dems began their conference.

The new, tough, take-no-prisoners Charles Kennedy stubbed out his fag as if it represented the last hopes of the Tory Party. Then he strode out on stage to tell his fellow Liberal Democrats what brand of people they were. 'We are sensible, not supine!' he announced.

All politicians love a new cliché and that was a belter. You could use it, or a variant, almost any time. 'We are practical, not prone. We will be careful, but never cowardly. We shall be bold but not bladdered!'

It would be misleading to say that the conference was energized by this call to sensibleness. It is always hard to thrill an audience with an address that includes the speaker's thoughts on loft insulation, or includes a line such as 'Now this complex passage must be decided upon at an inter-governmental conference.' Mr Kennedy was facing a rabble – a thoughtful, caring rabble, to be sure, the kind of rabble that would ask politely if anyone needed to get home before adding another bus to the burning barricade – but a rabble that wanted to be roused.

Instead he gave them a rabble-dowsing speech. He is, to the Lib Dems, a little like the middle child. His parents think they love him just as much as the others, and they certainly tell him that they do. But in the end, he's the one who gets the book tokens rather than the Play Station.

The fact is that he doesn't do excitement. He is more like a Scottish dominie, of a type who may still exist in the

Highlands – precise and careful, speaking at note-taking speed, wanting them to be well aware of the benefits loft insulation can bring. At one time he sounded as if he was working his way through the coal-mining regions of Belgium and would be testing them later.

Finally he let his voice soar and threw away his notes so as to give them some ad lib, impromptu, wellie. 'We are going to fight for a better, a nude, united Britain!' Disturbing images floated into our heads. The Liberal Democrats, nude but united, naked and unashamed. Sensible but stripped, sensitive yet starkers, a birthday suit our birthright. A colleague tells me he probably meant a 'renewed Britain' but I doubt it – politicians only like new clichés.

26.09.03

The Labour conference followed the Liberal Democrats'. The rivalry between the party's two most powerful members was, as ever, on prominent display.

Gordon Brown produced another superb, over-the-top leadership bid yesterday. Michael Heseltine was famous for being able to find the clitoris of the Conservative Party. Gordon Brown is less subtle. He grasped the Labour's Party's ample bum and gave it a massive, eye-watering squeeze. There were no fine wines and Belgian chocolates. It was more ''Ow about it, darling, your place or Number 11?'

The only drawback was that he looked so miserable. The more passionate he became, the more sorrowful he seemed. To misquote the old *Punch* cartoon, it was as if someone had said to him, 'Enjoy your speech, Gordon. I shall have some bad news for you when you have finished.'

The clue was that this was a leadership bid came in the first line. 'Conference, I can report to you today that with a Labour government, led by Tony Blair, with Labour policies, there are now more than 1.6 million men and women who did not have jobs under the Tories, who now...'

He didn't actually claim that under Tony Blair it only rains at night, but he was heading that way. In fact, praising Tony Blair at the very beginning was a demonstration of how ruthless he intended to be. He was clearing the decks for a thunderous announcement, a demonstration that he ought to be prime minister, an evangelical bishop rather than a milquetoast curate, hellfire from Elmer Gantry rather than *Thought for the day*. (Later he told us, 'TB is a curable disease.' We didn't need an Enigma machine to work that out.)

At the start he looked merely regretful, as if he had just been told that the clutch would cost £400 to replace. Then he began to look glummer. He gripped the lectern ferociously as if it were responsible for all the evils of the earth. He stopped talking about the mere economy, a topic that dwindled into insignificance as he portrayed a nation united, united in its Labour values, united in agreement with its Chancellor. Britain, Labour, Gordon Brown – the three formed a mighty trinity! As John Lennon said, 'I am he as you are he and we are all together,' or something along those lines. He is the Eggman, he is the Gordon!

'These are great causes worth fighting for, and worth campaigning for. Showing why a Labour Party, if it did not exist, would have to be created today to fight for justice, dignity and fairness in Britain!' he declared. (Translation: 'It does need to be created today, and under my leadership.') 'Labour needs not just a programme, but a soul!' he announced. As the cheers rolled around the hall we realized that he was the party's conscience, guide and saviour. 'Have confidence that Labour values are the values of the British people! The Labour Party – best when we are boldest, best when we are united, best when we are Labour! Unlike that Tory at Number 10!'

Of course he didn't say the last bit, but it might as well have appeared above his head, written in letters of fire. But at this point the misery on his face was too terrible to be ignored. What could have happened? Had his wife put his trousers in the wash without removing the winning lottery ticket? The previous night Channel 4 had shown *The Deal*, about his relationship with Tony Blair. Perhaps he had forgotten to set the video.

Or had he just got round to reading the Prime Minister's promise to go 'on and on'?

30.09.03

As always, Tony Blair spoke on the following day, the Tuesday.

It will be remembered as the conference speech at which Tony Blair almost cried. It was a classic New Labour moment: the leader moved to tears by his own rhetoric. We've had the self-cleaning oven and the self-basting turkey. Now we have the self-watering speech.

That came at the end. Even before he came out, Labour's achievements were flashed up on the giant screen to delirious cheers. Matrons back in hospitals! Free fruit for five-year-olds. Crime down, inflation down, a chicken singing in every garden, a bluebird in every pot! The delegates gave him a three-minute ovation just for turning up. He looked delighted, then realized that he had to look earnest as well. So he was smiley and serious, glittering and grim, happy yet haemorrhoidal.

He took a risk. 'So, what do we do? Do we give up on it, or get on with it?' and at least half a dozen people yelled 'Give up!' None of them was Gordon Brown, unless he has added ventriloquism to his skills. It was the last dissent. Behind me one man was clapping so hard I feared his arms might fly off. I looked round and saw it was the junior minister Ben Bradshaw. He was actually having to flap his arms in the air to cool his hands off. This is the kind of loyalty New Labour needs.

His message was clear. 'We have been crap, but you have been crappier!' (I paraphrase, but that was the gist.) Why was this? Well, back in 1997 they had thought things would be easy. 'I know many people are disappointed, hurt, angry,' he said, looking disappointed, hurt, angry. But it was also the party's fault. They were (famously like Gordon Brown, he didn't add) psychologically flawed. Their psychology had been, deep down, that someone else was the governing party, 'and we were the ones championing the grievance'. Snap out of it, he was saying.

And there was going to be no nonsense about squeezing the rich until the pips squeaked. 'It wasn't just the rich that were squeezed, it wasn't the pips that squeaked, it was us!' he said. What did that mean? Nobody knew. But it was aimed at Gordon Brown and that is all that mattered.

Next we were back with Iraq, and the letters from people who had lost sons there. One had sent him a 'beautiful letter...though their son was dead, they still thought it was right'. His eyes began to blink. 'And don't believe anyone who tells you that when they receive letters like that they don't suffer any doubts...' Blink, blink, blink. A red rim formed round the eyes, and the voice began to choke.

My colleague Steve Bell saw it all from immediately below. He reports that Mr Blair wasn't blubbing, and Steve did not leave the hall drenched. But both men were slightly moister than when they had arrived.

01.10.03

You would have thought that the doubts might be stimulated by getting a letter from people who had lost a son and thought it had been in a pointless cause. But even the caring and sensitive Blair could not bring himself to read out a letter that suggested he might have been wrong. This was, incidentally, also the speech in which he declared that he had no reverse gear.

*

As ever, the Tory conference followed.

The chairman of the Conservative Party conference, who is not to be confused with the chairman of the Conservative Party, invited the mayor of Blackpool to make the annual speech of welcome. 'Councillor Lily Henderson, Mr Mayor!' he cried.

Mr Mayor turned out to be a white-haired old lady. So perhaps it was a slip of the tongue, except that he said it twice more. Or possibly she was Lily in the same way that Lily Savage is. After all, we are in Blackpool, home of the Funny Girls transvestite nightclub in which men are men, and so are all of the women. (On a visit there we enjoyed listening to a disc jockey called 'Zoe'. 'She' picked on members of the audience she claimed to fancy. 'Remember my name – you'll be screaming it later!')

Or it could be that in Toryland, mayors are always called 'Mr' whether they are male, female, or in between. Next the chairman of the Conservative Party came to the platform. To add to the confusion, he was a woman too. Theresa May,

178

for it was she, wore a black trouser suit and zebra-skin shoes – her full dominatrix gear. A frisson ran through the audience, though it was quickly apprehended by the stewards.

Her speech was entitled *Building on Success*. Yeah, we thought, and next year's will be *Living on Thin Air* or *Playing Cluedo on Mars*. As usual, her theme for the day was that the Tory Party was no good. Useless. They should be ashamed of themselves. They needed punishment. Discipline. They had to be chastized! A look of passionate longing could be seen on some of the older delegates' faces.

Speaking of which, it is hard to underestimate how unpopular Iain Duncan Smith is with his fellow MPs. They don't wish him ill – they just want him to have a long, and imminent, retirement. I asked one backbencher how he would feel if IDS were to fall under a lorry. 'Well, a huge wave of relief would go through the party from top to bottom,' he said, before explaining that the problem was that the leadership was now in the gift of the party membership, and there was nothing to stop them coming up with another stumer.

But I was unprepared for the suggestion made by another MP, a junior shadow minister. 'We may have to murder him,' he said. 'It's the only way we can get rid of him in time.' I am sure he was joking. Well, pretty sure. But if Mr Duncan Smith's body turns up, an oriental dagger sticking from his back, I fear I will have to reveal my source to the authorities.

07.10.03

Tory MPs in Blackpool amused themselves with a party game – how best to despatch their leader? One suggested a pillow over his face. Another wondered if a Portillo wouldn't do the same trick. A third wanted to hook up to the Blackpool illuminations and pop the end of the cable in his bath. Poor Mr Duncan Smith had to make his speech at the end of the week. It was his last as leader.

He was preceded by Boris Johnson, who made the annual fund-raising speech. He begged the delegates to give money to the party, and not to waste their money on 'the fleshpots of Blackpool…or those curiously ventilated undergarments'. It was, I feel sure, the first time that any Tory MP has raised money by talking about split-crotch panties.

IDS won the crazed, over-the-top ovation he needed. The Tory Party in the hall was ecstatic. They couldn't believe how wonderful he was, or how wonderful they were for having chosen such a wonderful leader. He got a twelve-minute standing ovation, a gigantic, foot-stamping, throat-shredding V-sign to the Labour Party, to the media and to all the MPs who have spent the week more or less openly plotting against him.

But the success came at a terrible price. It was like being hectored for more than an hour by a very angry Dalek, a Dalek whose batteries kept running down. His message was clear: 'Tony Blair is a liar. Tories trust the people. I can't climb stairs.'

He swerved wildly from being the quiet man to the angry man. 'Anger!' he kept shouting. 'Anger!' Gosh, he was angry. Then suddenly his voice disappeared. 'Listen…listen,' he whispered. 'You can hear…' No we couldn't. 'You can hear, steady as a heartbeat, the hurt and the anger. Of the people. Of this country.' This was the politics of road rage. At times he seemed to be raving. 'The quiet man is turning up the volume!'

He had a claque, a doughnut of supporters who had been placed around the rostrum, which in turn had been moved out from the stage into a point near the middle of the hall. They stood up to applaud no fewer than seventeen times in the course of the speech in order to create artificial standing ovations, though since little of what he said even merited a sedentary ovation, the effect was of an entire political party with a serious bladder problem.

10.10.03

The Hutton Inquiry finally finished taking evidence.

Court 73 had been cleared of the clutter and the computers, so it had a slightly forlorn air, like a classroom just before the summer holidays. You half expected Lord Hutton to look down on us and say, 'Just because this is the last day of term doesn't mean that we won't be working as usual.' The only witness was Sir Kevin Tebbit, permanent under-secretary at the Ministry of Defence and a grandee so grand that he makes Sir Humphrey sound like a bus conductor.

It has been a rough few weeks for Sir Kevin. He has just recovered from an eye operation, and yesterday the *Guardian*'s front page named him in connection with a bribes scandal. But when you are a senior civil servant as majestic as he is, it would take the arrival of the Turkish football team in full battle formation to put you off. Like so many of his ilk, Sir Kevin communicates in a language known as 'British', which is very similar to, yet tantalizingly different from English. British speakers use terms such as *acquis* and *ad referendum*, 'tantamount' and 'contingent' in the same way you or I might say, 'Yes, a cup of tea would be lovely, thanks.' It is their mother tongue. In Sir Kevin's language nobody ever 'thinks' anything; instead, they 'incline to the view'. Nothing is 'included'; instead, it is 'subsumed'.

He used words like 'lest'. Can you imagine anyone you know saying, 'I'll take an umbrella, lest it rain.' Or in reply to 'The Parkers have invited us round on Friday. Do you want to go?' saying, 'I don't know yet. Why don't you make a temporizing phone call?'

At first Sir Kevin seemed calm and alert, serene and superb. But when he was cross-examined by Jeremy Gompertz QC for the Kelly family his body language unravelled. Even as he was speaking fluent British, he was grabbing his elbow with one hand, moving his carafe around, raising his glass to his lips then thinking better of it, fiddling with his pen and almost never making eye contact with his interrogator. And we began to see why. It's clear that the boys at the MoD have, in retrospect, come to loathe Dr Kelly. This is their view: he blabbed to the press and, when he was about to be exposed, admitted saying a small portion of what he actually had said. As Sir Kevin told us, if he had known then what he knew now, Dr Kelly would have been in deep do-do. (I translate from the original British.)

But they can't say how much they hate him, because since his death David Kelly has become a secular saint, or perhaps a scapegoat bearing all the iniquities of the government. You are simply not allowed to be rude about him, except by implication.

We learned what Sir Kevin really thought from a conversation he had with a BBC reporter at a buffet supper given at the Italian embassy. He told this man that he had thought Dr Kelly 'a bit eccentric and a bit weird'. Not, he hastened to add, that he meant this to refer to Dr Kelly in general, in the round as it were. He merely meant that anyone who talked to Andrew Gilligan 'must be off his head'. This was an example of his kindly translating for us from the British.

I suppose the remark will come to be known as 'the salami slur' or the 'lasagne libel'. In any event it was one of those sudden revelations of what people really meant that have occasionally enlivened this inquiry.

14.10.03

The House of Lords began its long assault on the hunting bill. Or rather it began its long assault on the pitiful remainder of the old hunting bill which had arrived in shreds from the Commons. The government had wanted a complicated compromise that would have allowed hunting to continue, but under licence. MPs threw that out in favour of a total ban.

The peers were trying to put Humpty Dumpty back together again, or possibly to reassemble someone who had just been disassembled by Arnold Schwarzenegger. The first part of the debate was an interminable discussion of what was meant by the word 'intentionally'. They were worried that some people might be prosecuted for hunting by accident. As always, they were at their best describing their own strange lives.

For example, Earl Peel asked what would have happened if his grandmother were still alive, which of course she was not, and she had been walking through the woods with her two chihuahuas. What if the toy dogs had decided to chase a hare?

Well, I thought, it's most unlikely that they would dig the old lady up just to prosecute her. But you never know these days. The police are always on the lookout for easy targets to improve their arrest figures.

Viscount Astor wanted to know what would happen if

someone tried to follow a hunt on a motorbike. Not a common occurrence, I'd have thought – you don't see a lot of people in hunting pink riding with motorcycle gangs. And how would they get over those hedges?

Lord Eden described, possibly at greater length than was strictly necessary, a walk by the riverbank with his dog. They had seen many rabbits suffering from myxomatosis. Many of these were blind. 'They were caught and were dealt with appropriately,' he said, which sounded rather sinister, unless he meant that they were taken to Rolf's Animal Hospital. 'Aw, look at these li'l fellas, 378 blind bunny rabbits. Hey, kids, I'll just finish painting Picasso's *Guernica* over here and then we'll drown the lot.'

Round about this point, Lord Hattersley came in and sat on the steps to the throne, where, I must say, he looked very much at home. Clearly the debate was of some importance to him, since his much-loved dog Buster would chase a rhino if he saw one. Roy could be in gaol for years, so putting a dent in his promising writing career.

They got quite technical. Viscount Ullswater pointed out that 'The intention of the dog may be quite different from the intention of the owner, and should not be confused with the intention of the dog' – as a past Lord Chief Justice had said, when ruling in the case of Rex v. Rex.

22.10.03

The public administration committee held many sessions of interest – of interest to political anoraks like me. On this occasion they had summoned Margaret Thatcher's old press spokesman, Bernard Ingham. It had been Bernard's task to take over the job of being Mrs Thatcher when she was too tired, or just too busy. He radiated her self-assurance, her certainty, her contempt for those who naysayed her.

Brick-red of face, beetling of brow, seemingly built to withstand passing hurricanes, Sir Bernard resembled a half-timbered bomb shelter. He also gave the committee a master class in government public relations. He spoke in short, lapidary epigrams. I was reminded slightly of the Chinese general Sun Tzu, whose book *The Art of War* is still a template for military men. In the same way, all spin doctors should carry a copy of General In Gham's thoughts in their knapsack. Or their soft leather manbag.

For example, here is In Gham on Alastair Campbell and the old team from the Number 10 press office. 'There has been a hyperactive relationship with the media, suborning them and knocking them down. This has reaped the whirlwind I predicted.'

By good fortune, Sir Bernard's appearance came just before Tony Blair's monthly press conference. I popped over to watch the whirlwind being reaped. Would he follow the instructions of the Master? For example, In Gham tells us that 'It is the function of the government to govern. It is not the function of the government to fill newspapers.'

The Prime Minister had ignored these wise counsels. He did all he could to fill the papers. He began with a seemingly endless disquisition on public services, and followed with an eternity on top-up fees. He could have filled page after page of the newspapers, if any of them had the slightest intention of printing what he said.

In Gham is at his most perceptive when he says that it is important for governments not to create news. Indeed, they should strive for the opposite. Their aim should be to reach a kind of Zen purity in which they leave nothing for the papers to write about. 'The best lobby meeting I ever held was when the reporters asked me, "Is there anything going on?" and I said, "No" and they went away.'

24.10.03

Back among the Conservatives, the plotters – who by this time included almost the entire parliamentary party – had gained their heart's desire and IDS was on his way out. There was a special meeting of Tory MPs.

As MPs filed out of committee room 14 they looked almost stunned, as if they were the dead men walking, and not IDS himself. He had taken the precaution of pre-resigning, in absentia. The air of dull astonishment is one effect of regicide. Have we really done that? What have we unleashed? What is this madness, this fever?

They didn't look stunned for very long, though. Even as the reporters churned around in the corridor, men in suits were barking about David Davis's announcement. He was not going to run! An assassination and a campaign sinking, all in five minutes. One MP said darkly, 'One coffin out, one coffin in.'

'Still time for one more crisis before the election,' said another, cheerily. At Central Office, IDS made a brief and dignified announcement. He got in a single jab against his tormentors: it had been an honour to be the first leader chosen by the party membership – not, he implied, picked by this back-stabbing bunch of nonentities.

It must have been a horrible day for him. Prime Minister's Questions at noon; Labour MPs were almost as jumpy as the Tories. They were desperate to keep him. They had formed a jokey campaign called SIDS: Save Iain Duncan Smith. They cheered wildly when he spoke.

Tony Blair's best strategy would have been to have pretended he had been worsted. 'Ooof,' he should have said, 'I have no answer to that devastating question!' But Blair is not wired that way. He produced another roll of dodgy statistics, allegedly showing that crime is going down even though it is going up. IDS did as he always has done, and sat shaking his head and occasionally shouting across the table, like those crazy people you sometimes see on buses. Later he asked another question, about Europe, and a Labour wag shouted, 'We'll get back to you next week.' The leader pro tem was flanked not by hunters, but vultures. They would be happy enough to rummage with their snouts inside the corpse, provided someone else had made the kill.

Outside room 14 the corridor was beginning to fill up. Michael Portillo arrived, preceded by his lips. The press of the press was almost suffocating. Older Tories regard the intrusion of the press as like having the cameras in to their wedding night. Others adore the heaving mass, the hot contingency of hacks, the sense of being a part of history, however minor. IDS himself arrived, trying to look jolly. 'Is it one of those gladiatorial things?' he asked. Inside there was the ritual banging of desk lids. If turtles played rugby that would be the sound of a scrum collapsing. They emerged to say what a fine, brave and stirring speech IDS had made, but they said it with relief, for the better his performance, the more dignity they could allow him, the less guilt they would feel.

We went downstairs to hear David Davis announce that he was standing down to make way for Michael Howard. But more than enough MPs had come forward, he claimed, for he himself to have won, if he had run. So we were offered the cherishable sight of a man taking his hat out of the ring while simultaneously trying on the crown for size.

30.10.03

So Michael Howard was the only candidate. He held a press conference.

There he was, along with Norman Lamont, a reminder of why people voted against them in 1997 and why they will take the earliest possible chance to vote against them again. They held the press conference overlooking the Thames in the Saatchi Gallery, home of the wildest off-the-wall art to be found on anybody's wall. It was chaotic. It was, aptly enough, the night before Halloween. We arrived early and apparatchiks told us to get out of the room. Liam Fox, a top Howard booster, told us to get in. Young men in shiny suits, jobsworths without jobs, told us to get out again.

After such a build-up, surely the candidate would not merely appear on stage. He would have to be lying down in his underpants, on Tracey Emin's famous unmade bed, surrounded by empty vodka bottles and used contraceptives. (Sorry, that's just a quiet night in for the more louche Tory MPs. Not Mr Howard, of course.) We were just a few feet away from Damien Hirst's pickled shark. Oh, and a display by the artists Jake and Dinos Chapman. This includes a lesbian couple making love, except that the women share the same buttocks. How inclusive can you get?

I delved into the catalogue. The Chapmans also display *Fuck Face*, a model of a two-year-old boy with a penis for a nose and a vagina for a mouth. It was back to basics again. The room was packed and heaving. Michael Fabricant was tugging at his hair, to prove it was 'real'. And there were Julian Brazier, James Gray and other MPs who look as if they should only be allowed out on tonight of all nights of the year.

Fights broke out between some of the cameramen. As the masses heaved from one side of the room to the other, Mr Howard appeared. 'He's coming behind you!' the MC declared. 'Oh no, he isn't!' we were tempted to reply, since we have been to pantos which were more closely in touch with reality.

In the old days, we had press conferences and rallies. They were separate occasions. Now politicians bring their claque to the press conference. Do they imagine it works? Does anyone say, 'I had my doubts about that chap, but seeing all those strange people with bulging eyes laughing at his jokes, I've changed my mind'?

A man from the television asked an aggressive question, which can be summed up as, 'Are you still as odious as you used to be?'

'That's a very generous question,' he replied, and the claque fell about in a hysterical trance of delight, as if La Rochefoucauld himself had delivered one of his most finely chased epigrams. I suspect that the Tories are now so desperate to be united that they would unite behind John Prescott if he was all that was on offer.

And I shan't mention the sculpture, exhibited a few feet away, called *Two-Faced Cunt*. Except to wonder how any politician in the world, however desperate for a space to announce his candidacy, might want to claim the leadership of Middle Britain within ten miles of a work of art bearing that title.

31.10.03

The Prime Minister continued to resemble Hugh Grant more closely every day. Grant had just played a prime minister in a film called Love, Actually, *in which he fell for the Downing Street tea lady, played by Martine McCutcheon.*

We can spot the transformation through small gestures. The sudden smile, for no apparent reason. The shake of the head that precedes a self-deprecating remark. The overall manner that implies, 'Hey, I'm just a regular guy who happens to be Prime Minister – for my sins!'

But first we heard from that strange automaton that speaks only in jargon. 'The NHS, driving ever forward the choice agenda,' the automaton said, bafflingly. On it went: 'The choice agenda will be driven by the entire agenda.' Then we moved to top-up fees for university students. The vote has been delayed until the end of the month, but that doesn't matter, because 'there is a triple lock for fairness'. I felt as I sometimes do when a computer geek tries to explain something to me. I don't understand their language, and they are unable to use ours.

He offered us a new slogan. Thanks to the old triple lock, universities would be 'free at the point of study, fair at the point of need'. Who comes up with this stuff? Mandelson? The twice-evicted cabinet minister has always confused a snappy slogan with the more difficult task of actually persuading people. Anyhow, the gist was that he is going to force top-up fees through, come what may. As well as famously lacking a reverse gear, it turns out that he hasn't got any brake pads either.

Then suddenly he found his inner Hugh. Someone asked, reasonably enough, why we were having a 'big conversation' when he had no reverse gear. Was it a sham?

'Yes,' he replied to titters, though Hugh Grant fans know that's the point at which he runs his fingers through his hair and says, 'No, I mean, uh, ha-ha, no.' Someone asked about Ken Livingstone's possible return to the Labour Party. 'Ah doan think ah can add to what ah said to you last time – and ah can't quite recall what ah said then!' he said with that famous winsome smile, as in you win some, you lose some.

We took the chance to ask what he would like to find in his Christmas stocking. 'Some improving literature,' he said. Perhaps he meant a leatherbound copy of the 2001 Labour Manifesto, the one that rules out top-up fees.

We asked what he would say when he met the Rev Ian Paisley. 'Wish him Happy Christmas, I suppose,' he said with studied ingenuousness. He was becoming obsessively like the floppy-haired fop. Then suddenly he was gone, disappearing into a back room to snog the tea lady.

No, of course not! He wouldn't do any such thing. It's the lass in the post room he fancies.

03.12.03

Gordon Brown launched his latest leadership bid – sorry, his pre-Budget report – yesterday. As usual, this was largely devoted to Gordon boasting about the state of the economy. He does this by slapping himself on the back for the good news and leaving out the bad. I was reminded of those match reports you get in football programmes, in which each of the home side's goals is lovingly described and the other side's ignored, so that it comes as something of a surprise to discover that the other lot won 5–2.

But before that treat we had Michael Howard in a terrific bate. The new Tory leader was furious because the government has started to run ads on commercial radio about the top-up fees. He is certainly on to something, because you aren't allowed to spend public money advertising a policy which hasn't even gone through the Commons. But why should that stop this government? They do what they damn well please.

Even more appalling was the language that the ad uses. It's meant to be a jokey version of teenage slang. 'Ya cough up zip till ya blinging,' quoted Mr Howard, with the air of one removing the droppings of a diarrhoeic sheep from his shoe. In the transcript provided for us, the ad actually says, 'Ya cough up zip till ya minted,' 'minted' meaning 'comfortably off', whereas 'blinging' refers to jewellery. The ad goes on to explain: 'The mega news is that the darty government will help you through uni by shelling out the clam.' Listeners are exhorted thus: 'So, peg it man, don't veg it.'

Only a civil servant could come up with such a weird mixture of outdated, inapt and entirely non-existent slang. Can you imagine anyone, including a young person, having a clue what was meant?

Mr Blair failed to answer questions about the ad ten times, so we moved on to Gordon Brown. To paraphrase his report, the clam situation was well wicked. His darty politics had left the whole nation minted. He was blinging home the economic bacon. He produced a flurry of statistics, burying the House in a mass of numbers. They flew past our ears. 'In France 3.9, in Japan 6.9, in Britain only 2.4!' he exclaimed. His self-satisfaction knew no bounds. The mega news was that the economy had been growing continuously for the longest period since our toothless ancestors lived in wattle and daub houses, eating woad for supper.

The bad news – that he has had to borrow £37 billion, far more than he predicted and rather more clam than seems prudent – was gabbled through in the middle of another passage about the benighted state of all foreign economies. But none of this mattered. The nation was minted, unemployment was close to zip, and Mr Brown's Treasury was darty as darty could be. As the government's own radio ad puts it, 'Don't sack it, braw!'

11.12.03

The House was about to rise for Christmas.

We had a chilling glimpse of life in the Blair Yuletide household. He was replying to an assault by Charles Kennedy. 'Over the Christmas break,' he said, 'let's both look at his spending proposals, and discuss them when we get back.'

What a terrible scene that evokes! 'Daddy, will you play Death Raider III with me?'

'I'm sorry, Leo, I have to contemplate this Lib Dem plan to spend £400 million on refurbishing village halls. What a great big fiscal hole that is! I bet Fungus the Bogeyman would be able to live in that fiscal hole!'

'Darling, lunch is on the table! Come and carve the turkey!'

'With you in a twinkling, dearest heart, as soon as I have followed the trail of their proposed £2 billion investment in the railways!'

But not everyone seems to be looking forward to Christmas quite as much. Gordon Brown has been in

Eeyorish mood. I've never seen anyone look so morose. Like the celebrated stuffed donkey he seemed to be saying, 'Look at all the presents I've had.' He waved a metaphorical tail from side to side. You would think that someone who was about to celebrate Christmas for the first time with a cute little baby in the house would be more festive.

It's not as if Labour MPs weren't bringing him presents, or at least tributes to lay at his feet. The general tone of the questioning was: 'Is the Chancellor aware that thanks to increased government spending on health services in my constituency, doctors and nurses are having to drag perfectly healthy people into hospital just to fill the new beds?'

Oliver Letwin, the new shadow chancellor, clearly didn't want to dispel the air of holiday gloom. He spoke miserably about how a 37 per cent increase in spending had brought a 40 per cent increase in management staff but only 5 per cent more operations.

Paul Boateng, Gordon Brown's deputy, started to yell. 'This is an old canard!' he shouted – no, screamed. Again, I imagined Christmas in the Boateng household. 'Would you like some more of this leftover duck, darling?'

'No, that is an old canard! I insist you bring me a freshly cooked canard!'

Mr Boateng insisted that what the Tories called 'management staff' included 'painters, cooks, gardeners, cleaners and secretaries. Why does he not give them credit? And since it is Christmas, *us*?'

He collapsed in a heap of quivering outrage. Gordon Brown heaved a deep, deep sigh, like a man who has just unwrapped his third matching tie'n'hank set, when what he wanted was a bottle of single malt.

19.12.03

Once a month, questions to the Deputy Prime Minister precede questions to the Prime Minister. Mr Prescott, having few real responsibilities apart from overturning local planning decisions, often had to field topics too unimportant to appear in the portfolio of other ministers.

Robert Key asked about chewing gum and how it disfigured our streets. Would the government include something about spat-out gum in its anti-social behaviour bill? Mr Prescott chucked. 'There was a song,' he reminded us, 'about sticking it on the bedpost at the end' – a slightly mistaken tribute to Lonnie Donegan. He added, 'It is a very important issue, this, in fact, anyone going into any other regeneration area can now see it, it is quite disfigured by the casting away of chewing gum, I think it's a deplorable practice, I know it's controversial to say that, but we are looking at a number of measures, we can take action to clear it up because they do disfigure some very well-developed regeneration.' So now you know exactly where you can stick it.

Then it was Michael Howard's turn. He wanted Tony Blair to deny that he had leaked Dr David Kelly's name and admit that he would have had to resign if Lord Hutton decided that he had.

Fat chance. The Prime Minister was logic-chopping like a sushi chef with a new set of knives. He replied, 'I suggest you look at the totality of what I said.'

This was greeted with much loud mockery by the Tories, and who can blame them? George Washington, asked if he had cut down the cherry tree, could have said, 'Father, I suggest that you look at the totality of what I have done.' Or, 'Herr Hitler, did you not tell us that was your last territorial claim?' 'You must look at the totality of what I claimed.'

08.01.04

Reform of the upper chamber dribbled on constantly, like the leaky tap that keeps you awake but isn't quite noisy enough to make you get up and do something about it. Occasionally the peers would try to reform themselves.

The fun began with the introduction of two new peers. The ceremony, which at one time lasted for ever, has been shortened by New Labour, but is still superbly verbose. Rookies are offered not just a title, but get the 'name, state, degree, style, dignity, title and honour', with the 'rights, privileges, immunities and advantages obtaining'. As members of the House get younger, you half expect the clerk to lean forward to a newcomer and say, 'So, what's your name, state, degree, style, dignity, title and honour, little girl?'

Next they held a debate on the proposal to have their own Speaker, just like the House of Commons. Currently the task is performed by the Lord Chancellor, sitting on the Woolsack, but his job is being abolished. A committee has spent a long time pondering this poser, made more difficult by the fact that the House doesn't actually need a Speaker. In the Commons, he is there to keep order. In the Lords there is no order to keep. You might as well install a dinner monitor in the dining room of the Athenaeum. The House rules, such as they are, state (a) never speak when another peer is speaking, and (b) gently nudge your neighbour if he is snoring too loud.

So given that a new Speaker would have almost nothing to do, what would his responsibilities be? Some thought he or she should welcome foreign visitors to the House. He might have a 'pastoral' role, which implied shepherding visitors round the old place. As I watched Lord Falconer, condemned for the time being to sit in a scratchy wig, pretending to be fascinated by the debate, I thought there were plenty of things he could do while sitting on the Woolsack. Macramé work can be used to make serviceable plant hangers. He could write an erotic novel. He could make satirical comments on the debate with the help of glove puppets, or do cookery demonstrations.

He could jokily hold up numbers at the end of each speech, like judges in an ice dancing contest, or, if a peer has been particularly boring, could stand up waving a gun and shout, 'Eat death, noble lord!' before firing a paint ball at them.

Then they spent some time pondering what to call this new functionary. Lord Lloyd came up with various suggestions, including 'prolocutor', or 'the mouth of the House', as he put it.

'All right, matey, what's your name, state, degree, style, dignity, title and honour?'

'Mowf of the 'Ouse, and you won't forget it if yer know what's good for you!'

13.01.04

The Hutton report was published at the end of January. To the surprise – no, the astonishment – of those among us who had sat through most of the evidence, it largely exonerated the government and its ministers.

Tony Blair almost never does gloating. He can announce the successful conclusion of a war in the same tone that a vicar might use to say that the church fete has been postponed.

But yesterday he was gloating all right. How he gloated! He didn't just declare that he had been cleared, acquitted, vindicated, washed clean, shriven like the lamb, proved to be utterly moist, fragrant and smelling of roses, but he took the chance to prance and tap dance on the graves of his enemies.

A blizzard was promised outside. Mr Blair was the new Captain Gloats: 'I am staying here. I may be some time.' He was triumphant: Caesar returning from Gaul, Jonny Wilkinson from Australia, the gingerbread man whom no one could catch. As Labour MPs cheered and yelled and almost screamed their support he described in detail his exoneration. And rightly so. The gist of the Hutton report seems to be 'Blair without flaw – official!'

It is no reflection on Lord Hutton's personal integrity that, if the Prime Minister had been invited to write the report himself, it would have read in much the same way. He declared that the findings were 'extraordinarily thorough, detailed and clear'. It left no room for doubt. 'We accept it in full,' he said. You bet he did. Given that his old pal Charlie Falconer had personally selected Lord Hutton for the job, this was a little like a newly canonized saint praising the Pope's clarity of judgement.

His flail thrashed everyone who had ever attacked him. He had been accused of lying and misleading parliament, but the truth was now out. Anyone who repeated the lies about him should withdraw them, fully, openly and cleanly. They should also cut off their right arms and throw them onto the pyre. (I made up the last bit, but it does convey the flavour of what he said.)

Then we heard one of those marvellous circumlocutions favoured by British judges as a way of not saying 'lie' or 'invention'. Mr Blair quoted Lord Hutton as saying that Number 10's need for a powerful dossier might have 'subconsciously influenced…members of the Joint Intelligence Committee to make the wording of the dossier somewhat stronger'.

Quelle délicatesse! 'Darling, while I might have been in a hotel room with my secretary, subconsciously I thought I was working late at the office.' Or, to give a political example, President Nixon could have said, 'Of course it is possible that I subconsciously authorized the break-in at the Democratic national headquarters at the Watergate building.'

As for the dodgy dossier, if he had lied, which he hadn't, it wouldn't matter because no one had paid any attention. 'Only in retrospect was it elevated to the single thing that conclusively persuaded a reluctant nation to war.' Those who had made false accusations against him should now withdraw them. He was looking straight at Michael Howard.

The Tory leader found himself in the position of a barrister whose client had been caught near the body with a bloody knife, having promised publicly to kill the victim. You can only do your best.

He was met by a sound new to me in the Commons: hissing. This is the equivalent of throwing sharpened pennies onto the pitch. He ploughed onward. He said that the Prime Minister had misled the House anyway, over the naming of Mr Kelly. This was greeted by such a barrage of loud opprobrium that the Speaker had to beg for quiet.

Mr Blair replied. He snapped into non-gloating but still vindictive mode. 'Nastiness is not the same as being effective, and opportunism is not the same as leadership.'

As they say in the Foster's ad, 'Whoa, that'll hurt in the morning!'

Out on College Green, I did a TV turn with a furious Boris Johnson MP. 'This is a snow job of Himalayan proportions!' he shouted as the first flakes of the storm began to fall.

29.01.04

To my delight, Sir Andrew Turnbull, the head of the civil service, gave evidence to the public administration committee, which was then trying to understand the nature of Tony Blair's style of government.

I came to work by tube. At Hammersmith an elderly man got on and sat down at the opposite end of the compartment. His clothes were filthy and so was his face, but he took out a handkerchief and a mirror and began to clean himself up, with as much care as any Oscar nominee preparing for this coming Sunday evening. He would lick the handkerchief, then use it to smear away some of the dirt. Then he'd lick it again, and soon he had a face as shiny as any boy sent off to school by his proud mum.

The problem was the smell – that rich, foetid, gungy, dungy, runny cheesy, rotting maggoty pong of someone who hasn't had a bath for a very long time. It hit me around Baron's Court. A middle-aged woman swiftly moved down the train. A young girl looked horrified, picked up her bags and followed in the same direction. A man in a Barbour jacket rolled his eyes and marched briskly away. A couple of Japanese tourists were the next to arrive, and just as quickly depart. The ripe smell grew as if it would soon replace all the air in the carriage.

The man himself didn't seem to notice. By the time I got off at Westminster he was sitting, smiling and radiant, all by himself, surrounded by empty seats, while the other end of the carriage was packed to the gunwales, like the first rush hour train after a signal failure.

I was reminded of this incident soon afterwards when I went to hear Sir Andrew Turnbull give evidence to the public administration committee. Do not get me wrong. Sir Andrew, who is head of the home civil service, is a man of unimpeachable personal freshness. He may look unnerv-ingly like David Hockney, but you could eat your dinner off his face.

His effect, however, was similar to the man on the tube. His disquisition on the nature of the civil service was thoughtful and slow. Gosh it was dull. You may remember that he had sent a letter to Clare Short after her description of reading the private thoughts of Kofi Annan. [Ms Short claimed to have evidence that the British had been bugging the UN secretary-general's private office.] The gist of the letter had been 'Shut it, Clare.'

'One of my duties,' Sir Andrew said, 'is reminding ministers of their duties when they are in government, and when they have left government, under paragraph 18 of the ministerial code. That is not saying that there can be any action; I am merely acting as a kind of solicitor's letter.' The chairman, Tony Wright, pointed out that ministers' letters were usually sent under instruction. 'It was done with the agreement of the Prime Minister,' Sir Andrew said airily, as if Tony Blair had helped with the typing.

I cannot be sure what followed immediately, because I had fallen into a light slumber. I woke to hear Sir Andrew explaining that Clare Short was not exactly wrong when she said there had been inadequate debate on the war on Iraq, but not exactly right, either. 'There were discussions. What she felt was that she was not learning as much as she had an appetite for, and she is entitled to that view.'

First my colleagues from the press began to leave. Then the public. The sprinkling of committee members began to look desperate. Sir Andrew's smile grew wider.

Being boring is not, if you are the most senior of all civil servants, any kind of drawback. In fact it is a necessity. I had to leave myself, and I suspect that Sir Andrew, like the tramp on the tube, finally found himself utterly alone. He would have counted it a triumph.

05.03.04

Later, in 2007, Sir Andrew, as Lord Turnbull, became far better known and much more exciting when he accused Gordon Brown of behaving like Stalin.

*

Another monthly treat is questions for the minister in charge of agriculture, or the environment, or whatever it is called these days.

Margaret Beckett, the secretary of state, finally announced yesterday that the government would allow a strain of GM maize to be grown from next year. Some MPs were cross, to put it mildly. But I was fascinated, since it explained why *The Archers* these days is obsessed with race relations, gay sex and shotgun sieges.

There are those who believe this is because the programme is mainly heard by middle-class people in cities. They may think they want an everyday story of country folk, but in fact they want to hear their own lives reflected, and that means lashings of homosexuality, racial prejudice and violence. I suspect, however, that isn't the reason. The fact is that there is almost nobody left in the countryside who understands the reality of modern farming.

'Phil at home, Jill?' someone asks.

'No, he's in the back field, phasing out atrazine, in accordance with the new EU regulations, and on his birthday too!'

'Eddie Grundy, if you don't understand the nature of a 0.9 labelling threshold, you should get out o' my way and take your tractor with you. Some of us in Ambridge can remember the time when you told us "gene stacking" was what Clarrie was doing in the clothing aisle of the Borchester Tesco!'

Or, 'Whoi you got that whip and those handcuffs, Jolene?'

'Well, Sid, I think it's high time we introduced a new regulatory regime with rigorous and robust monitoring, you naughty boy!'

I may have confused some of the characters. *The Archers* is usually on in our house, though I don't always listen with as much attention as I should. But all the jargon came straight from yesterday's session in the Commons.

10.03.04

Much of what happens in Parliament is quite interesting. Much isn't. There is one monthly session that is without doubt the worst of the lot.

On my way into work yesterday I passed some train spotters at Waterloo station. They were taking pictures of the train I had just arrived on, specifically the driver's cab and the number on its side. 'But they're all the same!' I wanted to yell. 'Only the numbers are different. You might as well photograph a range of Tesco loyalty cards!'

Nothing could be more boring than that, I thought. But I was wrong. An hour or so later I was in the Commons for work and pensions questions. I have always avoided this event on the grounds that it would make watching paint dry seem, by comparison, the chariot race in *Ben Hur*.

Wrong again. In fact, it was so dull, so unimaginably tedious, so narcoleptic, so steeped in terminal ennui, that it had its own strange fascination. Take this reply from a junior minister, Jane Kennedy, to a question about the work of Scottish job centres. You have to realize that this is only the second half of what she said. The whole thing was almost twice as long:

'As far as the second part of my hon. friend's question, it is thanks to a combination of economic stability and radical labour market reforms that more than 1.75 million more people in the United Kingdom are now in work in comparison to 1997, and unemployment is at its lowest level for nearly thirty years. However, we are not resting on that, we are not complacent, we know that there is a lot more to do that is why the Job Centre Plus roll-out is so important. The new service is being delivered by integrated offices of the Job Centre Plus and making a radical difference to the experience that people who are looking for work have, as I have said before, we are very inspired indeed by the enthusiasm being demonstrated by the staff in its new role that they are embarking on in assisting people to find work through the personal advisers system. It is a massive investment...'

At this point the Speaker, having presumably woken up with a jerk, and realizing that he was not actually rolling around with Jordan on a desert island, spotted that the entire Chamber was in danger of falling into a deep and possibly life-threatening trance. He invoked the celebrated Chinese divine, St Fu, whose name instructs us to 'Shut The Fuck Up', though he did not put it in quite those terms.

Even then Ms Kennedy was not finished. Moments later she delivered a gushing mock apology: 'Mr Speaker, I do apologize for getting carried away by the good news about the core of our...' I didn't hear the rest, as my head had slumped back again.

And it doesn't help that the minister in charge of the department, Andrew Smith, has a voice like a sheep in an anorak. You would not be remotely surprised to find him snapping the rolling stock at Waterloo.

27.04.04

One of the most depressing features of New Labour was its apparent obsession with gathering facts about the citizenry, and its bewilderment that some people found this objectionable. The government had an able ally in its mission.

The home affairs committee was investigating the proposed identity cards, so it heard from a New Zealander, Mr Len Cook, who is the registrar-general for England and Wales. Mr Cook is working on something with the innocent-sounding title of The Citizen Information Project. He is a short man with a bristly moustache, so he looks as if Groucho Marx had been in a lift accident. He seemed rather like the world's keenest philatelist, whose dream it is to possess one of every postage stamp ever issued. In the same way, Mr Cook will not rest until he has gathered in one place the name and personal details of every person living in the United Kingdom.

What a vision! One massive supercomputer handling umpteen gigabytes of information! In my mind's eye I see it in a vast cooled hangar, in rural Wales perhaps. In an outbuilding many miles away, possibly in Bangalore, thousands of staff spend their days tapping in more information about us all. Mr Cook wanders happily around his gigantic machine, his own amiable humming blending with the gentler whirr as it eats up the colour of our eyes, our addresses, employers, criminal records, star signs and votes for *I'm a Celebrity*...

205

Suddenly he sees a bee fly into an entry port; there is a spark and a fizzing noise. Then a great shower of sparks. To his horror, flames begin to shoot out of the back. He watches in agony as his darling, his brainchild, the world's greatest database, burns to the ground.

We can but dream. Meanwhile, in the hopes that he would be able to build this thing, Mr Cook decided to knock MPs into a stupor by the use of jargon. 'The role of this stage of the project,' he told them, 'is project definition.' He left them to chew on that for a while, before saying, with tremendous gravity, 'A population register would add considerably to the ability of citizens to know who they are.'

This had the ring of truth. Suppose someone asked you your name: you could call a 24-hour number (calls cost 75p a minute, £1.20 at peak periods) and an electronic voice would tell you who you are. Invaluable for amnesiacs and drunks.

Just in case the committee was not entirely clear what he was on about, Mr Cook provided a helpful summary. 'The project is being taken forward within the Office for Government Commerce Gateway Review framework. The project passed through Gate 0 (strategic assessment) during the feasibility stage. The plans for the next development stage include Gate 1 (business justification) and Gate 2 (procurement strategy).' So that was clear. There was also much mention of 'synergy', something which is always called in aid when vast sums of our money are being spent on things we don't want.

Mr Cook provided a sheet showing what various groups thought of his plans. 'Soroptimist International of Yorkshire supportive of unique personal number but not of population register,' it said, and I felt a great rush of gratitude for those sturdy Yorkshire women who may be the only bulwark between us and George Orwell's terrible vision. (David Winnick MP asked Mr Cook if he kept a copy of *Nineteen Eighty-Four* in his office, and he seemed surprised by the question.)

The chairman, John Denham, asked with some weariness, 'Why, since we have never had a national database in this country, do we now have to have two?' It seems they will be 'different'. But both will be hugely expensive.

28.04.04

My feeling about the encounters between Tony Blair and Michael Howard was that they were unnervingly similar to courtroom battles between rival barristers. They might abuse and revile each other's case in public, but back in the robing room it's all backslapping and camaraderie. The anger, the spluttering rage they showed in the House had a formalized, scripted air. The Prime Minister had, by this time, created a whole bag of tricks designed to deflect criticism. In this case Michael Howard had scored an unanswerable point, though since it concerned a matter long forgotten, I won't trouble you with the details.

The Prime Minister did what he always does when someone has got him bang to rights. He simply ignored the question. It never fails. 'And I myself personally saw the Prime Minister strangle a little girl's kitten.'

'The British people are not interested in that. They are concerned with the highest-ever employment rates, low inflation…'

And there was a finale. Up sprang Sir Peter Tapsell, most grand of all the grandest grandees, a man whose every word hangs almost visibly in the air as it emerges from his mouth, like ectoplasm. Hansard writers fling aside their shorthand machines and notebooks, to begin furiously stitching a great tapestry, possibly entitled *The March of British History Led by General Sir Peter Tapsell*. He stands on the balls of his feet, leaning forward slightly, his face brick red with an outrage which, unlike that expressed by his leader, appears to be entirely sincere.

Labour MPs adore him. They love the way that he evokes a bygone age, like those periwigged servants you sometimes find at stately homes open to the public. They like his questions, about the gold standard, imperial preference and, for all I know, the repeal of the corn laws. They kept up a barrage of mock cheers which seemed to last for ever, until Sir Peter waved them down, like a conductor at the end of a concert implying that the orchestra should be allowed to leave before the pubs shut.

But his question did silence them. Did the pwime minister (Sir Peter has a slight speech defect) think that the murder and mutilation of 'hundreds of women and children' in Fallujah was an 'appropriate response' to the savage murder of four contractors? Once again Mr Blair simply ignored the question. He deeply regretted civilian deaths but it was necessary to restore order. He wasn't going to support the killing of innocents, but you wouldn't catch him denouncing it either.

I personally would like to see Sir Peter himself despatched to that troubled land. The arrival of a white-robed Tapsell of Arabia, like T.E. Lawrence only far more majestic, would stop the trouble-makers in their tracks.

29.04.04

In what seem very distant days, members of the public were allowed to watch their legislators at work without being sealed off from them, as if they were attending a football match in southern Italy. A screen had already been built, but the front two rows of the gallery were in front of it. Seats there were reserved for people who could be trusted not to cause trouble, such as peers and the personal guests of MPs. The system proved faulty.

Yes, I was there when the cloud of death swirled around the Prime Minister. Heavens, we were scared. Some of us actually left the Chamber, humming to ourselves to show that we weren't frightened. If the cloud had actually been anthrax, ricin or sarin, or even blackcurrant flavour sherbet dabs, it could have been a disaster for hundreds. But having walked out, I thought 'This is silly' and walked back in again. I was proud of my colleagues. The attendants were shouting at us all to get out, but everyone stood milling around trying to see what was happening. They were risking their lives to bring their readers the latest tragic events, or at least a jokey paragraph. They should mint a medal: a purple heart for the purple cloud.

Up till then Prime Minister's Questions had been slightly friskier than usual, with Michael Howard jabbing at Blair, Brown and Prescott. The Chancellor had seemed tense throughout the session. A Channel 4 show a few days ago demonstrated his body language and how he demonstrated silent hostile indifference during a Blair speech. So yesterday I made a careful note of all his 'tells' – tiny actions which reveal a person's true mental state. In 18 minutes he rubbed his face 13 times, stroked his hair 12 times, emitted a clearly fake laugh (8) and fake cheers (4). This was pretty normal. But the most obvious sign of disaffection came from the fact that he was studying a document – a speech possibly. While

Mr Blair was talking, he would scrutinize it with care, only looking up when an MP asked a question.

Mr Howard said that Brown and Prescott had 'stitched the Prime Minister up like a kipper!' Nothing out of the ordinary, except that there was a delegation from the Palestinian Authority watching.

At this point there was a commotion in the lower right-hand corner of the public gallery. I looked up and saw two men standing in front of the new £600,000 glass screen that is supposed to protect MPs. Which it does, but only from the people sitting behind it. Suddenly two objects flew through the air and a cloud of purple dust was swirling round the Chamber.

If you look at the tape (it's been on television around 974 times), you can see that Blair hears the noise, looks over his shoulder, then decides to carry on replying to the 'kipper' jibe – no doubt with another exhaustive description of the economic paradise we live in.

At this point, the first condom filled with flour – for that is what it turned out to be – biffs him in the back, skids off and goes on to spray all over Gordon Brown. What an amazing shot by the protester, throwing from hundreds of feet along a downward trajectory! And how marvellously apt! It had been aimed at Blair but it had exploded all over Brown. The protesters had thrown Britain's finest political metaphor.

The tape continues and the Prime Minister hardly seems to notice. Then the Speaker, purple smoke billowing in front of his face, announces that the session is suspended, presumably the pre-ordained drill for any form of attack.

John Reid leapt up to spread paper over the – what? Lethal biological poisons? Self-raising flour? But his colleagues said it was John Prescott who was the hero, gathering up and laying down more paper to stop the dust from spreading. There was something very British, very make-do-and-mend about all this. There is probably a yellowing advice leaflet in the cellar of a ministry: 'In the event of terrorist attack, lay down lots of paper.'

As I left, I bumped into a Labour MP who said he thought the Palestinians would be glad to get back to the peace and quiet of Gaza. Well, no, not really. They have real problems of life and death out there. Ours are just very, very silly.

20.05.04

The perpetrators were later revealed to be Fathers4Justice campaigners.

It was a historic day at Westminster. Lembit Opik, the Liberal Democrat MP for Montgomery, announced that he would be standing for the presidency of his party. This is not the same as the leadership. The president works on detail behind the scenes and composes embarrassing songs to perform at party conferences. The simple announcement of his candidacy cheered everyone up because Lembit is a great force for happiness. I was once asked to attend a Lib Dem party at which, I was told, the intention was for everyone to 'eat too much, drink too much and tell jokes about Lembit'.

Because of his name (his parents were Estonian) he is known as 'the human anagram', though none of them quite work: 'I like to b MP' is one; 'I kil to be PM' another. At his launch yesterday an enthusiastic party official, Ms Tessa Munt, said that she had already made '200 portions of rubber chicken' in his cause. She said that Lembit was first rate at 'touching the membership...he goes round the country touching people,' she said. This could be a brilliant strategy, provided he keeps ahead of the police.

Today Simon Hughes MP will announce whether he is running for the same job. We asked Lembit if he would subtly remind the voters of Mr Hughes's humiliating failure to become Mayor of London. He won't. When he worked for Procter and Gamble, he said, he had learned that it was more fruitful to point out the virtues of your own product rather than criticize the opposition.

How that man ever got into politics, we may never know. Lord McNally, his most prominent supporter, said that he hoped not to read any snide references in the *Guardian* to 'soft soap'. He said he was pleased that so far there had been no mentions of Lembit's campaign against asteroids, his appearances on TV quiz shows and cookery programmes, his awful paragliding accident, and went on to list every humiliation the poor man has suffered over the years. With a campaign manager like Lord McNally, who needs an opponent?

Moments later we were outside the Commons for a photo session. Bravely, in view of his concern about meteorites, Lembit was without a crash helmet. He was joined by his fiancée, the television meteorologist Sian Lloyd. This excited the cameramen no end. She nuzzled her head into Lembit's cheek and gazed up at his left eye, as if trying to forecast occasional showers in the North-East.

'Can we have a kiss, mate?' asked a photographer. 'What you do in your own time is your business,' replied the candidate, smartly.

Ms Lloyd had the patter down perfectly. 'I'm forecasting sunny days ahead!' she beamed. Did she approve of her swain running for office?

'I'm forecasting areas of high pressure, but I can't think of anyone who could handle it better.' As we watched them cuddle each other, I reflected that Mr Opik would not do half as well if he were engaged to Michael Fish.

25.06.04

There was something curiously prescient about Mr Lembit Opik's behaviour. Poor Ms. Lloyd was, in modern parlance, 'binned' by Mr Opik a couple of years later, when we learned that he had taken up with one of the Cheeky Girls, a pop duo from Romania whose one hit was titled 'The Cheeky Song (Touch My Bum)'. Simon Hughes duly won the presidency, not least because of his failure in London; the Liberal Democrats love a loser.

*

Channel 5 (or Five as we were supposed to call it) signed up Alastair Campbell, no longer Tony Blair's director of communications, to conduct a series of interviews. One of his subjects was his old colleague and rival, Peter Mandelson.

What a feast of misinformation, exaggeration, mendacity, half-truths, hyperbole, evasion and whingeing self-justification we were promised! And of course we got all that. But what was most striking was the way the pair circled round each other, waiting to strike.

They can't help it. It's in their natures. They were like two cobras rising from the same basket, twisting sinuously to the music. They knew they were of the same species, on the same side as it were, but could not resist the temptation to lunge at each other.

For example: Campbell said that Mandelson had acquired a 'huge' loan to buy a 'nice, swanky house in Notting Hill'.

Mandelson: 'It was nice, but it wasn't swanky. It was about half the size of your house in Hampstead.' You could almost see the fang marks on Campbell's neck. Later, Mandelson mused about the manifold failings of the press. 'If you don't talk to them, if you don't return their calls, they think you're…'

'An arrogant, aloof git?' offered Campbell, in a spirit of helpfulness.

Mandelson's first words on air were 'I don't think I'm a particularly loathsome individual' – so clearly he wasn't afraid to plunge into controversy.

Campbell had preceded the question with an avowal that Mandelson was – and is – one of his closest friends and 'a very capable minister'.

'So why,' he went on, 'does the Labour Party loathe you?'

That was a facer. Mandelson thought that it was probably because he was 'a bit of a loner, a bit remote'. He didn't need to hang around the bars and tea rooms, because he had the leader's ear.

'I didn't need anyone else. I was not a retail politician,' he added. Of course not. No one had suggested that he could be bought!

The fact is that both Campbell and Mandelson have always been courtiers, first of Neil Kinnock, then of Tony Blair. The monarch always thinks the courtiers are terrific, helpful guys. Those outside the circle detest them for their influence; they themselves are deadly rivals for the affection and admiration of the king.

'If I am being honest, which I will be,' he went on, 'I don't think I've anything to lose by being honest at this stage in my political career…'

It was a fascinating insight. He made it sound as if honesty was something you might take up at a certain age, like angling, or DIY. Alarmingly he kept talking about himself in the third person. 'There has always been a fight within myself, and sometimes with others, about whether Peter is going to remain Peter the Process Man, or whether Peter is going to be allowed to become Peter Mandelson, the politician and minister.'

Gosh, I wouldn't mind a ringside seat at that fight – it would be as exciting and unpredictable as Mike Tyson v. Kylie Minogue!

As a boy, I once had an instructional toy called the Visible Man. He had a perspex body so that you could see the organs inside. Mandy has the Visible Brain; you can see the synapses working together. The synapses have worked out that the future of the Labour Party is Gordon Brown. The Chancellor, who felt spurned and betrayed by Mandelson at the time of the 1994 leadership campaign, may soon be in power.

'Get in with Gordon!' the synapses were screaming.

'He has the qualities and skills needed to be leader... Gordon is a big person, he is a big politician,' Mandy told us with every appearance of something close to sincerity.

In fact Gordon could do no wrong. The news about his house loan ('It wasn't secret, it was unpublicized,' he said to snorts of laughter at the screening yesterday) had been leaked by Gordon's associates. 'That's not the same as Gordon,' he said, and at this point Campbell burst out incredulously, 'You really believe that?'

Yes, he did believe it. Why, he had spoken to Gordon himself on the very day, and had received some good advice. ('Don't resign.') But the real, deep well of bitterness began to gush over his second resignation, after the expose of the Hinduja passport affair. He blamed Campbell for briefing the media against him. He accused him of 'a rush to judgement', adding, 'I think, as my friend of twenty-five years' standing, you might have given me the benefit of the doubt, and you chose not to.' He had created 'a sort of elephant trap, into which I fell'.

Later Campbell told us in person that he thought Mandelson had not been bitter. If that was him being cuddly and forgiving, I'd hate to see him when he really is bitter. In fact, for either to claim that there was no ill-feeling between them was just a load of old cobras.

06.07.04

2004–2005

Michael Howard tried to get Mr Blair to say why so many of his ministers have resigned from office and then ratted on the government. Fat chance. The Prime Minister merely recited, for approximately the 978th time, the well-worn litany of his government's achievements. If he were asked why he was naked at the despatch box, daubed in woad and trying to limbo dance under the Table of the House, he would reply with a list of low inflation rates, A-level results and unemployment statistics.

So we were pleased to hear from Anthony Steen of Totnes, who is a Tory MP and plainly bonkers, though not thought to be a danger to the public. He asked if Mr Blair would visit Berry Pomeroy Castle, in Devon. The Prime Minister said he had no plans to do so. A wag shouted, 'Why not?' which is the kind of line that passes for humour in these parts.

It turned out that Mr Steen actually couldn't care less if the prime ministerial limo never crosses the drawbridge. He wanted to let loose a rant against the EU. Many castles were built in southern England, he said, to repel invaders – most of them from the continent. (True enough, we thought – how many came from Canada, or the Upper Volta?) Now increasing numbers of people felt their freedoms were being eroded by the EU. 'No longer are their homes their castles!' he concluded triumphantly, while dragging his question, kicking and screaming, back to the subject.

Mr Blair gave him a bland reply about the EU helping to prevent wars. Then he scrambled through his briefing book – a great red folder, bristling with multicoloured plastic tabs, which enable him to find any number of dodgy figures and facts in a few brief seconds. His researches enabled him to announce that the relevant website claimed Berry Pomeroy Castle was actually haunted, 'principally by a blue lady – called Margaret!'

Everyone laughed at this amusing fact. But in my experience you can't believe much that comes out of Downing Street these days. So I checked on the website and found that, like so much told us by Tony Blair, it contained an element of truth that had been twisted and pummelled into making a more convenient point.

In fact, there are said to be two female ghosts at the castle. Margaret is the White Lady. The Blue Lady is a quite different phantom, whose name is unknown. The White Lady, Margaret, was allegedly starved to death in the dungeons by her sister Eleanor after both women fell in love with the same man. 'She [may be] the source of the feeling of unease and horror some people experience at the castle,' the website says, so the name fits well enough.

Her particularly terrible death is matched only by the experience of the real Blue Lady. She is said to have been raped by her own father. When the child was born, he strangled it, though in another version, she killed it herself. They say she brings death to anyone unlucky enough to see her.

Either way, the girls seem to prove the dictum often quoted from our own Blue Lady: 'There is no such thing as society. There are individual men and women, and there are families.'

Though not all as warm and supportive as she probably meant to imply at the time.

09.09.04

Family was one of the buzz-words of the day. Back in 2003, Alan Milburn, who was Minister for Health, resigned from office in order to spend more time with his family. In September the following year he returned.

'Now that Alan Milburn is to spend more time with his government,' said the Labour backbencher David Taylor, in an unusually waspish welcome to the new Chancellor of the Duchy of Lancaster (and what other country in the world can boast such a selection of grandiose titles? For instance, Peter Mandelson has resigned from the Commons not to become a European commissioner, but to be Steward of the Manor of Northstead, which is technically an office of profit under the Crown and so disqualifies him from being an MP. On the other hand, with property prices the way they are, he might be tempted to borrow the money from Geoffrey Robinson to put in a conservatory, and rent it out while he is in Brussels.)

Anyhow, back to the subject. Just over a year ago Mr Milburn told us that he wanted to spend more time with his family. Things seemed to have changed rather fast. Presumably he has been dropped from his own kitchen cabinet.

These occasions are never easy. Most wives and partners hate to be butchers. 'Awfully sorry, Alan,' they say, 'but, um, I need your place I'm afraid…would like to thank you for all your hard work…some splendid achievements. We won't forget that lasagne in a hurry, ha ha! Do feel free to pop in any time you're up from Westminster.'

Perhaps he could take part in one of those reality TV shows, with shrewish wives shouting, 'Shut it! I'm fed up to the back teeth with you under my feet, moaning all day! Why don't you clear off and launch a new policy initiative?'

It is all very confusing. Earlier in the week Andrew Smith

said he was leaving the Cabinet to spend more time with *his* family. (Hands up everyone who can remember what they were doing when they heard Andrew Smith had resigned? Hands up everyone who knew who Andrew Smith was?)

Wouldn't it be convenient all round if he spent more time with Alan Milburn's family? He could give one of those heart-rending interviews we are familiar with these days: 'The last straw was when I had to attend some meaningless committee meeting, and realized I was missing Alan Milburn's daughter appearing as Peaseblossom in her school play...'

10.09.04

Pretty well every other year Tony Blair would speak to the TUC annual conference. This would always be billed in advance by the press as a great emotional showdown. But it wasn't; it was something quite different.

Tony Blair walked out onto the podium and was greeted by a complete silence. Roger Lyons, who was chairing the conference, said, 'Tony, we are all delighted to welcome you here today!' This was something of an overstatement, and it too was greeted with silence.

It wasn't an aggressive silence, a collective dumb insolence. Neither was it a hostile silence. It was just a total absence of noise. It was the same silence you might expect when one signer for the deaf replaces another at the side of the stage. Nobody objects, but equally nobody sees any reason to cheer. Or even notice.

The speech began, 'As ever, before a speech to the TUC, I am not short of advice!' This line was, presumably, supposed to be met by a warm, affectionate chuckle. Instead it was greeted by more silence. It was slightly eerie; if you ever put on the kind of ear defenders used by aircraft dispatchers, you realize that complete silence can be as loud as noise.

Most speakers put in lines meant to win applause, or 'clap traps' – which is the origin of the term. Tony Blair had 'shush lines', which might have been designed to make the audience, already as quiet as a mausoleum at midnight, even more somnolent than before, sucking any remaining enthusiasm out of the air, like a top of the range Dyson with fitted silencer.

He mentioned the Warwick policy which the government and unions agreed earlier this year. It was meant to favour 'social partnership' he said. 'So I come to praise Warwick, not to bury it!' he said. This jokette ('Alas, poor Warwick' might have been more apt) was met by another silence, except for one faint, almost imperceptible sound, a minuscule murmur, like a hamster having a bad dream. I reflected that if a fourteenth-century court jester had written that gag for the king, his head would have been in danger. In these more enlightened times, the author may get a substantial consultancy fee.

He decided to quote himself from 1990, and all the promises he had made then as shadow employment minister – the minimum wage, social chapter, maternity leave, etc. 'We have done every one of those things, as a Labour government!' he said.

At this point, a small claque, fewer than one in ten of his listeners, some no doubt employed in Downing Street, decided it was time to wake up. A faint rustling noise floated up from the hall, as if a few dozen people had simultaneously decided to open their crisps.

Lines designed to bring wild applause – praise for miners, more apprenticeships, cash for the NHS, help for working families – were received with the same dark sticky silence, like Wellington boots lodged in the mud.

Then it was over. A single man rose in a crazed, doomed attempt to start a standing ovation. And there was a solitary boo. I thought how astonishing it was that a Labour prime minister, speaking at a conference of the TUC, the very begetter of his party, could be received with less excitement than a vicar reading out the parish notices.

14.09.04

The bill to stop fox hunting was still making slow progress through the House. A group of protesters made use of the fact that nearly all refurbishment is carried out at Westminster during the recess. This had been shortened by the addition of two sitting weeks in early September, so there were still lots of workmen about the building.

When the first protesters ran into the Chamber it was like one of those occasions when a gang of drunken yobs arrive in a railway carriage. No one knows quite how to react, except you can see everyone thinking, 'Pray somebody do something, but let it not be me.'

Four of the young men had run in from the back, apparently from the No lobby at the end of the Chamber by the Speaker's chair. Another, the first to be grabbed, dashed in from the members' lobby at the other end, straight past the deputy sergeant-at-arms, who, with his sword, is the only armed man in the Chamber. He took an executive decision not to use it.

At first, stupidly, I thought they were workmen, arriving to carry out some small repairs, perhaps involving a dangerously rucked carpet. Clearly nobody had told them to wait, not just to storm in the moment they had finished that job in Cricklewood.

Then seconds later, when my brain clicked into gear and I realized what was going on, it seemed quite astounding, since they had emerged from places where even most of us who work at the Commons are not allowed to go. If a platoon of North Korean soldiers had arrived in lock step, it would scarcely have been more surprising.

It took the young men a few moments to work out their bearings – which was the government bench, which the opposition – but having figured it out they stood in front of Alun Michael and Elliot Morley, the relevant ministers. They were bending, twisted with hatred for these enemies. But in spite of having crafted brilliantly successful plans to get past the security system, they hadn't quite worked out what to say. They had the world to address – the television pictures would be shown everywhere – but they had nothing historic or memorable to hand. It's as if Gavrilo Princip, having reached the running board of Franz Ferdinand's car, had brought only a tomato to throw. One of them shouted feebly, 'It's totally unjust!' like a child told he can't have an ice cream.

Another – or perhaps it was the same young man; it was hard to tell in the melee – yelled, 'This government! You've mucked up pensions! You've mucked up everything!' True to a degree, but hardly as resonant as the words of the most famous parliamentary interloper, Oliver Cromwell ('Let us have done with you! In the name of God, go!') Even their T-shirts, the same as those worn by scores of the protesters outside in Parliament Square, were subtly naff, as if composed by someone for whom English was not a first language. Or even a second. The fronts showed Tony Blair with red horns, and the slogan adapted from the French Connection ads, 'FCUK your ban. I'll keep hunting.' On the back, weirdly, was Cherie Blair tricked out as the Queen, wearing a tiara, the words 'I signed the declaration' above her and 'God Save the Hunting' beneath.

But most MPs didn't have time to contemplate the nuances. This sort of thing doesn't happen much in parliament. In fact it doesn't happen at all. By this time, and I mean a few seconds after the incident began, MPs had snapped into action. They gave the young men some very cross looks.

Only Sir Patrick Cormack decided to become a have-a-go hero and grabbed one youth in an armlock. Heavens, we thought, if they had been terrorists armed with machine guns, many of the nation's finest legislators would be dead already.

Sir Patrick addressed one of the youths. 'Get out!' he yelled. 'I am furious! This is disgraceful!' At least he was doing something.

But it didn't matter. By this time a crack team of men in tailcoats and tights had arrived on the scene. They were the badge messengers, and what a proud sight they were, flying into the Chamber, fleet of foot, arms flailing! These men might be middle-aged, retired warrant officers for the most part, but they were tough.

One demonstrator was snatched by the ankle and forced to hop backwards to the door. Another was seized by the throat. A third managed to lie down at the end of the Labour benches, making it almost impossible for him to be budged. And then they were gone.

I suppose I should report that MPs were angry, seething, alarmed. No doubt many reflected that it might have been al-Qaida. But in the end many were laughing. They found it surreal rather than sinister.

Whatever you thought of their cause, you had to admire the cunning and resource they used to get into the place. And now it might encourage the authorities to take steps against real terrorists.

16.09.04

The protesters – who included the singer Bryan Ferry's son Otis – had dressed up as contractors' labourers to get into the House, and a pretty sorry mess it revealed the security arrangements to be. Of course there was never the faintest chance that the demonstration would change MPs' minds. If it had, it would have been an open invitation for anyone who didn't like a bill to invade the place. What happened was that the bill to ban hunting went through, but hunting continued afterwards more or less unchanged. A perfect British compromise.

*

The conference season began again the following week.

The Lib Dems are never any different. Their motions are still thousands of words long and are riddled with amendments, like raisins in a spotted dick pudding. 'There will be four votes, so get your cards ready – on amendment 1: there will be two votes on amendment 1, so the first vote will be on whether you are in agreement with the first part, which is now number 5. All those in favour?' said the chairwoman, and everyone knew exactly what she meant. The rest of us are more bewildered. If the Lib Dem style of voting is ever adopted by the Commons, nobody would have a clue what they were voting for and could discover, quite by accident, that they had halved income tax, brought back hanging and taken us out of the EU.

Every conference has a catchphrase, and this one's is: 'It will send a clear message.' This translates as: 'There is nothing we can do about it, but at least we know what we are talking about.' One young man used the phrase three times in one speech, thus sending almost as many messages as Western Union in the same time. How lucky they are to have an MP called Vincent Cable.

It was also the day of the *Guardian* lunchtime fringe meeting, chaired by a junior member of the paper's staff, i.e. me. I noticed that there were several members of the House of Lords present, having got there under the popular 'attend twelve Lib Dem conferences and win a peerage' programme. Many of them had copies of the *Orange Book*, a work of radical Lib Dem re-thinking that is so controversial that its launch here was cancelled. People hissed when it was mentioned. I expect that some readers had hidden their copies inside a copy of Richard Desmond's *Hot Asian Babes*.

Sarah Teather MP, who has clearly learned a lot about her party in a short time, said that if God had been a Lib Dem, the Ten Commandments would have been the Ten Suggestions. Ming Campbell added that if the Greater London Young Liberals had been at Mount Sinai they would have moved the reference back. The discussion turned to secondary drinking. Could it do as much harm as secondary smoking?

Sir Ming said that as a young barrister he had once, along with the late Sir Nicholas Fairbairn, a celebrated toper, defended a man who had fired two shotgun cartridges into a crowded pub. The two lawyers had had a few drinks, then a good lunch, and had gone on to Barlinnie prison to meet their client.

After outlining the defence, they asked if he had any questions. 'Aye,' he replied, 'Sir Nicholas, would ye mind breathing on me again?'

21.09.04

This was a time when the party was winning several by-elections. They had come to believe that they could win almost anywhere, including the Labour seat of Hartlepool, recently vacated by Peter Mandelson.

The Liberal Democrats went gently berserk yesterday as they welcomed the victor of Hartlepool to their conference.

Jody Dunn isn't quite the victor yet – the election is not for another week and she is still behind in the polls – but that didn't bother this lot. As far as they were concerned, she might have taken the seat, become leader and, while she was at it, won the Olympic 400 metres. They had made careful preparations. There was a Jody Dunn poster on every seat in the hall. As the moment arrived, stewards shepherded people into empty seats to make it look as if the whole place was packed, rather in the way that 'resting' actors sit down at the Oscars to fill the places left by stars who have gone for a pee. There was even an instruction sheet for delegates who might not be used to displaying artificial frenzy. 'Please wave placards at the end of the Jody Dunn speech when indicated by Ed Fordham, who will be standing in front of the stewards' table. Please ensure your placard is the correct way up and displayed towards the stage.'

Which left one important question: who on earth is Ed Fordham? (A colleague told me he was Jody Dunn's press officer.) But even these instructions were too complicated for some delegates, who waved their placards in the wrong direction, and even upside down. Still, as I said, Lib Dems don't do unbridled enthusiasm.

Then she was among us, trim and excited in a charcoal suit. 'This is a special day for me!' she said. 'For the first time in two months I have had lunch, and at lunchtime!'

This is not a boast I could make myself, but I also wonder

if it is strictly true of Ms Dunn. I have glanced over her blog and discovered that it is extremely food-intensive. Long accounts of canvassing are interrupted by 'I squeezed in a baked potato at lunch (just!)' or 'The day ended with an exceptionally healthy meal of chips and garlic sauce.' There are frequent mentions of cake, and a heartrending description of how she yearned for a cooked breakfast but could find only cheese salad in her fridge. There are cheerier moments, though. 'Had a nice Chinese earlier this week. We enjoyed a 69 and then went for a meal.' (Of course she didn't write the last bit. I made that up. It's a very old joke, and Ms Dunn is happily married with four children.)

Ms Dunn then bade the entire hall to follow her back to Hartlepool, a cry greeted with loud though not ecstatic cheering. I suspect they found her slightly scary. I know I did.

One by one her children came onto the platform and were hugged both by her and Charles Kennedy, who did the politician's trick of pointing out someone in the audience: 'Look, there's my imaginary friend!' At which point the candidate left the platform, possibly in search of a kebab.

(Later the conference debated its new stance on law and order, which is to be tough, but in a caring, sensitive way. Their slogan will be: 'Bring back the rope – provided it is made from sustainable recycled jute.')

23.09.04

As ever, Labour came next.

People are saying that Gordon Brown's address to the Labour conference was a leadership bid. Nonsense. It was a leadership speech. In his mind, he already is leader, taking us on to new heights of economic glory. He is becoming the

Kim Jong Il of the Labour Party, its beloved leader. Now and again he had a word of praise for Tony Blair, but it was flung over his shoulder like a 20p piece to a busker.

The great oration was preceded by a short, heart-warming video entitled *A Fish Called Cameron*. [At this stage, David Cameron was an almost unknown backbench Tory MP.] The film was meant to call attention to working family tax credits. A Glasgow mum explained how the extra money had changed her life. At the end we saw the newly pros-perous family buying a goldfish in a plastic bag for their little boy, who named it Cameron.

Under the Tories, it was implied, working-class people could not afford to feed their pets, except on torn-up copies of the *Sun*. Now, thanks to Gordon Brown, the poorest people can buy fish food so luxurious that they could deep-fry it and eat it for supper themselves. In the last century, politicians worried about the gold standard. Now we are reduced to the goldfish standard.

This heartwarming film over, the Chancellor raced to the podium and started talking, or rather gabbling. There was no time to lose! He was the Incredible Hulk, bursting out of his clothes. Even his scarlet tie was bulging. Now and again the audience tried to clap, but he had no time for that. They couldn't even waste time cheering him on! His hands were in constant motion, flapping up and down like a goldfish in its plastic bag. They were held out, as if describing the one that got away. They chopped up and down, like the teeth of a piranha devouring the rotting flesh of Tony Blair's policies. Then the arms would be flung backwards, as if a kung fu hero was despatching half a dozen enemies who had crept up behind him.

He was yelling, shouting, bawling at us. Sweat poured from his temples. His words were crushed by the steamroller of his own rhetoric. 'Flourish' became 'flush'. 'Our peace-time history' became 'our piss-tie hizzy'. Sometimes he needed to make several runs at a sentence before getting it right.

He had to tell us – the great successes of the government had been his – his, he told us! His! 'Visions, values, commitment!' He tossed in 'no short-termism, no easy options, no irresponsible pre-election promises!' That could have been the low point of the speech, since the Labour Party is full of people who love easy options and irresponsible election promises. That's why they joined.

Then suddenly he was in elegiac mode, and we were with a man who had lost a baby daughter and who had just seen his mother lowered into the earth. 'We are not isolated individuals, but we depend on each other. Except Tony Blair!'

Of course he didn't say the last bit. He didn't need to. We knew what he meant. And somewhere, another grateful goldfish was thanking him for its own survival.

28.09.04

Next day it was Tony Blair's turn. It was, we were assured, his last conference speech before the next election, so the keynote was, naturally, triumphalism.

The Prime Minister had almost reached the end of his speech. The demonstrations had more or less stopped, the conference had received him well if in rather torpid fashion – you had to remember they were missing *Countdown* – and he must have been relieved to have hit the home stretch. So it's little wonder that in the penultimate paragraph his voice slipped and he announced that Labour would 'deliver better lies for working families'.

Better lies! Prime porkies, finer fibs, masses of hand-milled mendacities! Under New Labour hard-working families would get the untruths they deserved, exciting new terminological inexactitudes. The ultimate triumph of Campbell and Mandelson!

I suspect that the problem is that the Labour conference likes the idea of Tony Blair, double election winner, more than it likes the man himself. So when he was announced, just after lunch, the rhythmic clapping started, led by clapping leaders all around the hall, while drum and bass music throbbed out as the achievements of the next Labour government – not this one, the next one – scrolled across the screen. 'Crime cut by 15 per cent, shorter waiting lists, inter-active whiteboards in every school' – as if these miracles had already occurred. Newer and better lies for working families!

The noise, the commotion, the sheer tumult, like 3,000 drunken and drug-addled teenagers clubbing, was over-whelming. I wonder what Mr Attlee would have made of it if his speech had been greeted in this way. He might have assumed he was back in the trenches at the start of a German push. Then I realized we couldn't even see the leader. He wasn't there. He was getting a seven-minute standing ovation not for saying anything, not for what he might be about to say, but for simply existing. For being Tony Blair!

After that everything had to be an anti-climax, and so it was. There were those chunks of clunky prose, like an old Morris Marina rattling past: 'When the two, courage and conviction, combine their strength and take on the challenges...what was a challenge becomes part of the new consensus.' Someone wrote that? Did they know what it meant?

'The present is thrown out with scarcely time to become familiar; before a new future emerges to assert itself.' Another vowel, please Carol!

And this curious assertion that Conservative governments would turn out to be 'the punctuation marks, not the sentences in which our history is written'. So what were Churchill and Thatcher? Commas, semi-colons?

Then the promise of a ten-point programme for the third term. Short of spraying the hall with Novocaine, there is nothing a speaker can do to bring down an audience's mood faster than offering a ten-point programme. So the demonstration – around a dozen people shouting at once – perked things up no end.

And the apology for Iraq wasn't really an apology at all. OK, he said, there were no weapons of mass destruction. But there might have been. He wasn't going to apologize for the overthrow of Saddam. He was sorry, sorry he had been so far-sighted, so solicitous for the welfare of Britain and the world.

None of this mattered. Gordon Brown's reception the previous day had been much better. But his stomping and shouting and sweating looked awful on TV. Blair's downbeat style must have worked much better. But the Chancellor's audience was the thousands in the hall, while Blair's was the millions at home.

29.09.04

As ever, the Tories came last. Their conference was in Bournemouth and was addressed by Churchill's grandson.

Nicholas Soames, the shadow defence minister, was made manifest on the platform. Shadow minister? Never was any politician less shadowy. This week he hosted a lunch in Poole, where for just £49 guests could enjoy luscious seafood and wine. But it is a measure of the way Gordon Brown's stealth taxes are wreaking havoc among the hard-eating families of Britain that the champagne was non-vintage, and the Chablis only première, not grand cru. However, we can all be reassured. Within one day of a new Tory administration, we will all be able to afford first-growth clarets and the finest Pol Roger to wash down our crustaceans.

Soames was magnificent, a vast, florid spectacle, a massive inflatable front-bench spokesman. You could tow him out to a village fete and charge children 50p to bounce on him. They could have floated him over London to bring down German bombers. He wore a regimental striped tie – the Old Masticators perhaps – a striped shirt and a gorgeous, lustrous suit that may have been woven from the pubic hairs of ten thousand angora rabbits. This is not a man who merely gets dressed in the morning; instead he is swathed.

He had assembled a tremendous fighting force of sonorous words. 'Supreme gallantry and astonishing endurance' slipped from his lips as easily as half a dozen Colchester natives might slide in the other direction. Soames is never in the presence of a mere Queen, but of 'the sovereign'. He does not speak of ancestors, but of 'forebears' (unlike Goldilocks, who had only three bears).

As he worked towards his climax, we could almost hear the tattoo of the drummers in the military band. 'You may be absolutely assured that an incoming Conservative government will pay the premium on the most important policy our country can have – the policy which enables us to deter or defeat those who wish to do us harm.' As the delegates cheered, he stepped into the hall off the platform. Ten minutes later it stopped shaking.

Next we got another illustration of how the Tory Party doesn't quite get it. They held a question time session with luminaries such as Boris Johnson, Tim Rice and Malcolm Rifkind. Boris declared that young people would soon realize they formed the 'hip, happening, chic and cool party' because they believed in freedom of the individual.

Then, less than five minutes later, they were discussing, quite seriously, whether it would be a good idea to reduce crime by imposing a curfew on young people. Their slogan would presumably be 'Vote Tory and be under house arrest!' How hip and happening can you get?

07.10.04

The conference had a musical leitmotiv, which was Elvis Presley's recording of 'A Little Less Conversation, A Little More Action'. I wondered if the Conservatives had noticed that this song was not about hospital waiting lists, or improved schools, but quite explicitly about shagging.

*

By this time, a year and a half after the Iraq conflict had begun, Tony Blair was under increasing pressure to apologize for having led the nation in on a false prospectus.

Michael Howard said that he had not accurately reported the intelligence to MPs. 'Will you now say "sorry" for that?' Here is the Prime Minister's reply:

'I take full responsibility and apologize for any information given in good faith which has subsequently turned out to be wrong. What I do not in any way accept is that there was any deception of anyone. I will not apologize for removing Saddam Hussein. I will not apologize for the conflict. I believe it was right then, is right now, and essential for the wider security of that region and the world.'

This is the Tony Blair school of etiquette, in which you say you are 'sorry' while making it clear (a) that you are not to blame, (b) that it wasn't your fault and (c) that even if it was, you would do it all over again.

We can see how it works if we take a more domestic example.

'I am sorry that I spilled gravy all over your trousers. I hope you will accept that there was nothing intentional about this. Had I known that there was a tear in the carpet, I would not have put my foot into it while holding the gravy boat.

'But there is one thing I will not do, and that is to apologize for the gravy itself. The whole House will agree that gravy is a vital part of any meal involving roast meat. Meat without gravy is intolerably dry, and the British people will never accept dry meat. The Rt. Hon. gentleman has conspicuously failed to tell us his own attitude to gravy. Let me remind him that under the last Tory administration, of which he was a part, the standard of gravy fell to its lowest level ever. And with hospital waiting lists dramatically down...'

At which you just want to scream at him to stop. Oddly enough, the sharpest shaft came from Bob Wareing, a short and plump Liverpool MP who has been around the place, largely unnoticed, for more than twenty years. He opposed the invasion of Iraq, and stood up to say that if getting rid of Saddam had been the real aim of the war, how was it that in February 2003 Mr Blair had offered the dictator a chance to stay in office by meeting the UN demands? This was greeted by loud cheers from the Tories and Lib Dems, delighted to see a Labour MP, and such an unexpected one, wield the scalpel so deftly.

Mr Blair flannelled. 'The reason we had to change regime was that it was obvious he was not going to comply.'

Hmmm. 'Had the gravy boat been empty, my hon. friend would have had no need to complain. But it was because with gravy the beef is moister, a more digestible meal, a meal that the British people deserve...' And so on, no doubt for several years.

14.10.04

Now and again, the Speaker, Michael Martin, who had been an old-fashioned Scottish Labour MP before his promotion to glory, would show alarming signs of independence. Once he actually told the Prime Minister off for harping on about Tory policies rather than answering questions about his own.

What has got into the Speaker? Yesterday Charles Clarke, the education secretary, was trying to persuade us that our children are not only doing better in school but are performing so well that our system, like that of ancient Athens, has become a cynosure for all other nations. Why, Mr Clarke told us, he had been to a school in Yorkshire where he had simply walked in and found the children learning their multiplication tables on a whiteboard. (This is what we used to call a blackboard, only it's white.) 'And that was an entirely random event!' he said, as if a primary school, learning that the education secretary might be in the vicinity, would arrange for the children to be throwing paint at each other.

Then Barry Sheerman, a Labour MP who loves this government with what I can only call a tender ferocity, pointed out that Norwegian educationalists were coming over here, wanting to know how it was that, while spending so much more money than us, they failed to achieve results as glittering as ours. Mr Clarke eagerly agreed. Yes, and German politicians were coming here for precisely the same purpose. And ministers had even been invited to Madrid, to help improve teaching in Spanish schools!

Colin Challen of Morley wanted to add his hosannas. He had, he said with a winsome smile, done some homework of his own. Apparently the young folk of West Yorkshire are being educated to within an inch of their lives. 'I found that funding per pupil was up by 37 per cent since 1997!' he told us, with the air of someone attending a spiritual revival meeting and seeing a dozen people get up from their wheel-chairs and dance. 'There are 940 more teaching assistants! And as for support staff...'

Suddenly the Speaker's new rasping sandpaper voice cut in. 'Could the hon. member send these discoveries to the minister, in writing?' he asked.

There was a moment of shock. The Speaker is not supposed to speak like that to supportive Labour MPs. Mr Challen sat down, rather hurt, like the class swot who has just been told that nobody gives a flying fart about his class project.

What is the explanation? Mr Martin is teetotal, so this errant behaviour cannot be due to strong drink. Possibly he has a bulge in the back of his jacket, like George W. Bush, and the person who is telling him what to do has been on the sauce. But that is only a theory.

Then things got even more bonkers. In a discussion on healthy eating in schools, Stephen Twigg announced that the government has redefined carrots as fruit. What? Even New Labour cannot defy nature like that. Ronald Reagan once famously redefined ketchup as a vegetable, to make inner city diets sound better. But what next? Will they redefine hamburgers as spinach, chips as broccoli? And E's at A level can be redefined as A's, so impressing all those German, Spanish and Norwegian educationalists no end.

24.10.04

There were periodic attempts around about this time to get rid of the Prime Minister.

The Impeach Tony Blair movement held a meeting followed by a press conference at the Commons yesterday. It was magnificently chaotic. The meeting was private, but people listening intently at the door reported a row between the MPs involved and the various writers, artists and luvvies who had been invited to join them. The MPs wanted to do all the talking at the press conference but the luvvies wanted to get the odd word in themselves. The compromise agreed was that the various national treasures would be allowed to talk to the hacks, but only after the formal press conference had finished.

This was disappointing. Some of us had gone along in the hopes of hearing Harold Pinter, one of the keenest supporters of the move to impeach the Prime Minister. We had hoped he might recite one of his famous short poems:

'Bombs hurtle down
They split open the heads of babies
George Bush fills the skulls with shit
The shit of shitty damnation.
Thank you.'

Or words to that effect.

Sadly Mr Pinter was unable to attend, though he sent his best wishes. Instead we had the rock musician Brian Eno, the novelist Iain Banks, the famously left-wing actor Corin Redgrave and the famously right-wing author Frederick Forsyth. There was also Monsignor Bruce Kent, who used to be in charge of CND.

The meeting was originally scheduled to take place in a room just off Westminster Hall, but this proved to be too small. So it was transferred to another room, which turned out to be even smaller. It was that kind of day. We reptiles elbowed our way in. After that, they squeezed in a few more. It was like the Northern Line after rush-hour signalling problems at Camden Town, though without the stiff-upper-lip politeness. A lawyer called Dan Plesch filled us in; they want to set up a committee which will consider the case for charging Mr Blair with lying over the Iraq war. The chances of this happening are, frankly, zero, but Alex Salmond pointed out that ministers such as Peter Mandelson and Beverley Hughes had been fired for much less serious crimes.

We nodded gravely and took notes, or rather would have done, if to do so would not – if we had been on the Northern Line – have caused several people in our immediate vicinity to shout, 'Get away from me, you pervert!' Finally we were allowed to talk to the luvvies. I asked Frederick Forsyth how he felt about sharing a platform with Bruce Kent. 'And with Corin Redgrave,' he groaned. Great ziggurats of cameramen, sound men, reporters and photographers began to totter round the tiny room threatening everyone in their way. Writers and performers who would gladly go to Wrexham for the chance to appear on hospital radio were fought over by the BBC, ITN and Sky. It was demented. If the whole of their campaign is organized like this, Tony Blair is safe for the rest of the century.

25.11.04

Every now and again, a leader of the opposition – and over the years Tony Blair faced five – thought he was getting on top of the Prime Minister. Just occasionally one managed to get the edge of his knife into the oyster. The feeling rarely lasted.

Prime Minister's Question Time was full of frolics and fun. Win Griffiths asked Mr Blair if he would meet the president of Indonesia, to talk about terrorism. The president's name is Susilo Bambang Yudhoyono, and Mr Griffiths got it right, spot on, first time. Mr Blair edged round the problem by calling him 'the president'. And how is it pronounced? As it's written, of course.

Mr Howard raised the question of how much violence we should be allowed to inflict on burglars. We're not talking about loveable old Burglar Bill here, with his striped vest, bag marked 'SWAG' and genial chuckle. We are dealing with drug-crazed young hooligans with yellow eyes the size of lentils. Under the proposed new laws, we will be able to terminate them with extreme prejudice the moment they climb the garden wall, if not before. Somewhat to Mr Howard's surprise, the Prime Minister said he would contemplate a change in the law. 'I am very glad, Mr Speaker,' said the Tory leader in his silky 'A glass from this red decanter, Mr Harker? I think you will find it rather more interesting than wine' tone of voice. 'Once again, where we lead, he follows.'

No, said the Prime Minister, Labour had proposed the change first. 'He only jumped onto the bandwagon.' Mr

Howard leapt up as if he had just detected the first glimmer of dawn in the eastern sky. There was no time to lose. 'He talks about bandwagons! He joined Michael Foot's bandwagon to get into the Labour Party. He joined CND to get on in the Labour Party. He did over his Chancellor's bandwagon to take over the Labour Party! He is Mr Bandwagon!'

(No, that's the president of Indonesia.)

Mr Blair said, petulantly, that this was all because he had given an answer Mr Howard hadn't expected. So he should not indulge in 'rather absurd point-scoring', which is what politicians always say when there is no answer to hand.

All this put the Tory benches in very fine fettle. They started laughing in a curious and rather alarming way, like those mechanical clowns you used to find in old amusement arcades. They twitched and threw themselves about, holding their sides, shaking their heads and improbably going 'ho, ho, ho!' It was as if a party of department store Santas had been thrown into a pond full of eels, and someone had thrown an electric fire in after them. Mr Howard finished to a sound he has not, I think, heard before – Tory MPs yelling, 'More, more!'

09.12.04

Rory Bremner invented a line which he felt summed up the impression given by Mr Howard. He would say sibilantly, 'I'm not going to hurt you.' It's a line the government itself could have used in relation to many of its own policies.

The government's housing policy is in a mess. They have a strategy for dealing with this. Ministers have a row about how to tackle the problem. They then leak the row to the press, who can then be denounced for reporting the row in the first place.

Once one side or the other has won the argument, you produce a handsome, coloured booklet showing smiling people on the cover. We are going to get a lot of smiling people in the run-up to the election. You will see so many smiling people on party leaflets that you will be sorely tempted to smash some of them in the teeth, just to stop them smiling. The front of *Creating Sustainable Communities* shows a smiling old lady washing the dishes, a smiling gardener, a smiling boy in a wheelchair smiling at two smiling girls, and a mixed-race group having a meeting while smiling so much you assume they must have been diagnosed with piles then discovered later that day they had won the lottery.

There is also a spanking new train in a station which we can assume is full of smiling people ('A forty-minute delay due to points failure? Who cares?') and a flower-strewn water meadow of the type that will soon be concreted over to house more smiling people.

The next stage is for ministers to assemble a massive force of capital letters. This is then wheeled along to the House of Commons rather like one of those Roman catapults used to besiege cities. The capital letters are then hurled over the ramparts. Frankly you might as well surrender now and avoid having to eat rats later.

So John Prescott announced – and he can actually

pronounce the capital letters aloud – 'Sustainable Communities: Homes For All'. 'Market Renewable Pathfinders' were trundled towards the Tories, as were 'Choice-Based Lettings', the 'First Time Buyer Initiative', 'Move UK' (sometimes, bafflingly, written as 'moveUK', which appears to mean, 'If you can't find somewhere to live, clear off') and the great climax, 'The Sustainable Communities Summit' with 'English Partnerships'.

Mr Prescott read out the capital letters with great aplomb. He was on shakier ground when it came to the joined-up talking. 'The full amount of the receipts for the sale of the home, and I think that brings a level playing field …' which, of course, is about to be sold off to provide a Buyer Initiative or a roll-out of Sustainable Homes. The Deputy Prime Minister was enraged by Tory suggestions that he had leaked his plans, capital letters and all, to the press.

'I don't talk to the press, I can't stick 'em, quite frankly!' He waved crossly at us. 'Did you get that right?' A few syco-phants (and what an expense of spirit and a waste of shame is implied by being a sycophant to John Prescott) laughed, but we knew he was right – he doesn't talk to the press because he has people to do that for him. He was asked where the land would be found on which he could build all these homes for smiling people to live in. Some of it would be provided by 'the hospitals', and other parcels acquired from something mysteriously called 'the defence'. He went on: 'I think we've now consciously shown that it's far better policy, that's not every bit of land by government, but it's certainly some of it and particularly in regard to land by that, by homebuyers some of it, by, land, some of it owned by the government…'

So that was all clear. Whether the new policy will ever house a single person, smiling or grumpy, remains to be seen.

25.01.05

Tony Blair likes to start Question Time with words of condolence about someone who has recently died – a firefighter, perhaps, or an MP who has passed away in the previous week, or, increasingly often, a member of the armed forces killed in Iraq. I don't want to sound too cynical, but we in the press gallery do suspect that this instant memorializing may have the purpose of implying that any questions he faces are the merest trivial nit-picking compared to the questions of life and death he has to deal with every day.

We wonder what he might do if there were nobody to commemorate. 'We pay tribute to Tiddles, the House of Commons cat, who met her end chasing a feral hamster in the Ways and Means corridor last night. We extend our deepest sympathy to her immediate family and to 879 known descendants...'

It is all a matter of degree. Take yesterday, when after his words of comfort to the bereaved of the recent Hercules crash in Iraq, he was tackled by the Tory backbencher Julian Brazier, who wanted to know how he had replied to the sister of a wounded soldier 'when she wrote and asked how you had found time in your busy week to drop a personal line to Ozzy Osbourne when he fell off his quad bike, but not one member of your cabinet has written to or visited any of the 600 British soldiers wounded under your direction in Iraq?'

It was a good question, and one which rather shattered the mood of sombre contemplation. Unable to give the correct answer, which is 'Knowing who Ozzy Osbourne is makes me look cool and "in the groove",' he merely regretted that Mr Brazier had made his point 'in this way' before going on to a standard, boilerplate tribute to the courage of our fighting men.

This was a rarity: something of a Blair climbdown. Normally he would have said, 'Unlike the honourable gentleman, I am happy to pay tribute to Britain's magnificent rock stars who day after day perform sterling service for our country, facing terrible dangers such as breaking their backs on motorized toys, losing their nasal septums and choking on their own vomit – even, on some occasions, other people's vomit. It is typical of the Tory Party that they cannot join me…'

03.02.05

The Labour Party did have an extraordinary ability to claim credit for the most surprising things.

During environment questions yesterday, a Labour MP asked about the number of wild birds in this country. Normally the minister, Ben Bradshaw, would have made some anodyne reply. Instead he decided to take credit for the increase in our avian population. Bluebirds aren't just flying all over the land – millions of them are in great flocks, landing the bird poop of happiness on the windscreens of our humdrum lives!

'Thanks to the policies of this Labour government, wild bird numbers, after decades of decline, are now recovering,' Mr Bradshaw said. He even managed to keep a straight face, though the Tories were laughing their heads off. 'Bittern, corncrake and bunting are among the threatened species that are now recovering.'

It wasn't all good news. We had fewer sparrows and starlings. 'But I can announce today that from March, house sparrows and starlings will enjoy increased legal protection!' Precisely what this will mean for the sparrows and starlings he didn't say; possibly they will now be able to rescind legal contracts within the 28-day notice period.

Then came one of those cherishable parliamentary moments. Every MP was in transports of joy about the forthcoming royal wedding between Prince Charles and Camilla Parker Bowles. At least I assume they were; most seemed to have their ecstasy under a degree of control. But we were waiting expectantly to discover which MP managed to twist the subject round and offer the first loyal congratulations, thus winning the ancient title of Toady-at-Arms. It was the Tory James Gray. 'The wild birds in the garden at Highgrove, just outside my constituency, will join me in congratulating Mrs Parker Bowles on the exciting news of her forthcoming engagement!' he exclaimed.

I loved the idea of the happy birds twittering their delight at news of the royal nuptials. It was like one of those children's story books, in which larks, bluebirds, starlings, sparrows and possibly a few albatrosses hover protectively over Snow White as she makes her fearful way through the forest.

And of course Mrs Parker Bowles is herself a figure from a fairy tale, being the lovely princess and the stepmother at the same time.

Mr Bradshaw was not finished. Another Tory, John Randall, wanted to know what the government's policy on cormorants was. 'Cormorants have done very well over the past twenty years,' said Mr Bradshaw. 'Last year we decided to change the licensing regime on cormorant culling because of the damage they were inflicting on fisheries. Despite this, even if the licences were at their maximum, the cormorant population will be far higher than it was under the Tories.'

So, although the birds are now being massacred, they are still better off under New Labour and would certainly vote Labour if they could!

11.02.05

The government had great trouble getting its terrorism bill through Parliament. It is generally quite easy to get the Commons to do as they are told; the task is much more difficult in the Lords. This is also an intriguing insight into the way legislation works in our great democracy. The bill was of immense constitutional importance. Did that mean more time would be spent on it? Don't be silly.

The peers were going through the bill line by line. Except that they couldn't. So great was the rush to get the bill passed that nobody had had time to sort out the amendments. Their lordships would literally have no idea of what they were talking about. Some people would argue that they rarely have. But in this case they would not even have known what they were meant to be talking about.

When I say that some of them were apoplectic I mean it literally. When an elderly peer gets really cross you do wonder if it might be his very last explosion of rage. And cross is exactly what they were. The government benches proposed adjourning for a quarter of an hour ('during pleasure' as the quaint phrase has it, though just how much pleasure anyone might cram into fifteen minutes, especially at their age, I do not know).

The peers were so angry that they spent fifteen minutes debating whether they should adjourn for fifteen minutes. Then they were furious to discover that they were going to adjourn for fifteen minutes anyway, even though they had just spent fifteen minutes furiously debating that very topic.

Next they adjourned for fifteen minutes. When they came back they were even more irate, because it turned out they were going to have to debate a whole new bill. The Home Secretary had managed to get it through the Commons by promising great changes. They were going to have to make those changes. Lord Peyton called this 'an impertinence!' The lawyers were especially angry. One leathery old gentleman, whose name I regrettably did not catch, declared irascibly that 'There cannot be a derogation in escrow!' which is not the kind of talk you hear at the cheap end of the palace.

04.03.05

Tony Blair is famously religious, though he tends to keep quiet about it, except on the odd occasion when he implies that God will be his judge – a line which generally has the effect of closing down debate. Who can say, 'Look, old chap, in this case it looks as if God has got it wrong'?

The Prime Minister spoke in church yesterday. It was a very Blairite church. For one thing, it has changed its name from Christ Church, Lambeth, to church.co.uk. Not even church.org! It was a co., a plc. As we could tell from the leaflet they gave us when we arrived. It described the Faithworks Charter (which offers 'quality assurance in community care', as well as 'reviewing measurable and timed outcomes annually', and promises 'regularly to evaluate and monitor our management structure and output, recognizing the need for ongoing flexibility...')

Aaargh! Even the congregation is called 'clients'. It was like kneeling on a hassock for Question Time in the Commons – Jesus and the parable of realizing individual potential through optimizing best practice. The chap next to me said to his girlfriend, 'Save my pew, will you. I'm just off to check my emails on my BlackBerry.' He didn't come back, but another religious young man took his place. He boasted to the young woman who had just been abandoned that they had had Andrew Adonis from Downing Street to a social function. I couldn't bear to tell her that Mr Blair's favourite policy wonk did not entirely live up to his name, having been described as 'more Andrew than Adonis'.

There was a small sprinkling of dark faces in church.co.uk, but there was no doubt who formed the largest ethnic group – white guys in suits. They were not so much god-botherers as God's HR department. I expected a chap to come round and ask us to keep our mobile phones and bleepers on, so that we wouldn't miss any important messages. Instead he wanted us to switch them off, for fear they might interfere with the webcast. 'Thousands of people will be watching on their laptops,' we were told. This was utterly unlike St Augustine's, Hull, where I went to Sunday school, and where I was raised to fear the Lord, not to see Him as a partner and stakeholder responsive to my ongoing requirements.

Then the minister, the Rev Stephen Chalke, told us about his interview on Radio 4. 'They asked me if I was going to ask the PM about his faith – whether he is married up! They asked who I was voting for, and I said – us!'

Finally Mr Blair was among us. 'I hear you felt the media had got hold of the wrong end of the stick,' he said. 'Personally, I never find that!' The client base laughed cringingly at this sally. They were not going to be the WI. No slow handclapping here!

There was a slightly embarrassing question, sent in, of course, by email. Alastair Campbell had said that at Downing Street 'we don't do God'. What did that mean? There was a silence. It was as if a convocation of Delia Smith fans had been told that her team didn't do cranberries. They couldn't boo, but they leaned forward anxiously to hear his reply. He began to flannel frantically. 'I had a tremor of nervousness and hesitation when you said you were about to quote Alastair. I mean, what he meant, faith is important on a personal level but it can be very quickly misinterpreted. I mean, I don't want to be an American politician [who could he mean?] going around beating my chest, I think that's what he meant; politicians and religions have a lot in common, there are core issues, but if it ends up being used in the political process...'

It was all slightly embarrassing. We wished he could have been a little more robust and just said, 'We don't do God. And so far as I can tell, He doesn't do us.'

23.03.05

This was a busy period for news – or at least for events. The Prince of Wales got married – a day later than planned, since there were technical problems with the date he and his bride had originally chosen – and Tony Blair announced the election.

By a pleasing irony, the Commons was to debate two vote-rigging allegations. One was in Zimbabwe where, according to Jack Straw, 'there was much stuffing of ballot boxes with non-existent voters' (or ballot papers, as he probably meant). And there was more ballot-rigging in Birmingham, where local Labour leaders have managed to cope with the renascent Tory Party by Tippexing out their votes. Though admittedly nobody in the West Midlands has, so far as we know, been starved into supporting the regime.

Before all that we gathered in Downing Street. The dark green Jaguar was ready for the Prime Minister, as proud and silky as an Afghan hound waiting for its mistress outside a

Fifth Avenue apartment block. The door opened, the car oozed silently forward, and the PM emerged looking as pleased with himself as a landlord who's heard that the last protected tenant has just died. Or a tea towel manufacturer whose staff accidentally printed the date for the royal wedding as 9 April 2005. 'Ya gonna win?' someone shouted. 'Ya gonna lose?' shouted someone else. The car glided off towards the palace. We waited for half an hour. The noise level grew. A helicopter thrashed overhead, possibly poised to whisk the premier to safety. Feedback screeched from the mikes. Reporters tried to yell at spin doctors over the din. Someone taped a piece of white paper onto the roadway, presumably to let him know where to stand. It's a measure of the febrile atmosphere that when John Reid emerged from the famous black door, nobody could think of anything rude to shout at him.

'There's Tone now!' said a crew member, but it turned out that he meant 'tone', a technical TV term. Then suddenly he was back among us, so close that I could smell the thick orange makeup and the claggy aroma of Number 7 that's been gently warmed by skin and sweat.

He stood on the white paper, without his normal lectern or even his mug of tea. He told us that he had asked the Queen to dissolve parliament, 'which she has graciously consented to do'. I thought, wouldn't it be great if once, just for a prank, she did it ungraciously. If she stubbed out a fag, coughed and said, 'Orright then, but frankly I've 'ad it up to 'ere wiv you lot calling elections early just 'cos you fink you can win.'

Then he cranked up his election address. 'We should never stand still,' he said, while standing stock still. I went back to my computer and found an email on my screen from tony.blair@new.labour.org.uk. 'If you've been keeping up with the news,' he said rather unnecessarily – it is my job, after all – 'you may already know that I went to the Palace a few minutes ago to ask the Queen to dissolve parliament... you can help us to fight for every seat and for every vote.'

The miracles of modern technology! He must have used his BlackBerry to email me from the back of the Jag. I was touched and impressed.

06.04.05

2005–2006

Even when an election has been called, the Commons sits for a day or so to tie up loose ends.

Tony Blair looked and sounded terrible yesterday. His throat is sore. He is nervous and twitchy. His attention wanders. The man desperately needs a holiday. This is not good at the start of an election campaign.

Mind you, the election campaign has been going on for four years. This is just the final stretch. He is not Linford Christie, thrashing every sinew to propel himself down a 100-metre track. Instead he is Paula Radcliffe by the side of the road, wondering if he can summon up one last burst of energy, a single erg more to drag himself over the finish line.

He even lost at Prime Minister's Question Time – conceivably, though improbably, his last ever. Michael Howard must have marvelled at how easy it was. He kept quoting Gordon Brown: 'Why should we believe a word he says?' He had the Tories cheering like kids at a pantomime. 'Taxes – up!' he yelled, and they joined in on the 'up!' as they did with his cries for crime, immigration, waiting times, MRSA and school truancy. 'Take-home pay – down!' he shouted, throwing in pensions, productivity and manufacturing on that side of the scale. He began to sound slightly unhinged. 'Pensioners who can't find an NHS dentist are reduced to pulling out their own teeth!' he claimed, and I reflected that they could save a lot of money and trouble by just going up to John Prescott and insulting him.

But his greatest coup was to ask how many Labour MPs had pictures of their leader on their election addresses.

Tories roared with glee as half a dozen blockheads actually put their hands up, pointing up the contrast with the glum, silent, sullen cohorts around them. The PM said feebly that they would be better off with Michael Howard's picture on the leaflets, but he had clearly lost.

Soon afterwards he was at a joint press conference with Gordon Brown, designed to show what chums they are. The lighting was pink, scarlet and green. It strobed as the two great rivals strode in, as if the Relate people had decided to hold counselling sessions at a fairground. Inside we heard Bono singing 'It's a Beautiful Day'. Outside, a nice New Labour touch, it was pouring down.

Someone tried to ask the Chancellor a question. The PM didn't like that. He became snappish. 'Ah mean, ah know, we're in a sort of interactive state, but let's keep it interactive within limits.' He clearly loathed the questions. He wanted different questions. We were facing a 'big' choice, which sounded like a super-value, family-size choice, a Kentucky Fried Big Bucket O'Choice. He looked weary, unhappy, stressed. He badly needs that holiday, or at least a couple of days in bed. But he ain't going to get it.

07.04.05

The Tories launched their manifesto yesterday. All their pledges are on the cover, and rather badly hand-written, to make them seem more sincere. Voters are supposed to think, 'I think Tony Blair has done a pretty good job, all in all. But his pledges are neatly printed, and you can't trust that.'

Michael Howard turned up at the launch, all gleaming and polished and shiny, so it looked as if there was something of the bright about him. Members of the shadow cabinet were brought in to support him. They were plonked down, like computer equipment being delivered on little trolleys. 'Where d'you want this Ancram, guv? I've got a Letwin 'ere as well. Print and sign please.' They sat in a mute row and gazed up at their leader. He is a shade frightening. But this has nothing to do with his being a vampire; more with him being a lawyer, which is much scarier. He uses lawyers' words: 'It does not befit Mr Blair'; immigrants might be coming here 'for nefarious purposes'. These are not words normal people often use ('That next door's lad, he's a nefarious one and no mistake'). He speaks English as if it were a second language, taught by patient specialists so that even lawyers can understand. He was asked about Charles Wardle, one of his own former Home Office ministers who had attacked Conservative immigration plans. 'Producing Charles Wardle at a press conference is an act of such desperation that it beggars belief!' he said, in a language similar to but not quite the same as English.

'You did that!' several people shouted, and suddenly he remembered all those *Teach Yourself English the English People Speak* CDs, the ones that instruct you in the demotic, which, as far as politicians are concerned, means football. 'It's like producing Lee Bowyer to talk about proper behaviour on the football pitch!' he said.

('Hmmm,' you can imagine the voters saying, 'I have been tempted by the Lib Dems, but not only are the Tory pledges scrawled on the page, but they can remember things that happen in football matches. They've got my vote!')

He said that he proposed to address 'the simple longings of the British people. They don't ask for much.' This made us sound like hamsters. A few seeds, water, a little wheel to play on. It's not a lot.

'On May the 5th you can let the sunshine of hope break through the clouds of disappointment,' he declared. This line, from the later Wordsworth, or perhaps a Hallmark card ('With deepest sympathy on your coming election defeat. May the sunshine of hope break through the clouds of disappointment'), was too much for the hacks, many of whom began laughing in an unseemly and vulgar fashion. 'Imagine, five more years of it!' Mr Howard added. 'Five more years of smirking!'

He seems obsessed by the Prime Minister's smirk, and though it may seem a rather self-satisfied grin, it is not technically a smirk, which I think involves a certain relish for other people's misfortunes. A smirk implies *Schadenfreude*: Hubert Lane laughing at William Brown sitting in a puddle. But we are more conscious of smirking these days. You can see a little group of smirkers outside every office building, huddled together in the warmth, hoping for the sunshine of hope to break through the clouds of disappointment.

12.04.05

Labour launched its own manifesto yesterday. Or rather, it opened a coal hole and poured several tons of nutty slack down on the voters. Earlier this week the Tories offered pledges that amounted to just eleven words. Yesterday Labour produced a document listing a total of 279 different promises.

Yes, 279! Try fitting that onto your wallet-sized pledge card. Imagine what the Durham miners would have had to stitch onto their banners: 'High street chiropody check-ups!'; 'Protect biomass!'; 'Action on dormant bank accounts!' Or this: 'Car pool lanes for cars' (as opposed to what – for orangutans?)

I can see, through misty eyes, the men marching down from Jarrow, shouting, 'What do we want? New partnerships to fund workplace training! When do we want it? When time and conditions allow.' As they sailed for Botany Bay, the Tolpuddle Martyrs would have dreamed of a better world, with 'more flexibility in the structure of governing bodies' and 'every pupil offered enterprise education!'

Actually most of these pledges looked a trifle vague, being more in the nature of aspirations than promises. Labour proffers a lot of 'long-term aims', 'promotion', 'bearing down', 'fighting', 'enriching', 'leading reform' and 'tackling'. Lines such as 'opportunities for pupils in their strongest areas' is not what one's old English teacher called 'a verb clause'. It is a hope, not a commitment, rather like 'More sunny weather for all!'

Tony Blair started with a long meandering speech, which, without warning, would be suddenly interrupted by his colleagues. It sounded as if they were performing the recitative in some terrible socialist realist opera performed in Moscow in the mid-1930s. They all kept banging on about 'decent, hard-working families'. But what about lazy families? Don't they get a look-in too?

14.04.05

Early in the election campaign, Brian Sedgemore, once a member of the hard-line left-wing Tribune Group of the Labour Party, announced that he was joining the Liberal Democrats.

I had arranged to meet William Hague in the Fox Hall pub near Ravensworth, in North Yorkshire. I was early, so I took the chance to eavesdrop on the locals. Talk was of the election, and specifically of the bombshell just dropped by Brian Sedgemore when he defected to the Liberal Democrats. One man put down his pint, wiped his lip and said, 'When a giant like Sedgemore defects, it's time to tear up the whole political map of Britain.'

''Appen,' said his companion. 'It's like John Prescott said. The tectonic plates have shifted, mayhap for ever.'

'Aye,' said a third man, who left it at that. They fell to discussing Sedgemore's multitudinous achievements, his thunderous oratory, the life-changing bills that he piloted through the Commons…

No, of course they didn't! That was just my little joke. Everything after the first sentence was pure fiction! They weren't discussing the election at all, and they certainly weren't talking about Brian Sedgemore. Then, thank heavens, William Hague arrived, and I had someone to whom I could talk about Sedgemore. Our conversation on that topic lasted for about five seconds. The former Tory leader has other things on his mind. Richmond, his seat, is one of the biggest in the country and it has been Tory since before the Labour Party existed. In the nineteenth century pubs like the Fox Hall played an important part in elections, specifically through 'burking', which meant getting your opponent's supporters so drunk they were incapable of reaching the polls. It gives an older meaning to the current term 'spinning'.

We talked about this over halves of Titanic Lifeboat, not a description of Tory election prospects, but an ale. The campaign for real metaphors! Hague looks far more relaxed than he did four years ago, when he was piloting his party to their second catastrophic defeat. He has been round the country this time, thirty-three seats as well as his own, but he's enjoying his return to the gentle hills and villages of honey-coloured stone. And to his solid majority.

'Last time we had the highest percentage Conservative percentage vote,' he said, 'and the highest Monster Raving

Loony vote.' In less than thirty years since as a schoolboy he made his celebrated speech to the Tory conference, he has moved from wunderkind to party leader, then to elder statesman and man of letters, all in the time it takes some people to stop drinking alcopops.

There are 200 villages and hamlets in the constituency, and they must all be visited. We go round with the local county councillor, who rejoices in the name of Michael Heseltine (no relation). Many settlements are idyllic, inhabited by a mixture of older people and labourers, next door to well-to-do families in which the breadwinner commutes to Tyneside, Teesside and Leeds. Mercs and Range Rovers are parked in the street along with rusting Escorts.

'The wealthier ones are the less reliable votes for me,' says Hague, though the elderly vote seems pretty solid. One man darted out of his house in stocking'd feet to shake Hague's hand. A younger woman, who sounded as if she had been scripted by Central Office, said that you couldn't trust that Blair. Then we met a man in Dalton, who was walking his dog while wearing a pin-stripe suit and a striped tie. 'Your party needs to look at its management structure, particularly at leadership level. I am waiting for you to come back,' he said.

'Oh dear, no, I don't think so,' said the candidate with poorly disguised distaste, much as when, a few minutes later, he turned down a request from a woman who was mucking out her horses and said she would like a hand.

27.04.05

When Tony Blair first became Labour leader, my colleague Steve Bell noticed an important physical trait, to wit that he always has one mad staring eye. This became more marked over the years. What is particularly startling is that the eyes take it in turns. The phenomenon was particularly marked when it emerged that Lord Goldsmith, the Attorney General, whose opinion on the legality of the Iraq invasion had been required, had changed his mind.

Tony Blair arrived at the launch of Labour's business manifesto, before an audience of journalists and businessfolk. He made a few small jokes. 'Gosh, he seems relaxed,' you could almost hear them thinking. But we Blair-watchers knew the reality. We had noticed the eye. It was the right eye. The left eye has always had a somewhat manic gleam, while the right eye seemed comparatively normal. But yesterday that right eye told a very different story. It was the *Optic of Dorian Gray*.

It was dark and hooded. It was a very suspicious eye. Now and again it almost closed completely, rather like the eye of a boxer when the ref stops the fight. And when it was open, the right eye seemed to have a life of its own, acting independently from the rest of his face. At one point it actually blinked on its own.

The left eye travelled round the room, spotting old friends and sparring partners, Andy, Mike, George and Adam. But the right gazed balefully round at these same people, as if warning its naive partner, the left eye, not to trust them. The right eye is the Col. Tom Parker of the Blair face, the hard, cynical, calculating presence behind the popular entertainer. There is a vein above it. It wasn't throbbing yesterday, but it bulged.

And no wonder. The Prime Minister was facing the most difficult ('challenging' is the correct New Labour term) press conference since he got the job. The gist of his defence was that the Attorney General had not said the invasion was illegal, and no one had kept his opinion from the Cabinet. There were two members of the Cabinet on hand to nod in confirmation, though Gordon Brown rather spoiled the effect by, as usual, scribbling furiously while the Prime Minister spoke. The implication is, I suppose, that he is far too busy running the country to listen to Tony Blair blethering on, though I sometimes suspect he may be jotting down a to-do list: 'pick up dry cleaning, check MoT, launch desperate bid for power…'

At one point the Prime Minister, who sometimes talks about himself in the third person, though that may just be the right eye feeding him information, said, 'It was a decision this leader had to make for this country!' He had 'decided' to bring down Saddam Hussein, he told us, somehow forgetting the armed forces of the United States, who, we gather, may have been involved in some way too.

Then came a fine moment. Nick Robinson of ITN, perhaps a little startled by the Chancellor's apparent support for his oldest and deadliest rival, asked him, 'Are you saying that you would have behaved in an identical way to Tony Blair if faced with the same circumstances?' There was a pause which probably lasted around three seconds, but which seemed to go on for ever. The right eye turned to stare malevolently at Mr Brown, like some oriental jewel in a Victorian thriller, capable of taking over men's minds. The eyebrow above it arched in a V-shape.

Finally the Chancellor spoke, or rather barked: 'Yes!' The right eye suddenly relaxed and even seemed, just for one brief moment, to gaze fondly on Gordon Brown. Applause broke out from the business persons; they, after all, must know how much it cost Mr Brown.

'Well done!' said Patricia Hewitt, sounding as always like a doctor congratulating a small child on surviving a jab without crying. You half expected her to add, 'and for being such a brave boy you deserve this delicious Kunzle cake!'

29.04.05

The election was a good opportunity to get a first-hand look at a politician who was about to become an awful lot better known.

'David Cameron is coming here today, to push my campaign – over the edge!' said Stanley Johnson. 'Sorry, over the finishing line!' Stanley, the father of Boris, who could become the first man ever to follow his own son into the Commons, was in the Devon village of Chudleigh Knighton. He was refreshing himself with his campaign workers in a pub. 'We have campaigned in every village,' he said proudly; 'at least in every village that has a pub.'

David Cameron is the Tories' shadow cabinet member in charge of policy co-ordination, whatever that might be. He is tipped as a future leader. If they lose the election and decide to skip a generation, he could be there this year. He descended on Teignbridge like one of those American tornados that wreck trailer parks. He had been all over South Wales that morning, flown to Plymouth and been driven to the pub for lunch. Inside it was chaotic. Some nineteen people were clustered around him and Stanley – aides, agents, canvassers, hacks, photographers, drivers and hangers-on. Mad conversations began.

'And I spent an hour on the local radio station, talking entirely about nappies.'

'Who was the Stilton ploughman's, then?'

'I said I was all in favour of saving the planet, but had they ever tried washing a dirty nappy by hand?'

'Two ham ploughman's and one ham sandwich. Or is it the other way round?'

'So you see, reducing council tax is a massive issue here. That and slaughtering infected badgers.'

'Chicken salad? Somebody must be the chicken salad!'

'I did rather well in the pancake race, and one lady asked me, "Are you a practised tosser?"'

Cameron looks and behaves like a junior minister, and already talks the talk. 'I found that Cardiff was blue, and that Barry was blueing up…the momentum is in our direction. We're talking about what we're going to do in government, while the other two parties are talking tactics. "Don't let the Tories in by the back door," they say. After eight years, that's pathetic!'

We raced on, leaving behind enough food to feed a dozen hungry plough persons. Next we descended on the market town of Bovey Tracey, where Cameron raced up the high street introducing voters to the candidate, who didn't like to say that he had worked the shops some days before and yes, most of them had met him.

We passed a pub with a sign outside saying 'Eat The Rich'. Not natural Tory territory, perhaps, though it turned out to be the name of a rock group. A canvasser leapt out. 'We've got a swayer here!' he shouted. Old Terry was precisely that, literally and figuratively. 'Dunno how I'll vote,' he said unsteadily from the stool on which he was more or less seated. 'You could buy me a pint.'

'No, he can't, it's illegal,' said Cameron firmly. 'Old Terry, always pissed as a handcart,' the agent confided.

'Margaret in the fruit shop is *hovering*!' we learned, and faster than a speeding bullet Cameron was among the apples and cabbages to tether that vote. Once outside, he charged back down the street. An ex-policewoman came up. 'I would rather cut my arm off than vote for those lying scumbags who are in power now,' she said.

So not Labour, then, and indeed the party was a poor third last time. Stanley Johnson is just 3,000 votes – 5 per cent – behind the sitting Lib Dem MP, Richard Younger-Ross.

'We've got to go, David,' said his driver. We ran past a stylist's salon. 'I fight shy of hairdryers,' Cameron said. 'Hairdryers and banks. You should never disturb people when they are with their money.'

Finally the driver dragged him away. He grabbed the candidate's arm. 'Stanley, that was *huge!*' he said, a term which slightly perplexed Mr Johnson. He watched the next leader (or leader but one) with gratitude, but also some relief. 'We can slow down now. I don't know, people from London …' His voice tailed off as we went into a pub for an urgently needed restorative drink.

4.05.05

Mr Johnson failed to win the seat, though he went on to a successful career as a freelance journalist and environmental campaigner.

A few days later Labour won a third election by a smaller but still substantial majority. Michael Howard immediately announced that he would be retiring, making that four Tory leaders whom Mr Blair had seen off.

*

I had noticed a trend in election literature, by which candidates print more and more pictures of themselves, as if certain that the multitude of photos gracing their pamphlets would be enough to ensure victory. In some cases they were.

Oliver Letwin, for example, was thought likely to lose his seat in Dorset to the Liberal Democrats, though possibly thanks to the twenty-two pictures of himself in his address, some very large, he had a comfortable win. The shadow cabinet member Tim Collins did lose in Westmorland, perhaps sent on his way by the fourteen big pictures of himself that the Lib Dem challenger Tim Farron squeezed into his four-page leaflet. One showed him standing by a roadside, and was captioned 'Roundabout needed at Greenodd junction'. Forget Iraq, forget the pensions crisis – Tim will soon be in the Commons fighting for that roundabout.

In Welwyn, Grant Shapps won the seat for the Tories, with twenty-two pictures of himself in the main address, plus five more in the extra literature. Richard Beynon in Newbury beat the sitting Lib Dem with many pictures, one showing him personally ripping up ragwort. 'Richard has led a campaign against this poisonous weed.' But the Lib Dems did extremely well in Inverness, taking the seat from Labour. Danny Alexander's leaflet contains twenty-nine photos of himself and – this is very sweet – a picture of him a few months old, being carried along a beach by his dad. There's another of him with his fiancée, and one with a lobster.

It's not a universal rule. Sarah Teather held Brent East with only three pictures of herself, whereas in Dorset South Ed Matts failed to overturn the narrowest Labour majority in the country, despite offering twenty-eight pictures of himself, including one with a giant teddy bear.

But the worthy winner is Paul Truswell, returned again as Labour MP for Pudsey. His gallery is magnificent. There he is with schoolchildren, inspecting a road, giving a thumbs-up sign to a passing cart, Paul with a cat, with a bus, with a fishing net, looking fascinated as a member of the public points at another car. In this eight-page leaflet, there are no fewer than sixty-three pictures of Paul, an average of 7.87 per page. No wonder he suffered one of the smallest swings to the Tories, only 0.9 per cent, and on a whopping 67 per cent turnout.

14.05.05

One of the most startling results was George Galloway's victory for the Respect Party in Bethnal Green and Bow, where he unseated one of Labour's few black MPs, Oona King. Soon after the election, Mr Galloway went to Washington, where he faced a committee of senators who were investigating possible financial links between him and Saddam Hussein's ousted regime. He blustered, yelled and shouted at the senators in a way they had rarely if ever experienced.

George Galloway appeared in the House fresh from his triumphant appearance in the United States. Triumphant in his own eyes for the most part, yet there is no denying a certain sneaking admiration for his performance in front of the World's Greatest Deliberative Body, as it calls itself without any hint of irony.

We may be a minor power these days, and nobody much bothers to follow our debates, but when it comes to bombastic, browbeating, hectoring, bellowing rant and cant, plus half-truths delivered with the weight and effect of stone tablets hurled at the senators, then your traditional British MP is still a world-beater.

It's like our famous ceremonial. We do it so much better than anyone else that we haven't noticed that nobody else is doing it any more.

Mr Galloway conversed amiably with Gerald Howarth, who is Tory MP for Aldershot, and so represents many of the soldiers whom Mr Galloway accused of 'falling on Iraq like wolves'. It was this view, and his more or less open encouragement for people to shoot at British soldiers, that got him expelled from the Labour Party, though it didn't cause Mr Howarth to ignore him, or even manifest any resentment. Like the US Senate this is a very collegiate place.

He signed in, was given no fewer than five shakes of the hand by the Speaker (one or two more than most other MPs received) and then took the important decision – where to sit. He selected a bench on the opposition side, behind the Lib Dems, where he stayed for around two minutes. It was the political equivalent of a dog announcing its presence by peeing on a fence. And he was gone.

We can't wait for his first speech. No doubt he will denounce his fellow members as 'whores, poltroons, drunkards and lackeys of the baby bombers Blair and Bush', after which they will line up to buy him drinks.

20.05.05

In fact, Mr Galloway almost never turned up in the Commons chamber. He did however appear in the TV show Celebrity Big Brother, *where at the instigation of the actress Rula Lenska he acted the part of a cat and pretended to lap cream from her hands. This provided an important talking point in Commons bars for quite some time.*

The young pro-hunt protesters who got onto the floor of the Commons last year were convicted yesterday. The beak said, 'Your action caused some of those present alarm.'

Caused alarm? Since when was it a crime to cause alarm to MPs? They themselves do little else. According to the opposition the economy is about to go bung, and the streets will shortly be full of merchant bankers holding signs saying 'Will lick driveways clean for food.' Or else crime is out of control and you can't cross a Waitrose car park without hoodlums mugging you for the points on your loyalty card. The government is even worse. The planet is going to turn into a spinning ball of dust. We are about to suffer a terrorist attack that will make 9/11 look like a snowball fight. Or Saddam had weapons that could be deployed within…Well, maybe we shouldn't go there.

Alarm is what politicians trade in. If they abolished death, no one would buy any life insurance, and if politicians stopped alarming us, no one would see any reason to vote for them. The invasion by Lord Snooty and his pals caused some mild and transient anxiety, which is not the same thing at all.

Whereas the Chancellor might have felt some alarm yesterday. The alarmist turned out to be Michael Fabricant, who used to be one of the leading disc jockeys in the Brighton and Hove area, and who yesterday was wearing his summer wig. He asked Mr Brown about Treasury borrowing. The Chancellor reeled off figures which he implied were mere loose change, but which worked out at around £1,000 per household per year.

Mickey, who is busily reconstituting himself as an elder statesman, rose and pointed out that the current deficit was over £5 billion more than the Treasury had forecast. 'The fiscal position has deteriorated sharply over the past five years,' he said. 'The Chancellor will probably brush this off and say, "Hey, whatever!"'

The place dissolved in laughter. It would be impossible to imagine anyone less likely to say, for any reason, 'Hey, whatever!' It is one of those remarks you know will never be remarked. Like Tony Blair saying, 'I'm sorry, I got it wrong.'

Or Michael Howard: 'Tory MPs can say what they like. It's a free country.'

John Prescott: 'The press have a job to do, and they do it bloody well.'

Nicholas Soames: 'No, thank you, I've had more than enough.'

Mr Brown rose to a merry chorus of 'Hey, whatever!' He lashed back with a list of previous Tory deficits. Then he produced a quote from one of Mickey's election addresses. This had called for more spending on Staffordshire schools.

Mickey rose in his place, his hairpiece quivering and flashing like a disco globe. It was a sight that would cause more alarm than Otis Ferry and any number of public school yobbos. 'I said fair funding, not more funding!' Mickey yelled above the hubbub. 'And my majority went up by 50 per cent!'

The effect on the Chancellor of this noise and rage was so alarming that when Mickey showed him his election address near the Speaker's chair, Mr Brown gave him a great big old hug – which certainly alarmed me.

23.05.05

Andrew Robathan, a Tory, asked the Deputy Prime Minister what he was doing to foster a culture of respect. 'Respect' is the buzz-word of the moment. It implies not gobbing on passers-by, not binge drinking while getting pregnant at the age of twelve, not taking photos with a mobile while your friends throw up on bus passengers, and certainly not wearing hoodies.

To Mr Robathan's great regret, the question was not fielded by John Prescott – indeed he answered only one question in the whole half-hour devoted to his department. I had a vision of purring civil servants oh-so-delicately putting him off.

'Not perhaps your strongest suit, Deputy Prime Minister,' one of them would say. 'Maybe we should pass this on to Yvette…Mmm, this certainly is a fascinating one. I'm sure you could answer it magnificently! But young Miliband might be a tiny bit out of sorts if you don't let him tackle this.'

Prescott looks down the list and sees he is rostered only for a single question, on Pathfinder Initiatives, whatever they are. ''Ere,' he says, 'what's this?'

'I'm sure you will manage it with your customary flair and brio, DPM. Now, how does a biscuit sound?'

Mr Robathan ploughed on against an understrapper, Phil Woolas. When it came to 'respect', wasn't it important to show leadership? Did he think that the DPM thumping people in the streets and swearing at MPs in Commons corridors helped to foster a culture of respect?

This reminder of the moment in 2001 when Mr Prescott filled in a young farmer in Rhyl who had assaulted him with an egg delighted the Tories but brought Mr Woolas close to tears.

'I thought it was particularly unfortunate that the young thug who attacked my Rt. Hon. friend, who is of course of pensionable age…' The notion of John Prescott as some frail senior citizen stooping along the pavement, only to have his pension ripped from his hands by mullet-sporting hooligans, was silly enough to keep the House burbling with laughter for quite some time. Mr Prescott glowered aggressively at this mirth. He is someone who is actually capable of strutting angrily while remaining seated.

09.06.05

In the summer of 2005, David Dimbleby presented an admirable
television series called A Picture Of Britain, *reflecting the way*
our landscape has been seen by artists down the years. One point he
made is that the notion of what constitutes beauty in natural
scenery is constantly changing, and this was reflected in environ-
ment questions.

A few years ago we were all moaning about oil-seed rape, a
yellow blight, a scummy top dressing on some of our loveliest
countryside. But the other day, looking down on golden
stretches of Wiltshire shimmering in the sun, I thought how
beautiful it looked. In a few decades my grandchildren will
complain how set-aside and the policy of growing all our
food in developing countries means that England is now
covered in ugly, random trees and messy hedgerows. 'When
I was young, this used to be a sea of glorious yellow!' they will
tell their own children.

Under Margaret Beckett's watch, the landscape is forever
in flux. Often it is for the worse. Yesterday MPs and
ministers depicted a land covered in corpses – of animals and
suicidal farmers, unable to carry on after being reduced to
penury by the EU. The countryside once evoked by
Matthew Arnold and Rupert Brooke now looks like the
Somme after the first day.

There was the usual chuntering in jargon, which also
changes month by month. We heard about 'regulatory
windows' and 'improving transparency in the dairy supply
chain'. ('Whoi, that Daisy, she's all skin and bones!' 'Aye,
mayhap she be. But come Michaelmas she'll be completely
transparent!')

Someone asked about the 'haddock permit'. One
imagined folk being stopped by community support officers
on the way home from the chippy. 'Excuse me, sir, do you

have a permit for that haddock?'

'No, it's still at Swansea. But I do have a licence for this deep-fried samosa.'

The main discussion was on bovine tuberculosis, which is driving farmers to ruin and death, and which might by solved by a mass cull of badgers. 'This whole debate is being dominated by badgers!' said one MP, the first time anyone has made that point since Norman Lamont was sacked. With majestic contempt, the junior minister, Ben Bradshaw, pointed out that it was quite impossible to tell which badgers were infected until they were dead. The Tories came up with no reply to that, though a Labour MP, Nick Palmer, said sardonically that they merely reflected Tory policy on all matters rural – 'If in doubt, kill something.'

Then Vincent Cable rose to talk about the ridiculous amount of paperwork farmers have to cope with. It turns out that 100,000 of them have each received ten documents, including a total of 357 pages – accompanied by an explanatory note that said, 'Replace throughout the word "increase" with the word "decrease".'

10.06.05

The French and Dutch both voted against the new constitution for the European Union. And a summit meeting designed to sort out the common agricultural policy had failed.

Tony Blair does not normally do angry. Show him a European Union that is wounded and his instinct is to cover it in Savlon and kisses. So his stroppy, pull-yourself-together manner yesterday surprised and delighted MPs, mostly Tories, who did nearly all the cheering when he reported on the failure of the EU's weekend summit.

(It didn't do an awful lot for Sir Sean Connery, who was in the Strangers' Gallery. Britain's most famous ex-milkman seemed neither shaken nor stirred, but merely peeved, like Mr Blair himself.)

It did not make sense, the Prime Minister said, for 40 per cent of all the EU's spending to go on 2 per cent of its output. The budget was not 'fit for purpose' – a phrase new to me, which manages to sound both resonant and ungrammatical. The presidency proposal, 'from Luxembourg', he added, perhaps to remind us of another reason why we could safely ignore it, had fallen 'way short'.

(Why do we lack a rude word for the Luxembourgeois? Since 'krauts' and 'frogs' and 'rosbifs' are all named after popular foods in each country, maybe we should describe them by their favourite potato dumplings, as in 'Clear off home, you filthy grompernkniddelens!')

Mr Blair was not finished with the devious dumpling-munchers. The terms of the review had been 'so vague as to be meaningless'. The Tories loved that, not only because they were thrilled to hear the Prime Minister in Eurosceptic mode, but also because for him to complain about vague and meaningless language was like a natterjack toad moaning about rough skin.

Did Europe's credibility demand a deal? asked one of them. 'No!' he shouted, and that was, I think, the only single-word reply he has ever given in the Chamber.

He expanded on the EU's shortcomings. 'People support the concept of a European Union; what they don't like is its present reality.' The Tory sceptics could not believe their good fortune. Even Bill Cash, a man whose monomaniacal devotion to the Eurosceptic cause would bore to death the entire population of dumpling-downing Luxembourgeois, seemed pleased. So did Sir Peter Tapsell, who welcomed Mr Blair's admission to 'the Eurosceptic club', though being Sir Peter, he managed to make it sound as if this was, as clubs go, closer to the Order of the Garter than the Ovalteenies.

The only person Mr Blair was rude to was Alex Salmond of the SNP, which is Sir Sean's party. Mr Salmond, who always seems to get right up the prime ministerial nose, like a particularly large and painful bogey, complained about his 'style'.

'It's the budget we're debating, not fashion,' snapped Mr Blair, at which Sir Sean pulled a long, thin, but incredibly strong carbon fibre cord from his watch and abseiled down from the gallery to kill him silently with a hidden blade.

Well, it would have been spectacular if he had.

21.06.05

On 7 July, suicide bombers set off four explosions in central London, three on tube trains, one on a bus. Some 52 innocent people lost their lives.

'The British people will not be cowed and the terrorists will not win,' said David Davis, and for once it was his quiet, downbeat delivery, without ostentation or displays of instant fury, that made the words both effective and affecting. The flat refusal of the Commons to let the terrible events going on a few short miles away halt proceedings in Parliament at first seemed silly, then became rather impressive.

A small number of MPs had managed to get in for the start of business, which was questions on the environment and food. Surely, we thought, they can't be talking about the EU sugar regime, or single farm payments, or bottle banks?

But they were, and just as seriously as if this was just another morning, while outside the sirens swooped and rose, overlapping each other, wailing and whining – the now familiar soundtrack to terrorism.

They may have been talking about bovine TB but most members were staring straight ahead, and you could almost see that worm of doubt and horror inside all of us, the worm that curls up and dies only when we know that all our loved ones are safe.

Next, business questions. The House is to debate funding for the Olympics, and we were reminded that the euphoria of Wednesday had been ripped apart and shredded, like a mortar attack on a wedding. At one point a great shout of laughter went up when Derek Conway started asking about the Cat Protection League and the Dog Trust, or possibly the other way round. At first this seemed tasteless; then less so. Perhaps the ability to laugh at pointless jokes is as much a part of our democracy as anything else and so worth defending?

A few MPs slipped out to see the hollow-eyed Prime Minister on TV from the world summit in Gleneagles. The rest of the Cabinet was on the front bench, though Charles Clarke was not yet ready, and the Speaker suspended the sitting for twenty minutes – just time for a quick, horrified glance at the news channels.

The Home Secretary finally arrived. He rose to a complete, almost eerie silence. What he had to say was very brief and wholly factual. He limited himself to one boiler-plate condemnation of the attacks ('criminal and appalling acts') before reciting a short dossier of required information: the Metropolitan police were in charge, the health services were working well, public transport remained shut down. Again, there was no grandstanding, no implication that the nation needed to have its resolve stiffened and its sinews strengthened. We will not, he was implying, defeat terrorism by running around like headless chickens or squawking geese.

Mr Davis spoke about the 'unspeakable depravity and wickedness…this is not just an attack on our capital, but on our way of life.' Londoners, he said, had a long tradition of coping with terrorism – they had done so before and would do so again. The point was echoed by Charles Clarke: it was, he said, almost a truism that over the years London had demonstrated its resilience and would do so again. Then, as if it was a normal day, they started the planned debate. Which, as it happened, was about the defence of the whole world, and not just the defence of Bloomsbury.

08.07.05

The country responded with impressive stoicism. The House got an even bigger shock a few days later, when it turned out that all four bombers lived and had been raised in Britain.

*

A fortnight later, Ted Heath, who had been prime minister from 1970 to 1974, died.

The Commons paid tribute to the former Tory leader. Tony Blair recounted his first meeting with him, soon after the 1983 election.

'What party are you?' asked Heath.

'Labour,' said Blair.

'Well you don't look it. Or sound like it.'

This got a big, ironic laugh.

Charles Kennedy recalled sitting next to him for years, on the opposition front bench, just below the gangway. Once

William Hague was chivvying Blair, who was just back from a Third Way conference with other world leaders. 'The PM's Third Way is more a case of two fingers!' Hague had said. Heath had turned to Kennedy and remarked, 'Such a vulgar little man.' Which was unfair, since Hague is actually quite tall. You feel that, as with the Teletubbies, there is a full-sized actor in there.

The problem, which nobody addressed directly, is that there was a Good Ted and a Bad Ted. The Good Ted was warm, genial, outgoing and surprisingly full of fun. The Bad Ted was a miserable old grump. You never knew what you were going to get. Bill van Straubenzee, a very moderate Tory MP who was a friend of Heath's – or at least as much of a friend as people were allowed to become – lived near him and wanted to repay some of the hospitality he had received at Heath's home in Salisbury Cathedral Close. He wanted to invite other people, and couldn't be sure if he would get the Good Ted or the Bad Ted. It was a semi-formal lunch party – sports jackets and ties – and Heath turned up in a turquoise and orange Miami Dolphins sweat shirt. He was a great fan of American football and rarely missed the Superbowl.

On the eve of poll in the second 1974 election, a colleague and I had been despatched to cover what was left of his campaign. It was late in the day, he must have known he had lost, so we went drinking with him in a pub. He was in wonderful form, his shoulders heaved, he always bought his round and he told stories about the great and the famous. Yet the next day he could be hideously rude. People who knew him well ascribed this to his bone-dry sense of humour, though it wasn't always taken that way.

Once John Nott, who was number two in the Treasury while Heath was PM, approached him in the division lobby asking for a word. He had hoped to warn him about the coming rise in inflation. Instead Heath brushed him aside. 'If you want to resign, put it in writing,' he said. Nott never really forgave him.

If he had made up his mind, he never felt the need to justify his point of view. 'There are those who believe that...' (you could fill in almost any policy position taken by Margaret Thatcher or John Major) '...but they are quite wrong. So that is that.' No further discussion was thought necessary, by him at least.

Every year he gave a dinner for a selected group of journalists attending the Tory Party conference. At one such occasion, near Blackpool, he was presented by the hacks with a jokey present of a chocolate bust of Margaret Thatcher. In front of the whole dining room, which included several cabinet ministers, he picked up his knife and smashed the bust to pieces.

By the end he was liable to fall asleep at table. Another colleague of mine recalls another one of the conference dinners. Heath was recently back from Cuba, where he had had a lengthy conversation with Fidel Castro. He began to recount almost every word of this dialogue, at immense and tedious length. Then suddenly and without warning he fell asleep. The guests were perplexed about what they should do. Then after ten minutes he just as suddenly woke up, and resumed the conversation from the exact point at which he had left it.

Towards the end of his life he had unwelcome links with the Chinese government. Watching him defend the massacre in Tiananmen Square was more than distasteful; it was shameful and it demeaned his record.

19.07.05

Summer passed, as it will, and we regrouped by the seaside for the party conferences. Labour was in Brighton.

Tony Blair praised the people of London yesterday for 'locking horns with modernity'. You could see the Labour conference uttering a single collective 'What?' It was a curious phrase. Does he see the people of London as stags, challenging modernity to become the dominant male in the herd? Or was it all a mishearing? Had he asked his speech-writers to come up with gardening advice, suggesting that we dock thorns with impunity, or tips for chiropodists – lop corns with dignity? Or had it been originally about Zen seafood cookery – we should chop prawns with serenity? Maybe he wanted to crack down on the sex trade, both obscenity and swearing – to mock porn and profanity.

I mention this at length because these peculiar constructions he comes up with stop you responding properly to the rest of the speech. It's like being in the middle of a bracing walk and getting your trousers snagged on the barbed wire. Your companion may be marching blithely ahead, but you are still trying to untangle yourself.

Take this. The successful Olympic bid showed that we were a nation 'not just with memories, but dreams'. All right so far – I suppose what he meant was: we don't have to live in a glorious past; we have a future too.

Then he went on: 'Such nations aren't built by dreamers.' So what are we supposed to do? Dream, or not dream? Clearly we must do both, dreaming, but not becoming dreamers. We are to snooze but remain wide awake. We must be alert, yet asleep, on the ball while flat on our backs. Fortitude and forty winks!

The theme of the speech was his great favourite, change. As a nation we must accept the need for change. We should 'turn a friendly face to the future', asking the future if it needed any help getting that buggy onto the bus, or if it wanted fries with that. Labour as a party had to change too. Indeed we must all face the challenge of change. That way, our country would 'rise with the patient courage of the change-makers'.

(An American colleague tells me that 'change-makers' are those machines that give you coins for coffee, or a subway fare. Our nation should be covered with them, all of them patient and courageous, even when they go wrong and people kick them.)

The only thing that is not going to change is the leadership of the Labour Party. There will be no change there. Why? Because of something he learned from Neil Kinnock, which is now 'so ingrained it is like a strip of granite running through my soul'. We did not learn what the granite symbolized (unless, of course, it is real, implanted by doctors to stiffen up his irreducible core). He did however give us a glimpse. 'It's about leadership. Not mine alone. Ours together.'

Once again, the mind found itself stuck on a fence. If a leader has to lead, how can he have co-leadership with the people he is supposed to be leading?

There was a weird and slightly embarrassing moment when he referred to Hugh Grant, who plays a Blairish sort of prime minister in the film *Love, Actually*, and takes the opportunity of a joint press conference to give the US president a piece of his mind. This scene was, I gather, sometimes greeted with standing ovations in the cinemas. The real Blair said that a lot of people would like him to do the same. But then, he said, he would have 'the next day, the next year, the next lifetime to regret the ruinous consequences of easy applause'.

The *next lifetime*? What on earth was he on about? Is he saying that if he had not joined the invasion of Iraq, then he would have spent eternity regretting it? We know he believes God will judge him. If that would have been such an appalling misjudgement, would he have risked the eternal flames?

But the speech had moved on before we could ponder this. The audience seemed to like it in spite of everything, and even stayed awake. They had no need to block yawns with difficulty.

28.09.05

The party conferences become more stage-managed every year. The main difference these days is the louder objections from party officials when the television companies broadcast less and less from the stage-managed conferences.

The Labour conference was to hold its big debate on Iraq. Did they discuss it? Of course not. Instead a furious woman from Unison stormed the platform. 'I want to know why I have been stopped from bringing a bag of sweeties into the conference! It is bureaucracy gone mad!' she said.

The chairwoman said that the matter would be referred to the Conference Arrangements Committee, where it will no doubt disappear like a dead rat in a Bastille dungeon. They will spend hours debating the issue, then will come up with a confectionery composite, which will be voted on by, say, 1.7 million block votes to 638,000. We looked rather puzzled at the whole situation, until a steward standing near my seat said, 'I'll tell you why they're banned, they could be used as missiles.'

Missiles! What has Labour come to? The party of Hardie, Attlee and Bevan is afraid that its speakers might be cut down under a fusillade of Fox's Glacier Mints and Fishermen's Friends? As Hugh Gaitskell might have said, 'I shall fight, fight and fight again, no matter how many liquorice allsorts you hurl at me!' Later I learned that an old woman, a notorious leftie, had had a bag of Mint Imperials confiscated, for fear that she might create mayhem by rolling them along the floor. (However, I managed to smuggle in three of those little Toblerone things, which being triangular and sharp-edged could be lethal, like a chocolate ninja blade.) The issue may seem tiny, but it is a reflection of the state of the Labour Party, combining bombast, vainglory and total paranoia.

We finally got on to Iraq. Dennis Skinner made a speech in which he harked back to the good old days, when he had gone on endless marches and the miners were perpetually on strike. Glorious days, days of struggle, chaos and power cuts. 'I was very happy, and still am, to participate in the class war. I say this, to every young person in Britain: fight the class war, not the holy war!'

He got a standing ovation. All over the land young men and women will be seizing their Werther's Originals and marching to the barricades. What the class war needs is tactics – and TicTacs!

We heard from Jack Straw, the Foreign Secretary. Most of what he said was received with the merest polite applause, like drizzle falling on a tin roof. 'We are there for one reason only – to help the elected Iraqi government build a secure, democratic and stable nation!' At this point an elderly man in the gallery shouted, 'That's a lie!'

Dissent? At a Labour Party conference? That was defi- nitely right out of order. Building democracy in Iraq is one thing; having it at home and appearing on television is quite another. Two burly stewards grabbed this frail old gentleman. And rightly so – he might have had a deadly belt around his waist containing a dozen sticks of Blackpool rock.

29.09.05

The frail old gentleman turned out to be Walter Wolfgang from West London, a Labour supporter for decades. Incredibly, he was held by the police under the Prevention of Terrorism Act, which ministers had promised would only ever be used against terrorists, and certainly not mere dissidents. Anyhow Mr Wolfgang received many apologies, and was even elected to Labour's National Executive – which may be a worse punishment than going to prison.

*

We moved steadily from the Labour conference to the Tory leadership battle. It was clear that the two main contenders were the favourite, David Davis, and the youthful challenger, David Cameron. Mr Davis's launch was fairly muted. Then we went up Whitehall to catch David Cameron.

The launch was held in a room lit by soft shades of blue. By way of refreshment there were bottles of smoothies. In the old days Tory events were held in panelled rooms where old men slept under copies of *The Times*. But this looked like an aromatherapy salon. New Age music oozed from the loudspeakers – sorry, the softspeakers. There was a claque, fashionably dressed. I wonder how many lived more than a mile from Notting Hill Gate.

At first he appeared before us on video. He assured us that he was an optimist, a glass-half-full sort of person. 'Tomorrow is another day,' he mused, and we pondered how many great lines from the movies he might provide. Then he appeared in real life, and it must be said that he was very good. He had memorized his speech and spoke away from the lectern, as if what he had to say was so urgent that no written script could begin to convey it.

Change! Dynamism! Commitment! Passion! 'Not ideology, but idealism! We have a dream!' (Not another bloody dreamer, I thought. Isn't Tony Blair enough? Last night I dreamed I had tea with the Queen and she gave me a ham sandwich. What use could that possibly be for the future of our great nation?)

Both candidates were articulate and clear about what type of person they are. They are a great deal more vague about policy: Iraq, climate change, taxation. But that is not what matters. Change is all that matters. Change, and copying Tony Blair. I began to feel nostalgic for Tories who changed nothing. Evelyn Waugh once complained that the Conservative Party had failed to put the clock back by so much as one minute.

My ideal candidate will not make that mistake. 'Our job is not to reflect the country as it is, but how it used to be. We must not be afraid to stand still! Opportunity for the deserving, not the destitute! Upper-class degrees for upper-class people!'

And Sir Peter Tapsell will want us to leave the EU and return to the gold standard. He is not the voice of the future, but the standard-bearer of the past. I hope very much he runs.

30.09.05

He didn't. But five people did. We decamped north to Blackpool for the next stage. David Davis employed some young women with fine embonpoints. Their T-shirts declared, unnecessarily, 'I'm for DD!' The other candidates were Ken Clarke, Liam Fox, Malcolm Rifkind and David Cameron. Each got a chance to speak.

For the first time ever Ken Clarke seemed, in his rough-and-ready way, to be wooing the Conservative Party. It wasn't exactly fine wines and jewellery offered on bended knee, more 'How does a Scotch egg and a pint sound?' while bellied up to the bar. But at least he showed he cared.

In the past he has given the impression that he knows he's the best, the only real choice; if his party doesn't agree, then that's their problem, not his, and there's a CD of some recently discovered Charlie Parker tracks he wants to listen to. Yesterday he got to work on them, pushing their hot buttons, stroking a few of their fears and prejudices. If Michael Heseltine knew where to find the clitoris of the Conservative Party, Clarke is less subtle; instead he gave them all a big, affectionate slap on the rump. It won him a huge standing ovation.

Next we heard from David Cameron. Most of the delegates had never heard of him, or rather never quite clocked him, and they seemed to like what they heard, especially as he wandered round the stage, speaking apparently without notes, as if the words were being wrung from every passion-sodden fibre of his being. He has learned Ronald Reagan's trick of being dementedly optimistic: 'We love this country as it is, and our best days lie ahead!' It's morning again in Blackpool! They even loved him when he started raving, like a malaria victim who is at the point where he may live or die. 'Let us dream a new generation of Conservative dreams!' he said, which may be the most meaningless statement uttered at this conference so far.

'Changing our party to change our country! It will be an incredible journey, with no turning back and no false stops and starts! I want you to come with me!' (Though of course if it's like a Virgin train service south, it will involve an engine failure near Wigan and delays due to planned engineering work.)

Anyhow, after two speeches that went better than expected, Mr Davis must be rather anxious today.

05.10.05

The Tory conference rose as one yesterday to claim a fresh leader, a man of vision, courage, strength and humour. Sadly for them William Hague isn't running this time, but his undoubted oratorical skills plus the fact that the British love – no, adore – a loser, means that he got a thumping great stander for his speech. If he were running again, he would probably win.

Which is more than could be said for David Davis, who remains the favourite, but who yesterday could watch his support begin to gurgle away, like oil from a leaky sump. It's not that he was awful; he was thunderously not bad, majestically all right, triumphantly OK, I suppose.

But he wasn't great. They expected more and they wanted more. They wanted to love him, not just to like him. They wished for him to point the way to a glorious future, and what they got was 'Mind if I come along for the ride?'

He is not a natural speaker. You can't throw away your best lines as if you were warning a child not to forget their bus pass. You could almost see them thinking, 'If we choose this guy we will have to listen to this stuff every year for years.' He was clearly nervous, and arrived on stage with a tight little smile. His habit of swallowing words, and letting whole sentences drop alarmingly, like a fat man sitting on a three-legged stool, caused him to talk about 'Margaret Sasher'; bombings became 'bongz'. When he finally finished, the conference wasn't quite sure it was over, so they dragged themselves to their feet one by one. Some didn't even bother to get up. He stood on the stage, hoping to milk the applause, but that cow was already dry.

06.10.05

And that, we later found out, was that. Having seen the terrible reports in the morning papers, Mr Davis's spin doctors worked the press room telling us it was a minor glitch, would be forgotten in a day or so, etc. But as all politicians know, once you lose momentum – what George Bush Senior used to call 'the big Mo' – you are probably going to lose the race. That morning David Cameron became the bookies' favourite.

Tories love their leadership campaigns. They have so many of them. They come round regularly, like Royal Ascot and Red Nose Day. And they particularly enjoy them because for a few short weeks their opinions actually matter. If you're a Tory MP, most of the time nobody at all cares what you think. You are never invited onto the *Today* programme. Your children tend to forget your name.

But now, no matter how marginal you are, how crazed your views, how obsessed you are by Europe, or homeopathic medicine, or the white slave trade in Buckingham, you count. You matter. You are courted. For a short time you are taken seriously.

Campaigner: Now, Jasper, David wonders if you have made up your mind who you are going to vote for next week.

MP: I shall vote for whoever has mad staring eyes like me, and an alarming tendency to gob at the end of a sentence.

Campaigner: Excellent, excellent. I shall pass that on to David. I am sure he will take it on board!

There are rather fewer candidates now. A steady stream of people, including Theresa May, Edward Leigh and Bernard Jenkin, none of whom ever had the faintest chance, have withdrawn from the race before they even entered it. It's as if I were to issue a grave and formal statement that I do not wish to be considered for the England rugby squad.

Yesterday Tory MPs attended a meeting. It was called the 92 Club, because they used to meet at 92 Cheyne Walk in Chelsea. Lucky it wasn't number 69. MPs breezed in as if it were a birthday party. 'We love it!' said the pocket-sized Alan Duncan. 'Rah, rah, rah from the back row!' My old chum Michael Fabricant arrived looking perky. We asked his leanings. 'I'm on the soft-focus wing of the party,' he explained. We asked what that meant.

'It doesn't mean anything. I've just made it up,' he said. That's what we need – fresh supplies of meaningless jargon to plug the gap when New Labour has gone. We met Bill Cash, the tall and gangling Eurosceptic. Was there any point in the meeting? 'Oh yes,' he replied, 'there is a huge point!' Though the point about a point is that it can't be huge; you might as well have a towering hillock.

Ken Clarke was speaking. There was a thunderous sound of desks being banged inside the room. MPs then scampered off for a vote, but returned to say that he had been dazzling.

'Did he change anyone's mind?'

'I don't know, but we all enjoyed it.'

Of course they did. For many of these people it may be the first time a journalist has asked them about anything. I fear that as soon as the election is over we will revert to regarding their views as being slightly more important than our cat's, but less significant than the greengrocer's.

13.10.05

David Cameron seemed likely to win. His great friend George Osborne was already shadow chancellor, the latest in a long line of ambitious politicians who had been thrown by their officers into the trenches to face Gordon Brown.

Mr Osborne put up a feisty performance at Treasury questions yesterday. It was all going a bit too well for Dennis Skinner, who yelled out something which I couldn't fully make out, but it seemed to end with the words 'white powder'. What could he mean? So far as I know, Mr Osborne has never been accused of trading in illicit self-raising flour, or taking tiny packets of icing sugar into the toilets of Soho clubs. Perhaps his fashionably tight trousers cause chafing, which would mean he had to slather them in talc. Mr Skinner, a former Elvis impersonator, probably put gravel in his underpants to improve his gyrations.

Actually this whole drugs thing is getting pretty silly. If David Cameron didn't at least try pot when he was at university, then he isn't fit to be prime minister, on grounds of terminal lack of curiosity. If, on the other hand, he used to hang about the High in Oxford, his face covered in sores, his eyes red slits and his arms punctured like a tea strainer hanging limply at his side, accosting passers-by for the price of a bed for the night for him and his dog, then that might cast doubt upon his judgement.

We moved on to the economy. Gordon Brown said proudly that there had been no apprenticeships when he had come to power; now there were 300,000 young persons in 'modern apprenticeships'. My mind, as so often, began to wander. What would a modern apprenticeship be like?

'I was in my fifteenth summer when I left the city academy and was 'prenticed by my father to Jeb Haythornthwaite at the old call centre that had stood in our village for nigh on three years.

'"Tek this, lad," said Jeb affectionately, as he handed me a headset, lovingly fashioned in fine grey plastic. He fitted it over my head.

'"Look at them foam ear-pieces," he said. "You don't see craftsmanship like that any more. That thar thang has been in the Haythornthwaite family since the dawn of this millennium. 'Appen it will see us through to 2006. It might even see me out, lessen they close this place and I move to the Tesco Express check-out in Little Burdale!"

'"Mr Haythornthwaite," I asked nervously, "what should I do if ever I call someone up to tell them that our double-glazing representatives will shortly be in their area, and they be eating their tea?"

'His old eyes twinkled with pleasure. "Bless you, child, they will probably fill your tender ears with language that would stop a charging bull! But it bain't half be fun. I once called an old biddy who told me that not one hour ago her husband had dropped dead of the staggers. Didn't stop me telling her about our new range of fitted kitchens, though!"'

14.10.05

The Tory election process moved on. MPs had to select a shortlist of two. The final decision would be left to the party in the country.

The Conservatives were in a state of bliss. Eleanor Laing, a supporter of Liam Fox (they do exist), said it was just like an election day. 'We love it!' she trilled. She did a little dance on the carpet. The plotting was demented. Rumours whipped around the Commons like empty Big Mac boxes in a gale. Davis supporters wanted Fox kicked out in the early voting so they would get his supporters in the next round. Were they going to risk tactically voting for someone else? The Cameron voters wanted Clarke to depart so that they could scoop up his support. Was this really a good idea? Rank-and-file Tory members see Clarke as a Eurofiend. Might he not be the easiest candidate to beat? It was like trying to solve a Rubik's cube in the dark.

All the MPs were marching round with mobile phones apparently stapled to their ears. This was an e-conspiracy. (In 1868, Disraeli wrote a short and charming letter to his sister telling her that he had been chosen as the new Tory leader. These days he would have texted her: 'I 1 X B' – I won, love Benjamin.)

It was one o'clock and the voting was about to begin. A handful of MPs was waiting outside, like hungry boarders hoping the dining room might open early. 'There should be a numeracy test,' said Ann Widdecombe. 'If you can read an opinion poll, why are you voting for anyone except Ken Clarke?'

'Ann and I have a lot in common,' mused John Bercow, once a right-winger, now a moderate, married to a *Guardian* reader. 'We support Ken Clarke, and we are choppers, not twirlers!' I feared this might be some terrible euphemism, but it turned out to refer to the way they eat their spaghetti.

Nicholas Winterton bumped – literally – into Stephen Pound, the chirpy Labour MP. 'If I were any younger,' Sir Nicholas mused, 'I would be standing myself.'

'If you were any younger, you wouldn't be a Tory,' said Pound.

David Cameron arrived, with his friend George Osborne. They were neatly dressed and resembled the 'suit you' pair of men's outfitters from *The Fast Show*. 'Ooh, sir, does she like it in the ballot box? Does she, sir? Ooh, suit you!' Michael Fabricant arrived. He becomes more camp by the day. 'I'm a whip,' he said. 'I'm supposed to be inscrutable. Someone in *The Times* called me "excitable". Well, I'm not. I'm exciting.' He makes Graham Norton sound like John Wayne.

Some members were very proud of the fact that they had voted in the way they had pledged. Others refused to say, often in the most pompous fashion. We wanted to yell, 'We don't really care how you voted! In fact, we don't know who you are!'

Suddenly it was five o'clock and the voting was over. The corridor was packed: heaving, sweating, foetid. There may have been 500 people jammed up against each other. Cattle cannot be legally transported in such conditions. 'They love it,' said Keith Simpson. 'It reminds them of student union politics' – not a remark you would have heard in the old days of the Magic Circle. Sir Peter Tapsell was around for those days. Did I detect a tear in that grand old eye? Possibly, because there can be little doubt that the Magic Circle would have chosen him.

Suddenly Edwina Currie was among us! She had returned, the Joan Collins of the Conservative Party! (Ms Collins is the Edwina Currie of UKIP.) Nearly 200 Tory MPs piled into the room, Edwina among them. She hasn't been an MP since 1997, but she got past a less than alert police officer. Moments later she was ejected, not like a pea from a pea-shooter, but smartish none the less.

Then the spinning began. It will continue for the next forty-eight hours. 'DD is now in freefall. He doesn't stand a chance. It's David Cameron's best possible result!'

'Excuse me, David Davis is top of the list and you call that a defeat? What planet do you people live on?'

'All those people who were pledged to DD are now going to break away. Liam is a shoo-in on Thursday, and he's going to win in the country, too…'

19.10.05

The result had been disappointing for the favourite, David Davis, for although he had come top of the ballot, his support was clearly oozing away. Ken Clarke was eliminated, a third failure in three attempts at the leadership. The vote on Thursday was to find the top two candidates, who would then be left to the mercy of the party members in the country. The clear leader in this, the last MPs' vote, was now David Cameron.

The result was announced at 5.30, and within seconds I heard a Davis supporter say, 'Fully 55 per cent of the party did not support David Cameron!' On the other hand, as someone also pointed out, David Davis had actually lost five votes, which was scarcely a dazzling performance, since all Ken Clarke's thirty-eight votes had gone begging. There must have been quite a few fibbers about – but then there always are.

Charles Walker said ponderously on the step outside the voting room, 'I am sticking with David Davis. I am a man of principle and honour, both of which are in short supply here!' And he meant it.

But he was not quite the most pompous person present. Sir Nicholas Winterton stormed out of the room and bellowed down the corridor, so loud that it must have woken several people in the House of Lords, 'If I had known what I think is going to happen now, I would have bloody well stood myself, and the party would have known what it was going to get!' He strode southwards, hurling over his shoulder: 'Meant from the heart! And from the head!'

The dramatic effect was spoiled by only two small matters: nobody had the faintest idea what he was on about, and by young Tobias Ellwood, the Tory MP doing the count for David Cameron, asking loudly, 'Who was that?'

Who was that? *Who was that?* That was Sir Nicholas Winterton, that's who that was! I honestly despair of some young people these days. If the Pope himself had been carried down the committee corridor on a golden chair, flanked by two dozen Swiss Guards, some of them might ask who it was.

The corridor collapsed in laughter, if only at the thought of Sir Nicholas's outrage if he ever learns that the question had been asked. I enquired of Mr Ellwood whether he had genuinely not recognized him. 'I'm afraid they all blend into one,' he said vaguely. That's a feeling many of us have. It's not racist; we all look the same to them, too.

David Cameron emerged and announced, 'I've got a sense of direction, and I'm going to take that sense of direction all over the country!' I groaned inside; not more impenetrable New Labour jargon, and from the Tories too. But then Mr Cameron's unspoken campaign pledge is that he is a new Tony Blair, as if we didn't have enough of them already.

21.10.05

The campaign for the Tory leadership took the two candidates, David Cameron and David Davis, out into the country. The idea was not just to impress members of the party in person, but to impress members of the party with the way they impressed voters who were not members of the party.

David Davis arrived at a 'drop-in centre' in Tooting, South London, the neighbourhood in which he was raised. 'I want to see the children who go to my old school given the same opportunities I had,' he said. Exactly the same applies to David Cameron. In these anti-elitist days many old Etonians are reduced to managing rock groups or selling dodgy real estate in Chelsea instead of running the country, their traditional role.

The drop-in centre, which provides advice to young persons, was festooned with colourful, jolly leaflets about sexual health. 'Don't let an infection ruin your erection!' one of them counselled. Mr Davis took a tour of the computer terminals. 'And these chairs are just for chilling, I assume?' he enquired. In the old days Tory leaders probably thought that a chilling chair was a traditional remedy for piles. I was reminded of the time, forty-two years ago, when Harold Macmillan fixed the party leadership for another Old Etonian, Lord Home. 'Alec, I want you to go down to Tooting and chill with the homies. And bring back one of those leaflets about how you can get gonorrhoea from a blow-job.'

Mr Davis met the youths who had dropped into the drop-in centre. 'So you want to be a social worker?' he asked. 'And you? Oh, you're just chilling.'

A young woman told him she hoped he would win. He said he wanted the Tories to get back into the inner cities. What could he do for people like her?

'There should be more bus shelters for when it's raining,' she said. He said he couldn't promise that. It's useful for politicians to learn what the public really cares about, and it isn't always crime, health and tax.

He moved past a poster offering to 'pimp your car'. 'It's terrifically embarrassing,' he said. 'I used to scoot down to the pub next door when I was still at school.' Innocent days. A magazine had on its cover: 'He wet the bed – and other drinking disasters!'

Then he gave a short press conference, devoted to barely disguised attacks on David Cameron. 'I do not believe in being an heir to Blair,' he said, adding, 'I have the experience and the principle to win back these areas for the Conservative Party,' which means, 'I didn't go to Eton.'

26.10.05

Question Time in the Commons is the event that starts almost every parliamentary day. Some topics are rather dull – work and pensions for example – others surprisingly amusing. One that seems a little pointless is questions on foreign affairs.

What busybodies our MPs tend to be. Foreign Office Questions reminds me of a bridge session in some suburban home at which everyone in the neighbourhood is discussed and found wanting. 'That Iran, she's no better than she ought to be!'

'Burma! Did you hear what she was up to the other night, and her husband in hospital!'

'Zimbabwe, frankly she's a disgrace. As for that Libya, well, I'll tell you what I heard last night...'

The only country we all agree is perfect in every respect is the United Kingdom, which is the home of prosperity, human rights and all-round decency, though the Tories tend to think that the Labour government hasn't made that sufficiently clear to the layabouts and deadbeats who constitute the rest of the world. In twenty-four tabled questions, they discussed – and generally demolished – seventeen different countries. Eighteen if you realize that nearly all the questions about the EU are really about France, which could use a good talking to. There was an affecting moment when Jack Straw, the Foreign Secretary, was instructed in effect that it was time he grabbed France by the lapels and told it that enough was enough, and if they didn't reform the CAP he wouldn't be responsible for what got chucked over their garden fence.

'I have talks all the time with our French colleagues,' he said. 'That's the easy part. The more difficult part is getting them to agree with our point of view.' He said it so sadly that I was reminded of Matthew Arnold's apt poem, 'Dover Beach': 'Its melancholy, long, withdrawing Straw'.

Next we heard from Michael Gove, a Tory MP who used to be a journalist, so speaks as if his words were of great consequence. He was outraged that, back in 2002, Tony Blair had entertained the president of Syria to tea at Number 10. 'Does the Prime Minister not regret coddling that dictator at a time when he was planning mayhem across the Middle East?' But world leaders must often talk to people for whom they might not greatly care.

'Another cucumber sandwich, you bloodstained tyrant?'

'Why, thank you. Two sugars if you would be so kind, vile agent of Zionist oppression!'

02.11.05

At this time terrorism was a subject of much anguished debate. In particular MPs were exercised by a clause in the terrorism bill which would make a criminal offence of 'glorifying' terrorism. The main debate on the bill had caused the government's majority to drop to a single vote, causing various disgruntled rebels to sing around the bars, 'One vote! One vote!'

As Clause 21 of the bill puts it, when it considers whether there might be people who could 'reasonably infer that what is being glorified is being glorified as:

'(a) conduct that should be emulated in existing circumstances, or (b) conduct of a description of conduct, that should be so emulated.'

I have looked at sub-clause (5b) (or 'mini-bee' as they put it in these parts) for quite some time, but I cannot begin to work out what it might mean. What in heaven's name is 'conduct of a description of conduct'?

MPs seemed to know, by instinct perhaps, that it wasn't a very good idea. Indeed they were pretty well unanimous, all except the minister, Paul Goggins, who sat peering through his glasses in a gogglish kind of way, trying to look like a statesperson and not a colleague of Postman Pat.

Everyone had an unkind word for the bill. Ken Clarke pointed out that many Irish people, even those who have lived in this country for decades, often sing songs that celebrate mayhem of one kind or another. Were they all to be arrested? Bill Cash pointed out that there were plenty of events, songs and books that glorify the Catholic martyrs. 'At my own school [Stonyhurst] there were thirty who were hung, drawn and quartered during the, um ...' We waited anxiously to hear when. During the past few weeks? Or further back, say ten years ago? If so, it would be proof that the government's desire to give more independence to headmasters was working. They could create their own tariff of lesser offences: for example, boys who chewed gum in class could be hanged, drawn and halved.

In other words, what on earth is the point of a law that can only be interpreted by common sense, unwritten common sense?

04.11.05

It was always intriguing to see how feeble some of the ministers employed by the government were. The ones who got jobs had to be utterly loyal, and when the whips had excluded from those the mad, the bad and the hopelessly incompetent, the remaining field was rather small. Some ministers obtained the contempt of Sir Christopher Meyer, who was for a spell the British ambassador to the United States, and published his memoirs under the title DC Confidential.

You may have read about Sir Christopher's harsh descriptions of some senior ministers. He called them 'pygmies' – including John Prescott, Jack Straw, Geoff Hoon and so on. Well, if Tony Blair has nothing but pygmies to put in his Cabinet, you have to wonder what the junior lot might be like. Homunculi, perhaps, or manikins, the vertically challenged. Tiny little people who would struggle to stay afloat in a washing-up bowl. Take Karen Buck, a transport minister. Yesterday she was asked about aircraft noise. There is a lot of it about, and the government appears to be doing very little about it.

Barbara Follett, whose constituency is near Luton airport, said that the noise levels were not even within guidelines laid down by the World Health Organization. She wanted them monitored.

Ms Buck replied with a burst of jargon, rather like the noise a plane makes when it touches down and the pilot throws the engine into reverse: 'On the point of designation, we have made it clear that designation will remain an option, but it is not a power that is triggered by numbers...the WHO as a long-term target and an aspiration, which is why we have adopted a multi-pronged approach to bear down on noise,' she gabbled, as if she believed that if she said it fast enough nobody would get a chance to ask her what on earth it meant.

She went on. And on. These mini-pygmies never know when to shut up. 'Using noise controls and encouraging measures such as noise preferential routes, and in the civil aviation bill we have the powers to clarify powers.' At one point she mentioned 'local control' and Edward Garnier, a Tory, asked what that might mean, since his local airport East Midlands, was actually owned by local authorities from Manchester. 'We will be monitoring this carefully and ensuring there is improved delivery,' she said. In New Labour-speak, 'improved delivery' means 'If we wait long enough the problem might go away.'

Noise control came up. 'The government is encouraging local responses...profiling local noise contours.' Ah.

Then she came out with what might be the scariest line of the session. 'Luton airport have brought forward their master plan.' A master plan! Heaven save us! She repeated that, 'The power of designation remains.'

Alan Duncan, a Tory front-bencher, yelled that there were people who simply wanted a good night's sleep. Fat chance. There is no management matrix that covers that. What he got was more blather about the need for a balanced approach. All of it proof that you can't send a pixie to do a pygmy's job.

09.11.05

Next day there came a vote on the terrorism bill, the one which would allow the police to lock up suspects for ninety days without trial. It was thought this would prove to be a close vote, and Gordon Brown, who had been on a trip to Israel, was ordered to come back to support his government.

It was the morning after Tony Blair officially became a bed-blocker. The man whose bed he was blocking, Gordon Brown, was off to Israel for this third flight in two days, so he left his team of understrappers to deal with Treasury questions. It must have been galling for the Chancellor. Normally he leaves the team to field all the questions about growing inflation or the appalling balance of payments figures, while he explains how he is in the process of ending world debt, and has made millions of children with stick-like arms and big pleading eyes praise his name.

It's a fine opportunity every month to demonstrate his old Labour credentials. Instead he was stuck, yet again, on a plane. ('Mmm, a choice of lasagne or chicken, I see, and another chance to catch *Curse of the Were-Rabbit.*')

The morning after any great and terrible event at Westminster is usually an anti-climax. You expect to see signs of the massacre, with blood on the floor, and bullet-holes in the wall. Instead, the scene-of-crime boys have finished, the cleaners have moved in, and everything looks almost normal.

At least it does to the untrained eye. I chatted to a Labour MP who is a loyalist, though his loyalty has been stretched recently. 'What a [bad word]-up!' he said. 'What a [second bad word]'s breakfast! Why didn't Charlie [Charles Clarke] stand up to him and say "[first bad word again] off, Tony. You [worst bad word of all]!"'

'There isn't a chance he can get this [same bad word]

education bill through now. If he tries, Gordon will have to turn up with the suits and tell him to [yes, same bad word yet again] off.' I should explain that 'suits' is political slang for senior members of a party who can be drafted into an informal lynch mob.

11.11.05

In the event the government lost by thirty-one votes, more than anyone had expected. Mr Brown's extra journey to the Middle East had been in vain. And he had to return, so missing Treasury questions, the following day.

John Prescott was asked about planning guidance for flood plains yesterday, and he told MPs, 'I shall be making a flood direction.' Even for New Labour that seemed a bit much. In millennia past only the Lord God could issue flood directions, whether to get Moses out of a spot of bother in the Red Sea, or at the time of the great deluge, where his flood direction to Noah was to build him an ark of gopher wood, pitched within and without with pitch, and the length of it 300 cubits, according to government guidelines PPS/35 and 37.

Still, ministers in this government have always confused issuing directives with getting things done, and that was again the theme of Prime Minister's Questions. Michael Howard wanted to know when we were going to see the green paper on invalidity benefit. Roughly every two months this is postponed for another two months. Mr Blair said it had been delayed because of David Blunkett's departure. Nobody believed him. It has been delayed because of the wrong kind of backbench rebels on the line.

Mr Howard moved on. Mr Blair replied. There was a great deal of noise. The Speaker told MPs not to shout the Prime Minister down. It was pointless. It was the Prime

Minister who was shouting backbenchers down, preventing us from hearing their merry abuse, badinage and cater-wauling, all vital to our freedom of speech.

Mr Howard moved into silky mode. 'Let me give the Prime Minister a word of advice,' he said. 'He and I are both on our way out.' MPs on both sides sarcastically waved goodbye to the leader of the other. 'He doesn't have much time left. He shouldn't waste any more, and should spend every minute persuading his own side.'

Branggg! Something snapped in Mr Blair. 'Here's some advice for him!' he barked. 'When he wins an election, then he can give some advice to someone who has won three!' Whooo! It was a deeply schoolboyish moment, and ever so slightly camp.

Meg Hillier, a Labour MP from Hackney, asked a lick-spittle question about the new 24-hour licensing laws. Her local council had alcohol-free zones, but also what they termed 'saturation zones' in which everyone is encouraged to sell and drink booze. It will probably make it into the estate agents' brochures. 'Situated in Hackney's much sought-after saturation zone…' they will write about some public toilet converted into executive maisonettes.

17.11.05

At last, seven months after their third consecutive election defeat, the Conservative Party had a new leader.

The two Davids, Cameron and Davis, were wearing crisp suits and silk ties. They dashed onto the platform together and stood gazing into each other's eyes with warm, admiring smiles. Then they started giving each firm and manly pats on the back, with strokes upon the arm. Suddenly we realized where we were. It was one of the first of the new civil partnership ceremonies. Except that Elton John will do it with so much more pizzazz, and bigger frocks!

The venue was fabulously crowded. It was the back of the Royal Academy. MPs, peers, the media and even one or two members of the public forced their way into the heaving throng. It made the Black Hole of Calcutta look like a deserted ballroom. The TV cameramen filmed the snappers. The snappers snapped the TV cameramen. All of them got shots of the press and anyone else who was forced into viewfinder range. It was a feeding frenzy with nothing to eat.

Cynical TV people divvied up the cynical questions they were going to ask the winner. 'Do you have any better chance than the last four?' was one. Or, 'Have you booked the hall for after the next election?' An official came in and muttered that there weren't going to be any big surprises, as if we didn't know.

The Cameron team emerged and sat on the front row. Ed Llewellyn, who has spent years helping Paddy Ashdown to run Bosnia, now back for the much tougher task of sorting out the Tory Party. George Osborne, the even more youthful aide to the youthful leader in waiting. And Samantha Cameron, looking pretty terrific in a white wool coat and a fashionable brown dress with brown tights.

Sir Michael Spicer, chairman of the 1922 Committee, announced the result, as he has so often over the past few years, but he'd only got halfway through David Cameron's score before being made inaudible by a gigantic roar. It was a very modern, Notting Hill kind of roar, a sort of 'ya-hoo, yee-haw', as if a lot of drunken young persons were drinking long-neck Budweisers at a barbecue.

DD made a graceful concession speech (as in most part-nerships, there has to be a loser). Then David Cameron talked about modernity, compassion and reform. He even dared a side-swipe at Margaret Thatcher, when he said, 'There is such a thing as society. It's not just the same thing as the state.' He tried a little joke. We needed to tackle carbon emissions, he said. 'I tried to make a start this morning by biking to work. That was a carbon neutral journey till the BBC sent a helicopter to follow me.'

It was a very modern, compassionate joke. Samantha joined her husband on the stage, and again he stroked her bump, now larger than when it got its first public pat two months ago at the Tory conference. Politicians have always regarded babies as props, but rarely can a child have been used so often while still in the womb.

Then a crowd of his supporters – all of them young, modern and compassionate – gathered on the grand staircase. Mr Cameron emerged and promised them a modern and compassionate Conservative Party. Will anyone stand up for the old, out-of-date, oppressive Conservative Party. Of course they will!

07.12.05

That happened on a Tuesday. Next day Mr Cameron was thrown into the deep end with his first Prime Minister's Question Time.

The new Tory leader had told us that he wanted the Commons to stop sounding like Punch and Judy. Instead what he offered us was Richard and Judy – cosy and warm, just right for settling down with a cup of tea and a biscuit. Though perhaps the questions were a shade more chal-lenging, and certainly a lot shorter.

Mr Cameron wanted to demonstrate that he was beyond old-fashioned name calling. Instead he wanted to co-operate with the government when co-operation was deserved. He wished to help Mr Blair on education. He yearned to be at his side on climate change. He needed to be in the prime ministerial embrace.

Mr Blair was less enthusiastic. He was like one of those handsome young men on the Dick Emery show, pursued by the star in drag. 'Ooh, you are awful! But I like you,' his female character would purr, as she twined her arms around him. A look of panic would cross the young man's face as he tried to flee.

Samantha Cameron was up in the gallery. She is to give birth in two months' time. They say that babies in the womb respond to their mother's anxieties. This one will be born as if he or she had just drunk eight cups of strong black coffee.

Prime Minister's Questions is a horrible experience for anyone who might be described as a human being. Mr Cameron had one big advantage: most of his own side were actually on his side. For Tory leaders that is an unexpected help.

He was called by the Speaker. 'The first issue the Prime Minister and I are going to have to work on together is getting the good bits of your education reforms through the Commons and into law.'

Hilary Armstrong, the Labour chief whip, started shouting, as she often does. She is the Commons bag lady, railing against anyone who won't give her a coin. 'That's the problem with these exchanges,' Mr Cameron said. 'The chief whip on the Labour side is shouting like a child. Now, has she finished?' he yelled at her. 'Have you finished? Right!'

It was a terrific coup de théâtre. He was ostensibly offering to help Labour, while actually pointing out how divided Labour was on the issue he had raised. But he had to please his own side too. So he picked on the weakest member of the government, who is in deep trouble for incompetent whipping. He had spotted the wounded wildebeest and was giving it a good gumming.

For Mr Blair it was a serious problem. If he accepted Mr Cameron's hand of friendship, it would be pushed behind his back to make the half-nelson of revenge. No Labour leader would want to do that. It would be like Liverpool and Everton getting together on match day and deciding that to agree a draw beforehand would save an awful lot of running around in the mud.

Mr Blair flannelled around. He couldn't agree with schools having the right to decide their own admissions. And what about investment? He was desperate to find anything to put clear water between him and this new, Blairite party leader.

Then David Cameron produced a line which was no less effective for having clearly been worked on a long time into the night. 'I want to talk about the future,' he said. 'You used to be the future once!'

This rattled the Prime Minister enough to cause him to jab a finger at the new challenger on the block. 'Sorry, I'm pointing my finger, breaking up the new consensus,' he said apologetically.

But there is no new consensus. It's just that Edward Scissorhands has taken to wearing mittens.

08.12.05

One constant theme of the new Tory leadership was drugs. Mr Cameron refused to confirm or deny taking them, saying that his private life before he entered public life should remain private. Which everyone took to be a confirmation.

Yesterday the new era of touchy-feely caring consensus politics was brought to a sudden halt after less than twenty-four hours by Dennis Skinner. Dear old Dennis! Those of us whose memories go back further than we care to remember, if you see what I mean, recall him as one of the grand old veterans of the class war. For thirty-five years he has sat just below the gangway on the Labour side, yelling imprecations across the Chamber, like people who shout at you on buses. He used to be one of the great sights of parliament, like Big Ben. Visitors would point him out to their children, hoping they would remember this moment for the rest of their lives, though the children are now grown, and neither they nor their own children are entirely clear who Mr Skinner is.

New stars have emerged. So he needed some spectacular gesture that would tell the world that, like Norma Desmond in *Sunset Boulevard*, Dennis Skinner was back!

The new leader of the Tory Party might be little more than half his age, and hardly out of his embroidered silk nappies when Dennis first won his seat, but the new generation had to know, had to be told, about the past. He was ready for his close-up!

It was almost the end of Treasury questions. George Osborne, shadow chancellor, and a close friend of the new Tory leader, had been silent for some fifty-five minutes, while Labour backbenchers rose to carol the greatness of Gordon Brown. Mr Osborne was trying to find out, with little success, whether the Chancellor had known before the election that, at 1.75 per cent, our growth rate would be far lower than expected.

Then up sprang Skinner. 'Is my hon. friend aware,' he asked balefully, 'that in the 1970s and a lot of the 1980s, we would have thanked our lucky stars in the coalfield areas to have growth of 1.75 per cent?

'The only thing that was growing then were lines of coke' – I confess that I assumed Mr Skinner was about to denounce Margaret Thatcher for stockpiling fuel supplies in order to defeat the mineworkers in the mid-1980s – 'the lines of coke in front of Boy George and the rest of 'em…'

He strode forward and pointed a dramatic finger towards young Osborne. The Speaker suddenly cottoned on. 'Order!' he shouted. 'The hon. gentleman must withdraw that remark!'

'That were in the *News of the World*' said Skinner.

'Order!' said the Speaker again, flailing desperately. 'He must withdraw that remark!'

Skinner: 'I'm not withdrawing it. It's true.'

So the Speaker went through the ancient ritual of 'naming' Dennis Skinner, by saying, 'I name Dennis Skinner,' and the miscreant walked out of the Chamber with that slightly rolling gait that indicated he had won yet another historic victory.

'He is withdrawing,' said the Speaker, with evident relief. 'He's taken my advice,' which was plainly untrue since Mr Skinner might be withdrawing from the Chamber but had not withdrawn his remark. He disappeared, no doubt to the tea room, where he could tell the younger members about his past glories.

09.12.05

313

Sir Christopher Meyer's book, DC Confidential, *the one that described several senior ministers as 'pygmies', was the topic of a grilling by the normally calm and level-headed Committee on Public Administration, which had dragged the author in front of them. In the event, the session came to resemble one of those writer appearances at literary festivals which are meant to win publicity for a new book.*

I have been to many Commons committees, but never one which included a debate on ball-crushingly tight trousers. Sir Christopher's book includes many racy allegations and vivid personal insights, such as the one about the prime ministerial crotch.

The committee was furious with him. They would have loved to strap him into cast iron trousers and really get his nuts into a knot. The chairman, the normally sane Tony Wright, wanted him stripped of his knighthood, if not his manhood.

Select committees are very strange. Show them someone who has lost the taxpayer billions, or almost destroyed the rail network, and they will murmur something mildly disobliging. But Sir Christopher, who had merely made a few personal observations about those set over us, drove them into a frenzy. Even Gordon Prentice, who can be almost equable when he tries, spotted a passing high horse and leapt aloft. At one point he accused Sir Christopher of mendacity. 'That is a lie! A lie!' he shouted, an allegation that would have had him thrown out of the Chamber itself, since an MP can never be accused of telling an untruth, whereas a retired diplomat can be accused of anything at all. 'That is not a lie. You will have to be the judge,' Sir Christopher replied.

'I will,' said his interlocutor gravely, and if he had had a black cap he would have pulled it on then and there.

The committee had been razzed up by Lord Turnbull, who used to be cabinet secretary and who had no time for Sir Christopher either. 'Patronizing and destructive comments about elected politicians, whom he was paid handsomely to work for…they were betrayed and sneered at.' He had even cost us all money, for who now would want to stay at an envoy's residence, knowing that their most intimate details, some involving their underpants, would wind up in a book?

They would, he did not add but implied, wind up staying in the Wisconsin Avenue Travelodge, in a room with a nylon carpet, costing $34.99 a night, including cable TV and continental breakfast buffet.

Then the villain himself arrived, and we almost saw the thunder flash, reeled from the smoke and heard the screaming children. Sir Christopher, scarlet of sock and pink of tie, leaned forward like a captured bird of prey.

Mr Wright got straight down to his task. The book was 'a wholly disreputable enterprise', he said. Anyone who had held his position could have written it, but nobody had been so dishonourable as to do so. His private benefit had harmed us all.

Sir Christopher insisted that he had got clearance from the Cabinet Office. That was not enough. Why had he not got clearance from the Foreign Office too? And since the Cabinet Office had clearly got it wrong about the clearance, why had he not queried the clearance? As if any author would actually appeal against a ruling that he was free to publish his book.

Grant Shapps absurdly said that that was like finding that a restaurant has not charged you for your main course and failing to point it out. They got nastier. Why had he talked about John Major in his underpants?

He had not, he said. There were no 'underpants, boxers, thongs or Speedos…it is a complete canard! His shirt tails I mentioned, not his underpants.'

The thong might be over, but the malady lingered on. What right had he to write about Tony Blair's 'ball-crushingly tight trousers'? Sir Christopher took a tactical decision to become angry himself. 'Is it impossible, unethical or intolerable that a piece of clothing – on public display – cannot be mentioned? At the time, I said to the Downing Street retinue, "Cor blimey, look at those trousers!"'

Mr Wright groaned. 'It gets worse,' he said, and for a moment I thought he might need smelling salts.

Sir Christopher said that he could have written far more revealing material (whether about nether garments or matters of state he did not say) but had chosen not to do so. Mr Wright, by now recovered, seemed to switch sides, saying sarkily, 'I didn't see a strapline on your cover: "This book could have been franker."'

We learned that the popular romantic novelist Barbara Taylor Bradford, a friend of the Meyers, had helped to make the book more exciting. Perhaps that accounts for the tight trousers.

As I left, I noticed Sir Christopher sitting at a table behind a pile of his books, signing them for MPs. (No, I didn't! I made that up! It was, as he himself would say, a canard.)

16.12.05

The year 2006 opened with the great Liberal Democrat plot against Charles Kennedy, their leader. He was accused of being an alcoholic. In fact, few of us had ever seen him drunk, though we had heard the stories, such as the one told by a very senior correspondent who had fallen foul of Mr Kennedy by asking his colleagues what they were going to do about his drinking. They had a kiss-and-make-up lunch, the reporter was a few minutes late, and arrived to find Kennedy already tucking into his second gin and tonic. My sense was that he was no alcoholic, since he could avoid drinking for long periods, but found it hard to stop once he had started. When he had resigned, various Lib Dems stood for leader. The campaign was fraught. Mark Oaten, the home affairs spokesman, had to withdraw when it turned out he had had a relationship with a rent boy. Simon Hughes, the party president, admitted to having gay as well as heterosexual relationships. There were accusations of odds-fixing, by which one candidate would arrange for money to be staked on him, so as to produce an artificial 'momentum'. Throughout all this the favourite was the former Olympic sprinter Sir Menzies 'Ming' Campbell, who was acting leader until the time of the election.

I bumped into a cabinet minister. 'What have Charles Kennedy and Julius Caesar got in common?' he asked. 'They were both stabbed in the back by men wearing sandals.'

For those of us who have liked and admired Ming for many years, it was a sad occasion. Ming rose at Prime Minister's Question Time, tall, elegant and calm, every inch the statesman from his glistening and superbly domed pate, to the old-fashioned yet highly fashionable flare at his trouser cuffs, the creases so sharp you could use them to slice cheese. He sat down looking a bit of an idiot.

Here's how it happened. He stood up to roars of sarcastic applause from all round the House. Tory and Labour MPs love to jeer whoever happens to be Lib Dem leader this week; it makes them feel so much better about their own failings. As usual, they kept up the barracking for quite some time. 'And a very happy new year to you too!' he said genially, before asking Tony Blair a workmanlike question about failing schools and hospitals. Why, he enquired, was the government making such a mess of public services?

The Prime Minister replied, as he always does, with a list of statistics so beautifully massaged they could have been used to tenderize Japanese Kobe beef. On and on he droned: '...all exam results at seventeen and eighteen are better than they were in 1997, every health service indicator...' It seemed to be neverending. It would have given Ming, you might think, enough time to mull over his second, follow-up question.

He did not. Instead he ploughed ahead with what was on the slip of paper in front of him. 'Perhaps the Prime Minister will explain why it is that one in five schools do not have a permanent headteacher...'

He paused briefly. The penny was about to drop and activate the slow, clanking mechanism of the average MP's mind. No permanent head? Why, that was the Liberal Democrats themselves! They could jeer again, and even louder!

Which they did. It began slowly – you could even make out Sir Ming saying, 'When the Prime Minister entered Number 10...' – but within moments he was under water, his words washed away in a huge, gurgling torrent of gully-clearing, livestock-drowning pleasure. It went on for fully thirty-eight seconds, which in parliamentary time is a geological epoch.

Ming bit his lower lip. He opened and closed his mouth. He could not decide whether to go along with the joke, or maintain his serious face – the mien of Ming. He plumped for serious. The Speaker tried to interrupt but the noise was too loud. Finally Ming said wanly, 'I just knew it was going to be one of those days…'

The Prime Minister said, with mock sympathy, that it was always difficult to find a head for any organization, particularly if it was a failing organization, and Labour backbenchers dutifully laughed at that.

Will Ming fail to get the job merely because Labour and Tory hooligans laughed at him? I doubt it. But it looked bad and soggy, limp and ill-prepared, and it promised more humiliations in the future. No doubt some of the other candidates will have a certain spring in their step this morning.

12.01.06

George Galloway was the Respect MP for Bethnal Green and Bow, a seat he won from Labour in the 2005 election. He was cordially loathed by many of his colleagues, and gave a hostage to fortune when he agreed to appear on the Channel 4 show Celebrity Big Brother. *This was the year before the race row involving Jade Goody and Shilpa Shetty, but it attracted quite a lot of publicity anyway.*

Imagine the anguish of MPs from all parties. They hate George Galloway. I cannot tell you how much most of them loathe him. If they heard he had fallen head first into a wood chipper operating at full blast, the Strangers' Bar would echo with the cry of 'More champagne, good host! And make it snappy!'

Which pleases him no end. He thrives on detestation in the way that Frankenstein's monster needed electric current.

The day another MP says, 'All in all, you're doing a grand job, George,' is the day he will curl up and die like a salted slug. Meanwhile his colleagues yearn for the moment when he is nominated for eviction from the *Big Brother* house, where he is currently incarcerated. No doubt many have already memorized the number that will be used to chuck him out. All that will stay their twitching fingers is the knowledge that the sooner he leaves the *BB* house, the sooner he might be back in their House – though on past form that's not very likely. Mr Galloway always seems to have pressing business elsewhere.

The Labour Party, which has never forgiven him for winning Oona King's seat in Bethnal Green, has set up a website where you can watch the amount of public money he has been paid while in the *BB* house. It is already over £2,000 and is increasing at the rate of 1p every seven seconds, which doesn't strike me as all that much, considering the amount of pleasure he has brought to his fellow MPs alone.

Take the scenes last week when he pretended to be a cat, licking imaginary cream from the cupped hands of Rula Lenska, while she murmured, 'Here pussy, pussy, pussy, yes, ooh, little pussy…you've got cream all over your whiskers!' (In the words of the Grolsch ad on TV, 'Stop! This porno film is not ready yet!')

You can be sure that this event will never be forgotten, and whenever Mr Galloway rises to repeat his grand denunciations of George Bush and Tony Blair, he will be met by a chorus of miaows.

Yesterday, however, brought a crushing disappointment to the serried ranks of his enemies. It turned out that Mr Galloway had signed several early-day motions, or EDMs, which are not for debate, but act as a sort of bulletin board for what's on MPs' minds. His included, aptly enough, one which sought to protect household pets, and others on profiteering by budget airlines and offering congratulations to Harold Pinter on winning the Nobel Prize.

But EDMs have to be signed in person. How could he do that while trapped in the *Big Brother* house? MPs figured that this was a tremendous chance to have him disciplined and – who knows? – even suspended.

Yesterday the Speaker brought the tragic news. He had investigated the matter and discovered that Mr Galloway had sent his signature through the post to the Table Office before going out of contact. His name had been properly authorized.

MPs laughed scornfully. But they could not disguise their disappointment. Once again Gorgeous George had escaped from the jaws of his enemies.

18.01.06

Along with terrorism and global warming, one of the great scares was avian flu. We were consistently warned that it was about to decimate the global population.

Now and again someone says something in the Commons that makes you jump up and ask yourself, 'Did he really say that?' Such a moment came yesterday at environment questions. This used to be a bucolic affair at which MPs discussed ancient country matters such as the green pound and sheepmeat regimes. But now the Tories are thunderously environmentalist, and so it has descended into a lot of fractious debate about carbon footprints and climate change levies.

A Tory, Nigel Waterson, asked why the rules against avian flu only applied to flocks of fifty birds or more. The minister, Ben Bradshaw, replied that larger flocks were 'more likely to create the size of viral load', which sounded terrifying in itself. But, he added, we had better levels of 'biosecurity' than they have in other countries, where the disease is endemic. Then came the mad moment.

'In Turkey,' he said, 'in some of those small backyard plots, people actually sleep with their birds, and have very, very intimate contact with them. As far as we know that doesn't happen in this country.'

There was a shocked silence, as if the whole House had been smacked over the head by a gigantic rubber mallet. That phrase, 'very, very intimate', could mean only one thing. Do Turks really do that? And if they do, might not some lonely British poultry farmers do the same, so endangering our entire population?

Mr Bradshaw seemed to be saying that the only way a human could get avian flu was by having sex with a hen. It certainly gives a new meaning to some old phrases, such as 'I'm seeing this really tasty bird'. 'Chick lit' becomes a form of pornography.

Bill Wiggin for the Tories revealed that he too kept chickens. Was he going to hit Mr Bradshaw for implying that he too was a pathological poultry pervert? The minister quickly said that he was sure that Mr Wiggin didn't have the same level of intimacy with his birds as the Turks did. 'He is no flock-fucker!' he meant, but did not quite say.

But it was too late. It all sounded very silly. But at least we learned that it was easier to avoid catching avian flu than we might have guessed.

3.02.06

William Hague returned to the front bench for Prime Minister's Questions yesterday, for the first time since he resigned as Tory leader in 2001. He was replacing David

Cameron, who was on paternity leave.

Paternity leave? The leader of the Conservative and Unionist Party on paternity leave? Can you imagine what Lords Salisbury or Liverpool would have made of that?

'May I inform your lordship that there is no requirement for your lordship to attend the sitting of the House today?'

'Why the devil not, Pettigrew?'

'Because her ladyship has been delivered of a child, your lordship.'

'Good God, Pettigrew, and why was I not told? And what in heaven's name has that got to do with m'duties in the House?'

'Your lordship was shooting with the Prince of Wales, and it was thought inadvisable to interrupt the sport. Shall I bring the nappies to your lordship to change now, or shall I have a footman deliver them to your club?'

In the past Tory leaders probably had only the vaguest notion of how many children they had, if any. But Mr Cameron, being a new breed of Tory, was at home breast-feeding or whatever it is that new men do on paternity leave.

Mr Hague, who so far as we know has no children, said that it was probably the first time that all three parties had been represented at PM's Questions by 'a stand-in for the real leader' – the reference being to himself, Gordon Brown and Ming Campbell. He made a powerful attack on the clause that criminalizes the 'glorification of terrorism', which has brought much anxiety to the terrorism debate. Mr Hague, who has moved from boy wonder to elder statesman with only the briefest period in between, said that a 'water-tight law to catch the guilty is better than a press-release law to catch the headlines'.

Mr Blair replied that the bill would not be diluted. Removing the clause would 'send the wrong message'. But as

American politicians often say, 'If you want to send a message, use Western Union.' Acts of parliament are meant to lay down what is legal and what isn't, not work as a legislative version of Clintons Cards: 'Labour is red, Tories are blue, I wouldn't think of glorifying terrorism, if you know what's good for you.'

16.02.06

British deployment in Afghanistan came up in the Commons again yesterday and we were privileged to hear from Sir Peter Tapsell. Whenever he stands up, crack teams of cherubim and seraphim rise to the rafters and start recording his work with quill pens on vellum. Sir Peter could also try speaking in verse, since his words are somehow reminiscent of Sir Henry Newbolt's great poem 'Vitaï Lampada', better known by its chorus, 'Play up! Play up! And play the game!'

In this work Sir Henry recorded first a school cricket match ('There's a breathless hush in the close tonight'), then a British defeat in the Sudan ('The sand of the desert is sodden red / Red with the wreck of a square that broke' – or as Sir Peter, who has a slight speech impediment, would put it: 'Wed with the weck of a square that bwoke'). The poet goes on to record the desperate British fightback: 'The river of death has brimmed his banks...But the voice of a schoolboy rallied the ranks.' We know what the schoolboy is going to say, and I suspect that being told to play the game would be scant comfort if you were lying on that sodden red sand with half a leg missing.

To be fair to Sir Peter, however resonant and poetical his words may sound, he does take the opposite view from Sir Henry on our battles against the savage hordes of the East. He rose in his pomp, the seraphim nudged each other to be alert, and he addressed the defence secretary, John Reid, thus: 'May I urge you, for the third time, to halt the despatch of small contingents of our forces to southern Afghanistan, to undertake incompatible tasks which could not be performed even by 100,000 twoops! Does he wemember that in the 1980s the Wussians did send 300,000 into Afghanistan? And, sevewal years later, they fled the countwy, leaving 10,000 dead behind, and they were soon followed to their gwaves by the Soviet Union itself!'

It was majestic. If Sir Peter were set to verse, the last line of each stanza would be 'Retreat! Retreat! And clear off home!'

28.02.06

Prime Minister's Questions, and up in the gallery, accompanied by a gorgeous, pouting Tory MP, was the lovely, lustrous-lipped, corkscrew-haired pop singer from Colombia, Shakira. She looked puzzled, and who could blame her? What, for example, might Rachel Stevens make of a session of the Colombian parliament?

Tony Blair began with a list of condolences. This happens almost every week, and almost every week it gets longer. He includes anyone who has died in Iraq or Afghanistan in the past seven days, and yesterday he even sent his warmest regards to the Speaker, who has had a heart operation. I have never been in a Glasgow hospital myself, but I gather they have a machine that can feed deep-fried Jaffa cakes on an intravenous drip.

Mr Blair didn't offer his deepest sympathies to the owner of the cat that has just died of bird flu on a Baltic island. Perhaps next week, when he has the name of her kittens.

But politics in this country has become embarrassingly

touchy-feely. For example, David Cameron, making his first appearance for three weeks since his paternity leave (he has been taking the soiled disposable nappies of discredited Tory policies and dumping them in the recycling bin of history), began by thanking the Prime Minister for the flowers he had sent for the birth of his child. 'I received flowers from Number 10 and from Number 11 Downing Street, so I am the first man in history to be bunched by both our prime ministers!'

'Bunched'? It was a new verb to me. Perhaps it is Notting Hill talk. 'Tamsin, it's my fiancée's birthday. Bunch her, will you?' Or, 'I've just had an email to say my father's died. Find out my mother's address and bunch her one, right?'

His subject for the week was education, and he wanted to know if Mr Blair's 'foundation' schools would have the same rights as 'trust' schools. The Prime Minister said they would.

'Good!' said Mr Cameron, in the manner of a school-teacher who has just been given the right answer by a willing but not especially clever pupil. You expected him to lean over the dispatch box and bunch Mr Blair.

02.03.06

In early March the Liberal Democrats announced the result of their leadership election. The three candidates left were Sir Menzies Campbell, Chris Huhne MP and the party's current president, Simon Hughes. They held the event in Transport House, the old headquarters of the Labour Party. As one American correspondent said, 'Transport House? Sounds like a brothel...'

The excitement was almost, well, almost present. In its Labour heyday, Transport House was the scene of much villainy, hatchet work and hatred – like the Kremlin under Stalin, with less blood but more bile. Frankly, the Lib Dems don't cut it. 'We are hard-wired to agree with each other,' said Lembit Opik MP. And he was right. They were waiting to acclaim the result whoever won, and acclaim their new leader, whoever he might be.

Lady Campbell, Elspeth, arrived in a jacket of swirly colours with names you only ever see in fashion catalogues: magenta, teal, cerise, taupe. She is very proud of her husband, a former Olympic athlete, whom she fondly describes as having been 'the fastest white man on earth'. Charles Kennedy arrived to huge applause. If there had been a write-in vote he might have won. Then Lord Dholakia, the past president, made two very Lib Dem announcements: would we please turn off our mobile phones (actually, the true Lib Dem position would be to remind us to turn them on in case we missed a call) and second, there would be tea and biscuits afterwards. In the old days Labour would have offered bandages and blood transfusions.

Lord Dholakia read out the scores, and we learned that Ming had won by a higher margin than anyone had expected. He paused, then raised an arm. Then he raised both arms. Then he realized he had failed to grab the arm of Chris Huhne, the runner-up, so he hoisted that as well. Then all three candidates raised their arms. They put them down again. They let go and they turned around. They were doing the hokey-cokey without even being drunk. It looked like a communal origami session. If you had given them a giant sheet of paper, they would have produced a nesting swan.

The three candidates spoke. Golly, they were supportive. We yearned for someone to say something like, 'You made the wrong choice, God rot you,' but no one came close.

Sir Ming, his arms having returned to their sides, rose to make a speech full of resonant phrases from the *Liberal Democrat Bumper Book of Resonant Phrases*. These are illuminated, I suspect, by a crack team of monks working on an island off the coast of Fife. 'This is not just a victory for me, it is a victory for all Liberal Democrats.' (My rule is that if the opposite of a remark is clearly fatuous, then the remark was not worth making in the first place: 'This is a victory for me, and me alone, and a humiliating defeat for the rest of you.')

'Liberal Democrats! The party of ideas and innovation!' (Or, 'The party of stultifying obscurantism.') 'We have a duty to pass on a world fit for our children to live in!' ('We must pillage the planet while we still can. What have future generations ever done for us?')

He finished to loud cheers. TV cameramen and photographers began to sway alarmingly, at one point threatening to crash on top of Shirley Williams. What a tragic, yet magnificent ending to her distinguished career that would have been! But this was a Lib Dem meeting, and the group disbanded, a little sheepishly. Then the new leader set off to party headquarters, a short walk away, followed by literally tens of people. It was rather touching – less a victory parade than a ramblers' club outing.

03.03.06

Towards the end of his premiership, Tony Blair came to rely increasingly on Tory support to get his more controversial legislation through. Take the education bill, for example, which allows schools more say over admissions and budgets and which infuriated many Labour backbenchers.

Most Labour MPs and almost all Tories supported the bill, though for entirely opposite reasons. This is possible because it is incredibly complicated, containing 228 pages, 176 clauses, more than 1,000 subsidiary clauses, and 18 schedules divided into 37 parts.

I opened it at random and found this, on page 134: 'A1 (1) This paragraph applies to any disposal by the governing body of a foundation, voluntary or foundation special school in England of (a) any land acquired under a transfer under section 20 (1) (a) of the Education Act 1996, (b) any land acquired under any of the following – paragraph 2 of Schedule 3; paragraph 16 of Schedule 6 (including that provision as applied by any enactment); paragraph 544 (c), 5 (4B) (d) or 8A of this schedule; any regulations made under paragraph 5 of Schedule 8...' And so on, and on. I know that legal language has to be precise, but I also know that head teachers are complaining like mad about the incredible amount of paperwork they have to plough through, and now this lot thuds onto their desks. Weighing three times as much as *The Da Vinci Code* – another farrago of meaningless nonsense and ill-digested data.

However, like the Dan Brown book, there is plenty in here for everyone – for the Tories, who want to vote for it to embarrass the government, and for Ruth Kelly, the education secretary, who found this particular haystack full of bright and shiny needles. Though, of course, like the mad Jesuit monk in *Da Vinci*, Ms Kelly is a member of the fundamentalist Catholic Opus Dei, which makes me suspect sometimes that she wears a garter made out of barbed wire, so that she may be chastized for her sins 24/7. Who, while wearing such a garment, would care remotely what the Tories thought about anything?

16.03.06

Around this time the 'cash for honours' row and the police investigation began to reach the headlines. Tony Blair remained his usual alarmingly calm self.

We went to Downing Street for the monthly press conference. We wanted to see how Tony Blair would cope with the worst day of his political career. But then he has worst days roughly as often as the rest of us go out for a curry, and somehow he always survives. Yesterday he had a shiny new cliché, newly forged by the lads and lasses in the Downing Street cliché mint. It is 'direction of travel'. Some people, notably the Chancellor, would like his direction of travel to be towards the back door of Number 10, as fast as possible. In fact he is talking about his programme to reform all public services.

'This is the direction of travel,' he told us, 'and there is no point in my hiding it!' That would be a difficult trick, unless the entire electorate was locked, blindfold, in the back of a van.

He did look tense, and I don't recall such hostile questioning, mostly about the loans for peerages affair. His point was that the lords and ladies being appointed were to be working peers, sitting on the Labour benches. As Labour supporters they would naturally want to loan millions of pounds to the party they love.

'If someone supports the Labour Party financially, that's not a reason to put them in the House of Lords. But it isn't a reason not to put them in the House of Lords,' he said, elliptically. Hmm. 'The fact that Mr Donald "Don" Corleone treated the chief inspector to an all-expenses-paid holiday is no reason why crucial evidence should go missing from the station. But equally, it should be no bar to the evidence being lost.'

17.03.06

The Budget came round. It was Gordon Brown's tenth.

'Is this the Chancellor's last Budget?' asked David Cameron. Tony Blair doesn't get caught out by that kind of question. 'You will be sitting on that side of the House for a long time to come,' he said. It was one of his famous non-replies. 'Oh, come on, don't be so coy!' said the Tory leader, to a chorus of 'whoo-whoos' from Labour MPs, who affect to believe that Mr Cameron is so limp-wristed that he makes Dale Winton resemble Mr Mucho Macho Man.

He rephrased his query. 'When's he off?' he asked.

Not yet, it seems. 'I shall be here for the time it takes to carry through the programme on which we were elected,' he said. Could be a few decades, we thought.

Then Gordon Brown rose. When it comes to himself, the Chancellor is never knowingly undersold. False modesty is the only kind he knows. Every year the contrast with the Prime Minister becomes more stark. In Blairland, as depicted in Prime Minister's Questions, old folk live in freezing poverty thanks to failed pension schemes. Convicted criminals roam the streets, hunting for fresh victims. Trained doctors and nurses are fired by the score and end up rootling for food in dustbins. And the honours system is so bent, it makes a find-the-lady scam in Oxford Street look like a church tombola.

But in Gordonworld, things are fabulous. It is colourful Oz, compared to black-and-white Kansas. British people are the second-richest in the world, behind only the Americans (a trick of the exchange rate, of course, but we don't mention that). Money is being tipped into science, into sport, into fuel for old folk. Bog Lane Comprehensive will soon be as well-funded as Eton, and achieving the same exam results. The economy burgeons daily. Children's lungs will soon be filled with air as pure as that which Adam breathed.

In short, it was like every other Budget Mr Brown has ever produced, a thunderous tribute to himself, an egomaniacal encomium, a personal panegyric. By an ancient and inexplicable tradition, the task of replying to the Budget falls to the leader of the opposition. David Cameron started at a screaming rant, then pumped up the volume. 'In a carbon-conscious age, we have a fossil fuel Chancellor,' he yelled. While he raged, Blair and Brown had what – since they were in public – appeared to be a friendly conversation, as if it was something they did all the time.

'He is an analogue politician in a digital age!' Mr Cameron screeched, making a noise rather like computers used to do when we all dialled up the internet. And why not: 'He is a dial-up politician in a broadband age'? Or, 'a hand-mangle Chancellor in a spin-dry era'?

'Mr Speaker, he is in the past!' Mr Cameron finished, and sat down with a tight little smile which, I regret to say, reminded me of our cat's backside.

23.03.06

Tony Blair tried to avoid being abroad on Wednesdays because that meant John Prescott, his nominal deputy, would have to take Prime Minister's Questions. This was always a hazard. As the Radio Times *used to put it in an off-putting way, 'It's the show where anything might happen – and probably will!' Meanwhile, it emerged that President Chirac was deeply disturbed at the use of English in French business.*

Tony Blair was still away, so John Prescott faced William Hague. It was magnificent. Forget Punch and Judy politics – this was Punch and Punch, Cannon meets Ball, a Roman ballista up against a cauldron of boiling oil up on the battlements. William Hague wondered why pensioners, who had got a £200 rebate on their council tax last year, weren't getting it this year. (Because there isn't an election this year, stupid.) Prescott thumped back: 'I am delighted to see that the Tories are getting through leaders so fast they have started from the beginning again.'

Mr Hague pointed out that the average pensioner was now going to pay an average of £250 more in council tax. Meanwhile, Mr Prescott had not paid any at all on one of his properties. Here is the Prescott reply:

'It is the overall policy of this government to actually consider the pensioner payments and the other matters that we give to them and to consider it in the round. That I think is what we have done, that is what we continue to do, and as for the argument about the payment of council tax, let me tell him, and he must know again in the comparison between our government and his government, that we gave in the response 39 per cent increase in real terms...'

Hague hit back with this oven-ready zinger: 'There was so little English in that last reply that President Chirac would have been happy with it.'

It is at moments like this that Prescott is inclined to whinge. 'I may get the grammar wrong, that's true, and I'll have to take the blame for that. It's my education, and I'm responsible for that.' Eh? And as for Chirac, hadn't Hague himself called the French president a 'cheese-eating surrender monkey'?

'If it's a choice between getting the words wrong and getting the judgement wrong, I'd sooner have my problem than his.' (No, the point made by the DPM's many critics is that he gets both wrong.)

He pulled out his little snickersnee. 'I thought we had finished with Punch and Judy politics,' he said. 'I knew I would be called Mr Punch, what do you think that leaves you?'

Girls, girls!

30.03.06

Tony Blair gave his latest press conference from behind a new short lectern in Downing Street, covered in a sort of brown material I can only call suedette, possibly from World of Suedette on the North Circular Road. He kicked off with a presentation on the NHS, which is apparently in rip-roaring form. He would be showing slides with the help of someone he described as 'my gorgeous assistant, Ben Wegg-Prosser'. This humorous notion, of Wegg-Prosser (known to us all as Oofy) as a sort of political Debbie McGee, came as a surprise. He is perhaps the ultimate Labour apparatchik, and is not noticeably glamorous. Instead he has a scowl that could halt a Dalek at fifty paces.

Anyhow, Oofy pressed the buttons and up popped slides about NHS waiting lists. They were very small numbers, the Prime Minister assured us. Too right; they were so small as to be invisible. 'Those are facts!' he barked. We peered at them like eye patients being asked to read the bottom line. I just made out '1,378', '43,000' and '24.6' – impressive figures to be sure, and figures that would have been even more impressive if we had had the faintest idea what they referred to.

'When care is commissioned, there is an objective cost for what the operation will be,' he said bafflingly. 'The money follows the patient!' and I had a vision of cartoon pound coins and fivers with little legs and cheeky grins trotting loyally after a patient. He told us his recipe for a fine health service: 'Greater decentralization, greater patient choice and greater contestability of service.'

'Making people better' did not figure. But you can imagine one patient chatting: 'St George's is a bit of a long way for my daughter to visit, but they do have a really nice contestability of service there.'

'There is a difference between people's individual experience and their collective sense, which is often based on perception,' the Prime Minister continued. He was beginning to sound like a sage old hermit, offering wisdom to those who have the insight – the third eye – to make out what it means. 'All I ask for is a sense of balance,' he said. 'Their personal experience is their personal reality.' Branggg! He only needed a beard and a sitar, and he'd have rock stars queueing round the block. We switched to his plans for the House of Lords. 'I'll make up my mind on this when I have made up my mind, as it were.' As it were, as it was, and as it always will be. We were onto the Book of Common Prayer. 'When I am ready to say something to you, I will say something to you.'

Someone asked what this puzzling formulation might mean. 'It was meant to be a shutting-down answer, a dance of the seven veils. If I can give you some advice, I wouldn't read too much into what I am saying.'

A holy man telling us to ignore his holy writ! Someone asked if he might follow the example of the England footballer Alan Shearer, who is to retire because of knee injury. 'Knee?' he said. 'My knees are fine.'

As they would need to be, as I suspect that the new suedette mini-lectern is designed for him to sit cross-legged, beads round his neck, receiving humble plaudits – and cheques – from his disciples.

25.04.06

The Labour Party decided to attack David Cameron as someone who changed his mind a great deal. They came up with the idea of a cycling chameleon, which changed colour as it moved along. This was a fine example of a dead metaphor being dragged back to life. Some of these just don't work. If you paid someone to flog a dead horse outside party headquarters, for example, you would spread disgust rather than enlightenment. And in any case, many people rather like chameleons – the once a year that they are likely to think of them.

The Home Secretary has not had his best year, and it got startlingly worse yesterday at exactly 12.32 p.m. That is when he stood up to make a statement about the 1,000 foreign convicted criminals who have been let out of jail without anyone considering whether it might be a good idea to deport them.

The exact moment he rose, the Prime Minister also rose. Mr Blair then scurried out of the Chamber. The Tories bellowed and jeered and ranted and waved their arms in mock outrage and genuine merriment. At the worst moment in the political life of his Home Secretary, the man he has spent the best part of a fraught Question Time defending, Mr Blair was off – out, gone, history, *disparu*. Sayonara, suckers!

This was the captain abandoning the sinking ship, leaving the rats to man the bridge. Mr Blair, we were told, had to meet a group of Scottish businessmen. They must have been offering to loan the Labour Party an awful lot of money if he had to see them rather than give moral support to Charles Clarke.

I had been studying the Home Secretary during Question Time. He had adopted the defence hysterical, by which he demonstrates his insouciant concern for what the other side are saying by laughing in an exaggeratedly jovial fashion at everything. But his scalp told a different story. It was bright, crimson, almost beetroot red. Dave the Chameleon would have been deeply envious.

When he got up, however, his pate had gone pallid. The blood had drained away, heaven knows where. His manner had switched from forced jocularity to curt aggression. The release of all those prisoners was, he said, 'deeply regrettable' and his priority now was to set it right. He spoke for exactly 2 minutes, 41 seconds, which, given the seriousness of what had occurred might have been thought something of an insult. He parked his backside back on the bench to Tory cries of 'What about "sorry"?' but New Labour doesn't do sorry.

Later he decided to get angry. The ministerial scalp regained its vermillion hue. 'You have a long record of evading responsibility!' he shouted at Michael Howard, a former home secretary. Tories booed and jeered again.

Then Mr Clarke admitted responsibility. We were amazed. Ministers don't do that any more. But it turned out he had redefined the term. He was responsible, but not in the sense of being to blame. Instead he was responsible for putting right what he was not actually responsible for in the first place. That's modern politics.

27.04.06

In May, Labour did poorly in the local government elections, so Tony Blair did what prime ministers often do and held a Cabinet reshuffle. We wrongly assumed that John Prescott would be fired in the wake of his affair with a civil servant and his dealings with an American businessman who wanted to turn the Millennium Dome into a casino. He had also been photographed playing croquet on the lawn of Dorney Wood, the grace and favour house he was able to use at weekends.

Jeremy Thorpe once said, when Harold Macmillan butchered his Cabinet, 'Greater love hath no man than he lay down his friends for his life.' But Tony Blair laid down his friends, his enemies, his rivals, his slight acquaintances and possibly some people he met once in a pub but whose name he has forgotten.

And he did it in public. In the past ministers, sacked or promoted, have been able to skulk in and out of Number 10 by the back door. Yesterday they were paraded in front of the cameras, all manned by cameramen whose sense of *noblesse oblige* is not what it might be.

''Ere, love, you bin sacked?' they yelled at Ruth Kelly. 'Wha' yer got then?' they carolled merrily to others. Members of the Privy Council have to meet the Queen. Now the ritual includes meeting Her Majesty's Media. Unlike our sovereign, they do not see putting people at ease as part of their role.

'Wha' a terrible barnet!' they shouted at someone – I don't think he was an MP – who had teased his comb-over in front of a circular bald patch. John Prescott arrived at 7.45 a.m. He left just before eleven, looking cheerful – and no wonder, because he had expected to lose his job, but has actually held on to his title, his car, his driver and his country house (with croquet lawn), while shedding his entire workload. Lottery jackpot winners have settled for less.

What had he done in there for more than three hours? Perhaps Blair says something like, 'Look, John, the bad news is that I have to sack you. The good news is that Cherie has just made some of her delicious brownies, and I'd like you to stop here, have a cup of coffee and enjoy one – or two!'

Rumours were flying around, most of them false. Hazel Blears, the diminutive Mrs Pepperpot of the government, was going to be minister for social exclusion, no doubt waiting outside the Cabinet room with a bag of crisps and a bottle of lemonade, trying to listen at the keyhole without anyone noticing. She posed outside the famous black door while members of HM Media yelled, 'Gorra job, darlink?' Finally someone inside spotted her tiny frame outside and she was admitted.

Alan Johnson climbed from his car in dark glasses and a silvery suit. He arrived looking like a middle-ranking Mafioso, but left as education secretary.

Alistair Darling turned up with David Miliband, and we wondered how well the job would have to pay for Mr Darling to buy Grecian 2000 for his hair as well as his eyebrows.

06.05.06

Ms Blears actually became chair of the Labour Party. Ruth Kelly went on to become minister for communities, which covers 'social exclusion' and Mr Darling went to Trade and Industry. Charles Clarke was sacked as Home Secretary, and preferred to go the backbenches rather than take another cabinet job. He was replaced by John Reid.

In the old days policemen would give 'a clip round the ear' to any youngster who was caught 'scrumping' apples. These days we would be delighted if our young persons stole apples. Instead they are round at the newsagent's, trying to scrump cigarettes.

John Reid is an old-fashioned copper. He would love to cross the floor and administer a clip round the ear to members of the opposition. 'Come on lad, hop it, and don't let me catch you at it again!' He is also in the fine old tradition of Labour home secretaries, which consists of blackening the name of the previous holder of the office. This has to be done subtly, since British politics does not allow an outright attack on your own colleagues. Yet it must be absolutely clear what you mean. The criticism has to be obvious, but the language must sound like high praise. Take his response to a question about the under-reported foreign criminals.

Mr Reid said he 'thought' – longish pause – that he 'ought to pay tribute' to his predecessor, Charles Clarke, who was 'a big man in every way'.

'He took responsibility for a series of very serious mistakes, which ultimately he probably only discovered relatively lately.' There was near-genius in that word 'probably', which sounds judicious and thoughtful, but implied that we must consider the possibility that he knew all about the problem and merrily chose to ignore it.

'Relatively' translates as 'clearly he was very slow on the uptake. But we can't really blame him for being as thick as two short planks.'

'He took responsibility for beginning to remedy this, and we should accept that he dealt with the situation in a very honourable fashion.'

Ouch! He dealt with it competently, or effectively? No, he dealt with it in an 'honourable' fashion. Honourable is what we are when we are failing miserably, but decently. And consider the phrase 'I believe we ought to accept...' as if to say, 'Most sane people would laugh in his face. But I am here to suggest we take a more charitable view.'

You could perhaps call it praising with faint damns. It was a masterpiece of ambiguity, like those drystone walls you see in the north of England, perfectly assembled, without the onlooker having a clue how it's done. And if I were Mr Clarke, I would want to give his successor not a clip, but a bloody great clout round the ear.

16.05.06

John Prescott underwent months of mockery and vilification in the media. But he still had to face the Commons.

It must have been hard. Usually MPs are benign to a colleague who has suffered in the press. They dislike us journalists more than they hate each other. But they don't like John Prescott. That chippy, resentful, class-based routine gets right under Tory skins. They now have the chance to strip him down and sell him off for parts, and they're not going to miss it. He was treated like a supply teacher in a sink school at the end of term.

He tried. How he tried! He repeatedly told us how much work he was doing in his new job. 'The Prime Minister felt I was able to play a role...' (Role, roll, get it?) At this the Tories collapsed in heaps of fake laughter – or, more worryingly, genuine laughter.

Rob Wilton nudged them towards hysteria when he asked, 'What steps are you taking to ensure that staff working under you are not subject to sexual harassment?' 'Yeah!' they cried, like Texans at a rodeo. 'Keep the door closed next time!' a familiar voice shouted. It turned out to be my old chum Michael Fabricant, who has clearly put his project to become an elder statesman on hold for the time being.

Labour MPs had clearly been told to provide the Deputy Prime Minister with some breathing space. Anne Snelgrove said that the party and the country felt 'pride' at the role he was playing. This is not, perhaps, the first feeling people have when they contemplate him. Your average punter does not look you in the eye and say, 'I'll tell you what I feel about John Prescott. Pride! Aye, pride, and that goes for any right-thinking Briton!'

He thanked Ms Snelgrove for her kind remarks. 'Any more would be very welcome,' he said with a grin that was not just rueful but rue-sodden. But he did seem to be clawing his way to safety. His language was disintegrating, which with John Prescott is always a good sign. But then it all went horribly, dreadfully wrong.

Dari Taylor, a Welsh Labour MP who, tragically, was only trying to help, praised his work renewing neighbourhoods. 'Is he still going to have a hands-on in these areas?' she piped, and as the Tories began to collapse and wheeze, and hug themselves as if being attacked by a swarm of anacondas, his smile became grimmer. Finally Andrew Robathan dispensed with double entendre and asked whether, when he met world leaders, they would treat him with 'the same degree of ridicule as this House'.

It was a kick in the kidneys from a Doc Marten. But then Prescott and Robathan go back a long way, back to an altercation in the Tea Room. Mobile phones are banned there but Prescott was using his to talk, as it happened, to the Prime Minister. When Robathan complained he was treated to a blast of Prescott invective that he has never forgotten, or forgiven.

18.05.06

The imminent arrival of Gordon Brown concentrated our minds wonderfully on what the Chancellor actually said. The Home Secretary, John Reid, had appeared at a select committee and, in order to distance himself from future disasters, announced that his new department was not 'fit for purpose' – a gruesome and much overused phrase.

Here is what Gordon Brown said this week: 'We will continue to reform our public services, matching national objectives with other drivers of change – competition and contestability and local choice and voice, including publicly real-time data across the key public services.'

Imagine having to listen to that every day! Think of those *It's Your Call* election programmes. 'Mrs Purdue, whose hip operation has been cancelled for the third time, it's your call to the Prime Minister.'

'Well, Mrs Purdue, I am sorry about your delayed operation. But if you study the real-time data and take into account contestability issues...'

Mr Blair can obfuscate too. Yesterday he explained why the Home Secretary had the hardest job in government. At health, people wanted to get better, and nurses and doctors were anxious to help them. In education, teachers, parents and even children were united in wanting good grades. Whereas, 'When you're home secretary, your client base, if I can put it like that, wants the opposite. They are against what you're doing.'

I see what he means, but it's still a wonderful thought: all those illegal immigrants, Albanian people-smugglers and knife-toting youths as a 'client base', as if they were on a mailing list for John Reid's shop-at-home catalogue. Barristers refer to some miscreant in the dock as 'my client', but will coppers do the same? 'You're nicked, chummy. But could you spare a moment to fill in this client satisfaction questionnaire? It shouldn't take long, and your name will be entered for the prize holiday draw.'

09.06.06

David Cameron made his big speech on the new politicians and family life. 'We have to big up Asda!' he said excitedly. I wondered whether other Tory leaders would have brought the same message. 'Swan and Edgar – respec'!' Or, 'Let us give due esteem to Sir Thomas Lipton's Emporium of Quality Comestibles!' as Disraeli never tired of saying.

It seemed to have something to do with the supermarket chain's family-friendly working hours. 'We need to big it up, talk about it, promote it, and get others to do the same!' he said, and sounded so enthusiastic that it was easy to forget that Asda is owned by Wal-Mart, one of the world's most rapacious chains, whose policies towards their staff are more ferocious than family-friendly.

He planned to change utterly the old Tory attitudes to the traditional family, or, as he put it, 'Not only is our war against lone parents over, but the weapons have been put permanently beyond use.' As so often with Mr Cameron, the imagery is slightly alarming. One had a picture of Tory politicians who had once launched ground-to-air missiles against single mums burying the stuff in County Sligo, where General de Chastelaine can't find it.

In a tribute to the importance of the Tory leader's speech, the Labour Party had sent along an actor in a big blue chameleon outfit, in a clumsy attempt to depict him as all things to all men. I told the chameleon that he was a dead metaphor and immediately felt a pang of regret. Chameleons have feelings too, or so I suppose. At least he didn't turn red and flick a long sticky tongue in my face.

Mr Cameron bounded in, his hair slightly and perhaps carefully tousled. His speech had been sponsored by Vodafone. The commercialization of politics, once a joke, is gathering pace. Why not have all debates sponsored? The BAe Weapons Systems debate on Iraq, perhaps, or the Guinness Licensing Hours bill.

He is a great one for soundbites that somehow make your teeth itch. 'There is more to life than money,' he told us, adding that 'No man is an island.' If he had said, 'All you need is love,' he'd have had the hat trick.

The most eagerly anticipated line of the speech came when he said that men ought to be present at the birth of their children. And failing that, at the birth of other people's children. (No, of course he didn't say that! But he will next week.)

He seemed to be drawing back. 'I am not trying to force men into the delivery room,' he said. And, of course, if you pulled out a sharp object to cut the cord, John Reid would have you banged up, pronto.

21.06.06

Jack Straw congratulated the government yesterday for the recent hot weather. 'There has been a lot more sunshine since Labour came to power in 1997,' he said. It was a joke, but a curious one, since the government does believe that its actions can slow global warming. But then, some years ago, John Prescott claimed credit for the fact that there had been no hosepipe bans.

Yeah, right. As always, Mr Prescott was all promise and no delivery. If he had claimed responsibility for Halley's comet, at least it might have turned up on time – though perhaps not, if the DPM's Strategic Heavenly Body Planning Authority had been in charge.

Every month questions to the Department for the Environment, Food and Rural Affairs reveals more horrors lurking in our once lovely, peaceful countryside. If Kenneth Grahame had written *The Wind in the Willows* today, nearly all the characters would have been annihilated. Ratty would have been poisoned by pest control officers. Sonar equipment would have driven Mole from his cosy hole in short order. If the pair had gone to visit Mr Badger in his home, with its twinkling pewter plates and roaring log fire, they would have found their host slumped at the door, dead from a shotgun blast fired by a farmer convinced he was harbouring bovine tuberculosis. Only the endangered Mr Toad would have been protected.

As for the fish that glide past Ratty's boat, they would be dead from koi herpes virus, which, we learned yesterday, is the piscatorial equivalent of foot-and-mouth disease. The junior minister, Ben Bradshaw, called this 'a challenging situation', which is New Labour talk for 'We haven't a clue what to do about it.'

MPs urged farmers to forgo their traditional crops and sow 'biomass' instead. These are plants that can be turned into fuel. We are to grow our own petrol! Mike Penning had tabled a question asking, 'What level of perfluorooctane sulfonate is allowed in drinking water.' He was, sadly, not present to put it.

But I found myself writing another bucolic idyll set in modern Britain. 'As a boy I ran through the heat of summer across waving fields of miscanthus grass, carrying a bag of dead badgers to Mistress Miliband's cottage. There I would have slaked my thirst under a black plastic bag full of hay…' *Perfluorooctane Sulfonate with Rosie* would have been a good title.

21.07.06

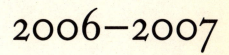

2006–2007

Six months after taking over leadership of the Liberal Democrat party, Ming Campbell had not really set the world alight, so there was much excitement when Charlie Kennedy returned, if not to reclaim his throne, at least to give it a longing look.

Not a lot happens at Liberal Democrat conferences, which is perhaps why Charles Kennedy taking a short stroll, an event that might not over-excite the media, or even Mr Kennedy's dog, became a magnificently bonkers, toweringly crazed, frenzied whirligig of chaos.

It was of course deliberate. Aides had put out a paper announcing that the erstwhile leader would be walking from his hotel to the conference centre, a distance of perhaps 150 yards. This was meant to create precisely the effect it did create, which was to block the pavement in front of the Metropole Hotel in Brighton with a massive claque of hacks. There were nine TV crews, plus innumerable cameramen and reporters, and even a few curious passers-by, who can have had little idea of what was about, quite literally, to hit them. Mr Kennedy emerged with his wife, Sarah, and set off on a trek that would normally take one minute, but might yesterday have daunted Sir Ranulph Fiennes.

The media clamped round him in a gigantic scrum. The Kennedys tried to move forward. Now and again they would make a little progress, inching forward in a new version of a twelve-step programme. Then they would be blocked again, as cameramen climbed onto the backs of TV crews, and the chaps with the long furry microphones in turn climbed on top of them. What the Americans sometimes call a 'goat fuck' formed and dissolved, before lurching down the street and re-forming a few yards away. At this point he was in danger of missing his own speech.

Warnings were shouted, a few of which were heeded. 'Bike!' somebody yelled just in time, or else one unhappy child would have returned to find his bicycle a pea-sized lump of mangled steel. The GF moved backwards, so those facing them had to act like coxes. 'Lamp-post, lamp-post!' and on one occasion, 'Mind that cement mixer!'

Mr Kennedy, it soon became plain, adored every tottering moment. 'You are making me feel very nostalgic,' he said, beaming. 'As I said at the general election, you have got to take care of yourselves.'

'Are you taking care of yourself?' asked someone, a reference to his drink problem. He ignored them. 'Does this sort of attention make your heart sink or swim?' asked someone else. The answer to that was obvious: he wasn't just any old Lib Dem backbencher now – he was Bonnie Prince Charlie marching on Derby.

We juddered dangerously across a side street. 'For the party's sake, I am not going to upstage anyone,' he said. Suddenly, almost impossibly, we had reached the conference centre. A voice boomed, 'Charles, when you stop drinking, we want you back!' It must have been as warming as a generous measure of Islay malt.

Of course he had upstaged someone – himself. The speech had been carefully choreographed with the new leader's staff. There would be no handshake. (Ming is definitely not Charlie's old china – in fact Charlie blamed him for briefing against him in his time of crisis.) The new leader would not even be on stage, but at the front of the audience.

Mr Kennedy appeared to the first standing ovation of the conference, led by Ming. He had no notes, but wandered round the stage as if delighted to be able to move freely. He wanted to give a 'personal thank-you' to all the many thousands of people who had sent messages of support (translation: 'Even in defeat, I am more popular than the rest of them') and to the thousands who had no interest in party politics (translation: 'I can reach out to the masses beyond, unlike these dreary tossers').

He went on, perhaps, for a trifle too long, but they stood again at the end. The message from the conference seemed to be: 'We are desperately sorry that you had to go, but, ahem, we don't actually expect you back.'

20.09.06

At the Labour Party conference, Gordon Brown made what was meant to be his last conference speech as Chancellor, and indeed his last as premier-in-waiting, in which he praised Tony Blair. Sadly for him, it all went suddenly pear-shaped.

Not since the Potemkin villages were demolished after Catherine the Great had gone, not since the old Crossroads motel, has a facade come down so fast. It was a magnificent moment for us connoisseurs of political disaster. Gordon Brown was midway through a paean of praise for his old rival. 'I've worked with Tony Blair for almost ten years!' he said, waving one of his much chewed fingers towards the Prime Minister, as if we might have forgotten who he was.

The words must have been wrung from him like entrails on a torturer's wheel. Then he said, 'It has been a privilege to work with him...' He was not to know that at this very moment, Cherie Blair was walking through the exhibition stands just outside the main conference hall. The

Chancellor's voice boomed out from innumerable speakers. It was Mrs Blair's terrible luck that at the moment she muttered to herself, 'That's a lie!' she should be close to a reporter working for Bloomberg, the financial news agency.

Number 10 quickly denied she had said anything of the sort. It claims that she actually said, 'I need to get by.' More cynical observers than me point out that nothing can be thought to be true until it has been denied by the Downing Street press office, but that may be unfair. Possibly she said, 'My mouth is so dry,' or 'Will someone swat that fly?' On the other hand, it is scarcely likely that the press office would agree: 'Yes, the Prime Minister's wife thinks that the Chancellor is a fibber who makes Pinocchio look like George Washington.' On the other hand, Mrs Blair's distaste for Mr Brown is well known – if she could have planted leylandii between Number 10 and Number 11, she might well have done so. And the Bloomberg people have no reason to make it up. What she thinks is unlikely to affect the Dow Jones average, or the value of the Thai baht.

Mr Brown, unknowing, raved on. 'The most successful ever Labour leader and Labour prime minister! Always in tune with the aspirations of the British people!' They had, admittedly, had their differences, and those differences had distracted from what mattered. 'I regret that, as I know Tony does too.' This translates as 'I have been an asshole, but then so has he.'

Mrs Blair scurried off to a fringe meeting, happily unaware of the chaos she had created by saying she could murder a pie.

26.09.06

This blunder by Mrs Blair created what we in the trade call 'an embarrassment', although it was rather unconvincingly denied. The next day her husband made what we were promised would be his last speech to a Labour conference.

Did we detect a small but manly tear, a mini-sobette, staining the prime ministerial cheek? Apparently not; the glistening we saw was only sweat. One sensed that he would have loved a great big gulping six-Kleenex sob, but all we got was a slight catch in the throat. Deputy sales managers have left with more emotion. And they get a clock, or a travel voucher.

The speech was well delivered and well received, but it was boilerplate Blair. He could have delivered it at almost any time in the past twelve years. The gist was, as it always is, 'I'm right; if you don't agree with me you're wrong. And the voters know it.' He read them a crisp, businesslike lecture. There were the usual verb-free sentences, seventy-nine in all, which in the past implied commitments without making promises. Now they evoke achievements that may or may not have occurred: 'The end of waiting in the NHS. Historic. Transforming secondary schools. Historic.'

And there were those strange, clunking sentences that make you ask what on earth he could possibly mean, though you haven't time to work it out because the speech has raced on. 'The USP of New Labour is aspiration and compassion reconciled.' Eh? 'Ten years ago, if we talked pensions, we meant pensioners.' What was that about? 'The danger is in failing to understand that New Labour in 2007 won't be New Labour in 1997.' Run that past me again, will you? 'Ten years later, our advantage is time, our disadvantage, time.' Lost me there, old cock.

Even the single mad staring eye was back. Yesterday it was the left eye that gleamed over us. Sometimes it is the other. But the two eyeballs, obliged to live next to each other, have often been at odds. They are obliged to work together, but there is no denying that it has been a strain.

The organizers had tried to whip up a frenzy, which they almost, but not quite, achieved. Before he arrived there was a 'spontaneous' demonstration in which members of the audience held up hand-written posters: 'We love you, yeah, yeah, yeah', 'Too young to retire' and simply 'Thank you'. It was like waiting for Stalin, but Stalin remodelled as a West Coast counselling guru. We were shown a video in which ordinary people gave thanks for the existence of Blair. One old lady said, 'I'm grateful for the £200 allowance. It's better than a woolly hat.' And to think that the British are accused of having a poverty of ambition!

Then he arrived and ran to the podium. Party leaders have to run now, to prove how fit they are. He sprayed thanks around to everyone, including the party, the British people, his agent and his family. At least, he said, he didn't have to worry about Cherie running off with the bloke next door.

I suppose that was a tacit admission that, in spite of her denials, she had indeed said 'That's a lie' while listening to Gordon's speech. Then he broke off for a story about his two elder sons, Nicky and Euan, who had been canvassing for Labour in a street where one householder gave them a volley of abuse. 'I hate that Tony Blair!' and so on. Then when Euan said, 'That's my Dad,' the man said he was very sorry and offered them a cup of tea. It was a heart-warming story meant to illustrate the innate decency of the British people, but it made me wonder why they bother to canvass next door in Downing Street.

He praised ministers who were 'asked to make way', which is to say, 'I sacked them.' Most had gone without bitterness. 'They never forgot their principles when they were in office, and they never discovered them when they left office.' 'Oooh,' went the conference. Charles Clarke, Clare Short, Frank Dobson – you know who you are. Take a bow!

Finally, the finale – quite short. 'You are the future now. So make the most of it.' He left to a thunderous storm of mild regret, a rolling cascade of ruefulness.

27.09.06

The star attraction once again was a former US president.

Bill Clinton reached out to the Labour Party, reached out and fondled it, told it how much he loved it. 'I have never seen a man flirt with 3,000 people simultaneously,' said one minister on her way out.

It felt like being drowned in a gigantic sundae, with slathers of ice cream, hot chocolate sauce and plenty of fudge. He told them they were fabulous, wonderful, adorable, and of course he would phone in the morning.

'Ah'm glad to be back here, ah lahk this Labour Party conference,' he began. Clinton can get away with saying 'ah' for 'I', unlike Blair, who sounds posey. 'The victory you won last year was good for the UK but also for the world as a whole,' he told them. Mmm, raspberry sauce!

'Your Prime Minister, your government, your party, have all been stunning successes,' he went on. I first saw Clinton speak at the Democratic convention in 1988 and he was terrible. Now he is brilliant. His arms reach out as if he would like to stroke everyone in the hall, tenderly and repeatedly. You might be sitting fifty feet back but he still seems to be making eye contact with you, personally. He uses long pauses, as if searching for precisely the right compliment for the gorgeous, quivering party in front of him. 'I say to all of you. Well done. You should be happy. And you should be proud.' Yum, toasted almonds on top!

The conference, so to speak, crossed and re-crossed its legs. He warned them of the terrible danger that would occur if they ever lost power. 'If you vote another crowd in, surely to goodness, they would keep everything you did right.' Longer pause, for the irony to sink in. 'Yeah,' he said, sorrowfully, and as one they felt his pain. He felt their pain. He wanted to kiss them all better.

He thanked everyone. He thanked Tony Blair, he thanked Cherie and the children. He thanked Gordon Brown for his 'brilliant economic leadership'. He thanked the party for giving all of them the chance to serve.

The gist was that their genius had changed the world, and it was all thanks to the Labour Party conference – yes, this very conference! 'You are the change agents in this great nation! You have been, and you will be.' Slurp, slurp, delicious sprinkles and bits of banana! They applauded wildly his applause for them.

Tony Blair was, he told us, 'proud but humble'. Yes, we might have added, and brilliant but useless, truthful but mendacious, level-headed yet crazed. He had been greeted with 'gratitude, devotion and love'. I tried to breathe but had the feeling I was gagging on whipped cream.

Then we heard about AIDS, and global warming, and the good work his dearest friend would be doing to tackle both. 'Be of good cheer! Take a deep breath! Be proud of what you have done, and keep in the future business!'

He finished with an African word he had learned. It was *ubuntu*. He didn't immediately tell us what it was. It sounded like one of those huge amalgamated unions you find in the modern TUC: the United Beaders, Upholsterers,

Needleworkers, etc. Or possibly it was a reference to the joke about the new district commissioner in Africa who is greeted everywhere he goes with cries of, say, 'Ubuntu!' This enthusiasm pleases him greatly, until he reaches a cattle compound where his guide warns: 'Be careful not to step in that ubuntu.'

It turns out to mean: 'I am, because you are.' No, I haven't a clue either. But the speech was a mighty success, compared to Alan Johnson, the education secretary, who was worthy but pedestrian later in the day. In a party that is by now charisma-crazed, he did his leadership chances no good at all. He simply lacks the ubuntu factor. And I'll bet they never have him over to address the Democratic National Convention.

28.09.06

John Prescott was also quitting as deputy leader. Prezza's last huzza came at the end of the Manchester conference.

How we will miss him, especially sketch-writers. At the end of his speech they even ran the tape of him hitting that Welsh farmer, and it got one of the biggest cheers of the conference. Most of the audience had given him a standing ovation before he even started. As much as anything, it was two fingers to the press. Straight away he addressed the one nagging doubt in their minds when he began with contrition for recent events. 'I know I let myself down, and I let you down. I just want to say sorry.'

Would they accept his apology? Of course they would. They love him and they know they are about to lose him. He did not disappoint. He began at a bellow and continued at a roar. He had a sore throat. With most speakers this would get worse as the multi-decibel rant went on. In his case things improved, as if the very words were acting like Dyno-Rod on his larynx.

We didn't get the full blast of Prescott vocabulary and grammar, because he was reading from a speech, but reading at such a pace that whole words, entire phrases, were lost in the system, like one of those office copiers that seem to have a permanent paper jam. Extractors became 'extrictors', Labour money 'baggan the regeneration of Manchester' and the MP who campaigned against slavery (a Tory, as he somehow never points out) became 'Wilby William Wilberforce', who sounds like a little boy from verse by A. A. Milne. But these were no more than reminders of the great days of Prescott, the days when with two quick jabs he could leave the language a curled heap on the canvas.

He took credit for the regeneration of British canals, once a symbol of our urban decline. Somehow omitted to mention that Defra, now hopelessly in debt, had just announced severe cuts in funding for waterways. But why spoil a good boast? The speech in any case had roared off down the canal, like a speedboat smuggling cigarettes.

Finally the peroration, a fierce appeal for party unity, delivered almost at a scream. 'Always remember who the *real* enemies are, the Tories, the Liberals. As Tony said, let's get after them. So do it for me. Do it for Tony.'

It reminded me of Ronald Reagan's favourite phrase, from the film about a dying footballer: 'Win one for the Gipper!' Were they going to be watching us from heaven? It sounded that way.

Then the video, one sentimental reprise of that punch, and Mrs Prescott up on stage, kissing the old man, and wiping away a final tear as the conference boomed and stamped and clapped for one last time.

29.09.06

David Cameron spoke twice to his first Tory conference as party leader. In his first speech he encouraged them to 'let sunshine win the day', which sounded like a cross between Morecambe and Wise and Polyanna – and to be at odds with Tory policy on global warming. His big set-piece speech came at the end of the week.

The leader tried to drive a stake through the heart of Thatcherism yesterday. Whether her supporters will pull it out like a cocktail stick from a sausage remains to be seen. But yesterday he won cheers from a Tory conference for gay marriage, single parents and the minimum wage, none of which featured on her agenda. He was even applauded for talking about social justice – this to a party which not long ago thought that social justice meant birching for hooligans, before or after they'd been strung up. There were those, he said, who accused him of lacking substance. 'What they really mean is that they want the old policies back. Well, they're not coming back. And we're not going back.' It sounded like a deliberate echo of Mrs Thatcher's famous line: 'U-turn if you want to…'

He did not need to add, 'and if you don't like it, you know where you can go. Ukip if you want to. The gentleman's not for kipping!' (Unlike some of the people gathered behind him on the stage, there to provide a backdrop of alert eager folk of various ages, all colours and both sexes. Unfortunately three of them seemed to be falling into the arms of Morpheus, so the camera angle changed until they were woken up, possibly with the aid of cattle prods.)

Tory opposition leaders usually spend much of their conference speech abusing the Labour government. He did some of that, but spent more time praising them. They had done many wonderful things, things the Tories would never want to change. Bank of England independence! The minimum wage – why, they wouldn't only keep it, they'd increase it! Education reforms! Afghanistan and Iraq – he grew dewy-eyed about our 'vital' presence there.

This man doesn't just admire Tony Blair; he seems to be in love with him. He recalled his campaign slogan, 'Education, education, education', and said his equivalent was going to be 'NHS – one of the greatest achievements of the twentieth century!' When he did attack the Prime Minister, it was from the left. Last week he had made a cheap joke about hoodies and had so betrayed 'one of the best things he ever said – tough on the causes of crime'.

There was, perhaps, a rueful touch – every great love has its bitter moments – when he opposed ID cards, and spoke about government decision-making being removed from the cabinet room and taken onto the Number 10 sofa.

Oh, how he yearns to be on that sofa, without Tony Blair but preferably with him. Perhaps he could be persuaded to stay on and join a Tory cabinet? He was beginning to sound like the terminally jealous Sebastian in *Little Britain*. John Prescott, John Reid, Gordon Brown – they might as well not have existed.

Now and again some members of the old Tory Party woke up, as if from a bad dream. The loudest applause came when he said that immigrants ought to be made to learn English. But the gist of the speech was: 'You don't need Tony Blair, for I am him – reborn!'

05.10.06

In early November, the Speaker bizarrely ruled that David Cameron could not ask Tony Blair whom he supported as his successor. 'Who will be leader of the Labour Party is a matter for the Labour Party!' he said, as if we were talking about a new human resources manager or a lift attendant. The topic was raised soon afterwards at Mr Blair's press conference, where parliamentary rules of order do not apply.

The Prime Minister devoted his monthly press conference to not answering questions, a job which he performs with distinction. He is able to not answer questions in a dozen different ways, sometimes managing to imply that it is an outrage that the question has been asked in the first place. But this does not matter. The main purpose of the press conference is not to provide answers to questions, but to give the press a civics lesson. Yesterday's lantern lecture was about identity cards. To help him he had invited along the immigration minister, Liam Byrne, who sat poised to answer our queries. Sadly, no one had any. Poor Mr Byrne sat silent throughout the whole hour, though at one point he shook his head. It was his only contribution.

As Mr Blair banged on about ID cards – apparently they will help us to buy goods online – I began to ponder. Does he imagine a world in which we will all remember our cards, every day? What will happen when we go to the doctor with a nasty rash and realize we have left our card in our other jacket? Which is now at the dry cleaner, where all that biometric information might be being wiped by the tumbling chemicals. Or your son used it as a makeshift screwdriver and warped it. Will you no longer exist? Would they one day invent an ID card that can be put on a chip and lodged inside your skull, so that shopkeepers will zap your head in order to confirm your credit card details? I wouldn't put it past this technology-crazed bunch.

And take this business of scanning your retina. Mr Blair has one mad staring eye and one sinister hooded one. Like the earth's magnetic pole, they change places now and again, though rather more often. Yesterday the left looked more bonkers, then the right. How will they tell which is which? 'Sorry, sir, your eye is saner than our records show. I'm afraid you can't buy this patio heater.'

Questions followed, but no answers. Adam Boulton of Sky News asked whether he approved of Saddam being executed. He didn't want to answer that, since it might have broken the fiction that it was an entirely Iraqi decision. 'So you're opposed to his execution,' Mr Boulton persisted. The Blair temper snapped. 'Adam, excuse me, that's enough. I will express myself in my own words, if you don't mind. And what did you have for breakfast this morning?'

That last, peculiar, rider may have been meant to add a note of levity and so diminish the impression of testiness. I recalled that Mr Blair attended Mr Boulton's wedding early this year. 'Do you take this woman...'

'Come along, don't put words into my mouth. I have made my position on taking this woman perfectly clear on numerous occasions.'

He also failed to answer questions about the criminal justice system, on the security situation in Iraq and on the sale of peerages. 'I don't think it would be appropriate for me to say anything.'

Finally, did he support Gordon Brown as his successor? 'I'm afraid that I have said I will speak at the appropriate time, and have nothing to add to what I said in the House of Commons last week.'

But last week the Speaker had prevented him from saying anything on the topic to the House of Commons. So it was a dazzling masterwork of evasion!

07.11.06

One of the issues much discussed at this time was apology – should we, or our leaders, make formal apologies for events in the past, such as the Irish famine and the slave trade – events for which we as individuals had no responsibility? There was also the exceedingly distressing murder of a Russian agent in London.

The Home Secretary made a statement about the death of Alexander Litvinenko. This was preceded by something far more serious.

Sir Peter Tapsell spoke. It was as if the amiable chuntering of *Thought for the Day* were suddenly interrupted by the Voice of God. The topic at Question Time was the trafficking of women. Someone raised the sort-of-apology Tony Blair had made for slavery this week. Ruth Kelly, the minister, spoke in the Prime Minister's support.

So far, so quiet. But suddenly, unexpectedly, up sprang Sir Peter. It was past the time questions should have ended, so we were all ill-prepared for this visitation. The crack team of French seamstresses, who sit, like firefighters, waiting to leap into action and stitch Sir Peter's words into a great tapestry for the edification of future generations, did not have time to race to the Chamber from their withdrawing room.

There was much loud cheering, mostly from Labour. Many might imagine this to be sarcastic, but I know it reflects the profound, atavistic respect with which Sir Peter is held on all sides of the House. Time passed, and as when a great wave has hurled itself against a rocky shore, there was a brief moment of silence. Sir Peter waited, and as the last ripples and eddies died away, he spoke.

'When are we going to get,' he demanded, his voice rolling and hurtling down his mighty frame like an avalanche gathering pace on an Alpine slope, 'a pwime ministewial apology. For King Henry VIII's disgwaceful tweatment of his wives?'

There was another pause. Then a great shout of laughter. Was the laughter at the joke? At Sir Peter himself? Or both? It is not given to us, even those who were laughing, to be sure. Sir Peter descended and sat quite still, black of brow and ferocious of forehead, for part of the gag is that he appears to mean every word. A few minutes later, though, I looked at him and saw that his mouth had curled into a private, almost secret grin, the smile of a man who set out to do a job and succeeded triumphantly.

Soon after that Mr Reid, his own voice soft and low – making it even more sinister than usual – briefed MPs on the latest news of Mr Litvinenko's death. Perhaps the scariest question came from Kali Mountford, who said that during the scrutiny of the civil contingencies bill 'we had tried to imagine the unimaginable. But we did not imagine this.'

You can see why. For decades we expected the Russians to send their nuclear payload over in rockets. Now it seems they can dispatch the lethal material along with the in-flight magazines, the duty-frees and the Plasticine-flavoured smoked salmon starters. No wonder BA staff want to wear crucifixes.

01.12.06

Every year, the Chancellor produces a pre-Budget report, which is, in effect, a sort of mini-Budget.

Mr Brown certainly paints an idyllic picture. You feel that his pre-Budget report should come in the form of a glossy, colourful brochure, advertising Gordon Braes, perhaps, a luxury timeshare in the Trossachs.

Of course there is nothing there yet. But there are endless promises. GDP growth is about to rise phenomenally. ('And that's where we are going to build the spa, with fully equipped gym.') Educational standards are going to burst upwards like a Saturn rocket, thanks to Gordon giving schools so much money that dinner ladies will use tenners to light the gas under the new, healthy-eating options. ('Over here will be a Michelin-starred restaurant, offering a candle-lit fine dining experience.')

In science, we will lead the world. Gordon's investment in stem-cell research means that millions will lead longer, healthier lives. ('That may look like rubble, but when you take possession of your chalet it will be an Olympic-size swimming pool with showers and hot tubs.')

You start to wonder if there is any way of getting home before the company bus arrives to take you to the airport. ('Thank you, very interesting, perhaps we'll come back when you've got something more to show us…')

This was, I think, the tenth pre-Budget report I have heard from Mr Brown. They are all almost identical. All the news is good. All the figures add up. All the statistics are favourable.

The mirage tends to dissolve when the other lot get their chance. George Osborne, the shadow chancellor, pointed out that his growth forecasts were falling, public debt was soaring, and unemployment was on the way up again. 'This is a man so obsessed by his next job that he has forgotten the 300,000 people who have lost their jobs!'

It does not lie in my mouth (as the lawyers say) to complain about people who make cheap jokes. I liked Mr Osborne's opening barb: that Gordon might still be Chancellor next year – if John Reid keeps him on. But there are many ways of attacking his climate change taxes, and merely quipping, 'People say he's just become green. That's unfair. He's been green since that meeting in Granita!' is not quite enough. And while it is amusing to point out that the famous restaurant has now closed and been replaced by one named Desperados, that does not do the business either.

Then we heard from Vince Cable, the Lib Dem spokesman. Mr Cable is so anxious to be fair and reasonable that when he does kick you in the slats, the effect is much more painful than it otherwise might be. He mocked Gordon's figures. 'He is the clever schoolboy who always gets ten out of ten in his tests – because he marks them himself.'

Ooof! I fear that dark clouds are gathering over Gordon Braes, the building work is behind time, and the estimates may be hopelessly optimistic.

07.12.06

There was one of those tempests in a teapot that so obsess the British, when participants in a popular Channel 4 'reality' show were accused of racially abusing the Indian actress Shilpa Shetty.

Racism in the *Celebrity Big Brother* house came up at Prime Minister's Questions yesterday. Keith Vaz, a man who carries round a simmering pot of anger, ready to throw at someone, demanded that Channel 4 demonstrate more care before broadcasting racist material.

Tony Blair duly condemned racism in all its forms. He added that he had not seen the show. That may be a mistake. This time next year he could be on it. ('Toe-knee iz clinning the toilit with 'iz tith!' the voiceover will say.)

It was probably the first time that Jade Goody had cropped up in the Commons, even by implication. You might argue that since she is a loud-mouthed overpaid boor, best known for her fathomless ignorance, and under the impression that people care what she thinks (but loveable with it), she would fit right into the old place. That would be unfair.

The row was also an important lesson for Gordon Brown. He was caught on a tour of India at the time. It must have been bewildering. The Chancellor leads a blameless life for the most part, his nose buried in Treasury statistics and Raith Rovers fixture lists. Suddenly he had to cope with the kind of off-the-wall, out-of-left-field stuff that prime ministers face every day. Mr Blair would have had a sound-bite all ready: 'She truly is the people's pillock' perhaps.

Back in Britain, during a surreal Question Time, Mr Blair had to deny that he had described Mr Brown as 'psychologically flawed'. This remark (actually 'he has these psychological flaws') is usually attributed to Alastair Campbell, but this week Lance Price, a reformed Number 10 spokesman, said that it might have dropped from the lips of the Prime Minister himself.

I suspect it came from neither. The remark is quoted in Andrew Rawnsley's book *Servants of the People*, and is attributed to 'someone who has an extremely good claim to know the mind of the Prime Minister'. The source is later described as 'this person' – in other words, no sex is specified. Which may be a helpful hint for political anoraks.

No matter. What a joy it was for the Tories that the Prime Minister had to stand up and deny in public that he had called his Chancellor a loony, a fruitcake, wired to the moon, three annas short of a rupee, makes Jade Goody look like Dame Mary Warnock, and so forth.

18.01.07

For some reason, Labour MPs are obsessed with golf clubs – the social organizations, not the things you use to hit golf balls. Most sane people can't stand them. Even many golfers can't stand golf clubs.

All those self-important committee members and bossy hon. secretaries, the anally retentive rules about what you can wear at precisely what time in exactly which location, the fusspot suggestion books ('Am I alone in thinking we should be provided with more custard for the jam roly-poly?'), their unique language ('What's your poison?' rather than 'What would you like to drink?'), the cartoons of forgotten past captains, the gilt statuette of some idiot in plus-fours and a Pringle pullover, labelled 'The Protheroe-Havisham Trophy', the old-before-their-time young men in tweed jackets, the notices everywhere about what shoes you are allowed to wear in the toilets – how horrible it all is!

(Every few years when I find myself in a golf club, I feel an urge to write extra rules up on the noticeboard: 'Members are instructed that it is strictly against club rules to use a JCB to remove balls from the bunkers. Urinating on the lounge carpet is a contravention of Rule XVII vi (c). Couples are reminded that they may NOT fornicate on the greens, but must restrict themselves to the fairways. By order, J. Protheroe-Havisham, Hon. Sec.)

I cannot understand why any woman enjoys a game of golf so much that they would actually want to set foot in a golf club, never mind belong to one. Yet their cause is constantly taken up by Labour MPs. The latest to ride to their rescue yesterday was David Taylor. He told the women's minister, Meg Munn, that the 'glorious game of golf' was a 'fifteenth-century gift from Scotland to the wider world', but that many clubs were 'stuck in the social bunker of that bygone era'.

Apparently in a lot of these places women are not allowed to use some of the facilities, and can't take part in running the club. Is that so? Calm down, my racing heart! Golf club members guilty of unthinking sexism? Who could have conceived it?

Was the minister, Mr Taylor enquired, 'up for the tussle with the antediluvian tendency in the sport...so that at last women and men will be on a par?'

Ms Munn ignored the dreadful puns and said she was taking it all very seriously. She was pondering how the problem could be addressed, which presumably means more laws.

Julie Kirkbride pointed out that some clubs did not admit women at all, including the Royal & Ancient in St Andrews, which is the governing body of golf. Ms Munn was evasive. She was not going to make any promises. In other words, we could assume, one fine day it would be illegal to discriminate against women in golf clubs, but not to keep them out altogether. It's a very New Labour compromise.

19.01.07

Older members may remember Frank Muir and Denis Norden's show on Radio 4. They always ended with appalling long-winded puns, which the listeners adored. Probably the most famous was the one about the Eskimo who tried to keep warm on fishing trips with a paraffin stove. Once it fell over, and burned a hole in the canoe, and he drowned. The punchline was: 'It goes to show that you can't have your kayak and heat it.'

My mind was wandering yesterday because the question session on 'communities and local government' was outstandingly dull. The cabinet minister involved was Ruth

Kelly, and we had hoped she might offer a few thoughts on why she, as a former Labour minister of education, had sent her son to a private school costing £15,000 a year.

Or about her position on gay adoption. The government is introducing a law to oblige adoption agencies to place some children with same-sex couples, but the Roman Catholic church wants exemption on grounds of religious belief. They hold that homosexual people are loved by God, but that it is a sin for them to have sex with each other. So God loves them all right, but He feels, on balance, that they should live in a state of constant, lifelong sexual frustration.

Ms Kelly has been flagellated by the media over these two issues, but as a devout member of Opus Dei, she may feel that they have saved her the trouble of doing it herself.

To give you some idea of how dull it all was, here is just part of an answer about local government funding from the junior minister, Phil Woolas: 'At the moment £17.5 billion is redistributed through the non-domestic rating system as opposed to £3.3–£3.5 billion through the remainder of the RSG. Of the £7.5 billion some four or five councils contribute nearly 10 per cent of it, and the redistributive effects of the NNDR in the absence of the schools budget form the RSG...' This sort of thing is what local government fans love to hear, and Mr Woolas's audience was small but enthusiastic.

I, by contrast, was fighting sleep. So I mused about question number 19, which had been tabled by Robert Flello (Lab, Stoke South). How would Muir and Norden have made use of his name?

Mr Flello has a healthy complexion and thick black hair, like someone whose forebears might have hailed from the sub-continent. I thought that he could have gone to visit, say, Mumbai, where his striking good looks would have caught the attention of local film-makers.

However, he lives in Stoke-on-Trent, and after standing around in 40-degree heat for several hours, he might well have fainted. A doctor would have been quickly summoned.

'Put him in a meat fridge, quick as you can!' he would have said.

'But why?' the director would ask.

'Because you know what they tell you in medical school, "Freeze a Bollywood Flello!"'

Awful, I agree, but a lot more entertaining than local government questions.

24.01.07

It was astonishing how little the subject of Iraq was debated in the House, as opposed to being merely the topic of occasional questions.

'And then there was the predictable incident of the Prime Minister in the Iraq debate,' remarked my companion. 'But the Prime Minister did not attend the Iraq debate,' I replied.

'That was the predictable incident.'

And indeed he was not there. Why should he be? He only took the most controversial military decision of the past fifty years, and naturally he preferred to be with the well-fed pussycats of the CBI than face stroppy MPs.

It was the first time the House had debated Iraq in government time since the invasion. As the SNP's Alex Salmond said to Margaret Beckett – who was making a rather unhappy speech in support of the Blair policy Mr Blair was too busy to defend – 'He was so anxious to talk us into this disastrous war, but so reluctant to explain how we are going to get out of it.'

'That is, frankly, rather a silly remark,' Mrs Beckett retorted. When MPs say that I always hear the unspoken parenthesis, 'and I can't think of any adequate reply.'

But then respect for Tony Blair has been disappearing as fast as candy floss in a gale. David Cameron said at Prime Minister's Questions – shortly before his hasty flight from the House – that the government resembled the container ship *Napoli*, currently wrecked off the Dorset coast. 'It is washed up, broken up and they are just scrambling over the wreckage.'

'I think that sounded better in the rehearsal,' said Mr Blair in a sneery kind of way, but Mr Cameron had caught the mood of all the House, not just the Tories.

Mrs Beckett looked for crumbs of comfort where she could – a reduction in violence here, a favourable opinion there – but she was not a cheerful Foreign Secretary.

She left the Chamber more or less at the moment Sir Peter Tapsell rose. 'By abstaining himself from this debate,' said Sir Peter, apparently reading from a vellum scroll, 'the pwime minister, one of the architects of the Iwaq catast-wophe, has demonstwated once again his contempt! For the House of Commons!'

He concentrated not on Iraq but on Afghanistan, and if he didn't refer to 'the wily Pathan', that's what he meant. His father had served in the third Anglo-Afghan war, roughly 100 years ago, and had vowed that no British soldier would ever have to serve there again. Afghanistan he said – no, he intoned – sorry, thundered – was not worth 'the bones of a single Lincolnshire marine!'

Then suddenly George Galloway was up. Mr Galloway last came to our attention when he pretended to be a cat on *Celebrity Big Brother* twelve months ago. It's a measure of how serious MPs felt that nobody was moved to say 'miaow'.

I am sure that in the meantime he has been working in the interest of his constituents, but if so he has been doing good by stealth, since it was the first time I had seen him there for many a month.

Mr Galloway begins at a bellow and works himself up into a rage. Stick a wind farm in front of him and you could power Bethnal Green. He spoke with relish of the fate of British soldiers in Basra if anyone attacked Iran. 'It would be like the film *Zulu* – without the happy ending!' Saddam's old chum boomed ghoulishly and, it must be said, with a certain feline relish.

25.01.07

As his period in office came towards an end, John Prescott had the added humiliation of having his monthly Question Time session halved to just fifteen minutes.

In a few short months, Mr Prescott has moved from national laughing stock to national treasure, a sort of cross between Les Dawson and Alan Bennett. Since he doesn't have a real job, all the Tories can do is taunt him with how little work he does, and how much he costs the taxpayer.

For example, William Hague asked how it was that, in spite of all the government's initiatives to cut spending, £645 had gone on changing the plate outside his office to read, instead of 'Office of the Deputy Prime Minister', 'The Deputy Prime Minister's Office'.

Mr Prescott replied, 'I hear the argument about £645, it wouldn't have paid for one sentence from the speech you give at the rate you charge.'

This was greeted by huge Labour cheers. But I did some quick calculations. Mr Hague's agent probably grabs what he can get, but if the former Tory leader and star of *Have I Got News for You* is offered £10,000 for a speech, which is about the going rate, and if he speaks for around half an hour, that means he earns around £2.20 a word. At that rate the new brass plaque would be a bargain at only £11. But if he were paid as much per word as the plaque cost, he would earn more than half a million pounds per speech. Even Mr Hague doesn't get that.

Next up was Tony Blair, who now has to face the torments of the rude boys, many of whom are now on his side. David Cameron asked if he didn't realize that it was 'all over'. David Haworth, a 'Lib Dem', wanted to know if he had 'taken the Fifth' on the cash-for-honours scandal, to avoid incriminating himself. Alex Salmond – the two men really don't like each other – compared him to Richard Nixon.

What must have really hurt was the parade of Labour MPs who took the opportunity to throw their own bit of rotten fruit. Tony Wright, usually the least smart-alecky of all backbenchers, asked silkily, 'Can it be true that we had to pay GPs a lot more money to do a lot less work, and now we have to pay them a lot more money to do the work that we paid them to stop doing?'

All sides laughed loudly and humiliatingly at this well-crafted jibe. It was the equivalent of the small boy saying that not only did the Emperor not have any clothes, but that he was naked, pot-bellied and criss-crossed with varicose veins.

01.02.07

Shilpa Shetty visited the Commons and was the object of much fascination.

In the Commons, they were debating Lords reform, the biggest change to our constitution for a century. Tony Blair was being told yet again that it was time for him to go. But few people noticed. Everyone else was obsessed by just one thing: Shilpa Shetty (proof that Andy Warhol was wrong; many people can be famous for as long as fifteen days) had come to watch Prime Minister's Questions.

The Bollywood actress and *Celebrity Big Brother* winner sat in the public gallery looking marginally more gracious and serene than the Queen does when she inspects the lads in the legislature. She had been brought to the place by Keith Vaz MP, who spent the day bathed in her luminescent glory.

The first question was about anti-semitism, which gave Mr Blair the chance to say how much he detested racism. No doubt she could relate to that. She might have been more puzzled by Colin Challen, a Labour MP, who is giving up his seat for the Chancellor's factotum, Ed Balls. It must have been puzzling for her that as Mr Challen spoke, Tories yelled 'Balls! Balls!' at him, like a bunch of middle-aged Jade Goodys.

David Cameron wondered where Gordon Brown might be. (Where he often is during Prime Minister's Questions: standing in front of a TV, shouting imprecations, like a drunk with a can of Special Brew.) Mr Cameron replied, in the modern demotic, 'If he's doing such a great job, bring him on!'

Minutes later, with hundreds of pairs of eyes on her, Ms Shetty glided from her seat and moved on towards the Prime Minister's office in the Commons. I have her own account to go on: 'He was really, really kind, and said I had conducted myself with the utmost dignity. He was very sad to see what I had to go through in the House.' How wonderful it must have been to receive a sympathetic message to which she could reply in exactly the same terms.

She was then taken to the dining room, where she and her mother were entertained by, among others, Tessa Jowell. The culture secretary was just as big a hit. 'Tessa was so kind. She holds a really important position, and I know she rooted for me, and I really loved her.' How rare it is these days that any minister hears such fragrant words!

In the Commons, Tories denounced the government's plans for deciding on Lords reform by means of the single transferable vote method. This idea was, they said, an 'outrage'. But many more people were gathered outside Portcullis House, where Shilpa was giving an impromptu and alfresco press conference.

The pavement was heaving. Several crews had flown in from India for this single event. It was lights, camera, over-reaction! London-based reporters for Indian papers and broadcasters were peeved. 'They are sending the big nobs over, just for this,' one said. An Indian passer-by was invited to ask a question. 'Will you marry me?' he asked.

Someone asked her if the House of Commons was like the *Big Brother* house. 'No,' she said. 'They are more polite in parliament, they can leave when they want, and they know what is going on in the outside world.'

They do? Possibly she had not spent long enough in there.

08.02.07

In March there was a debate on Trident. The government wanted to update the delivery system for our nuclear deterrent, and had the support of the Conservatives. But there was a great deal of unhappiness on the Labour side.

'I want to be remembered!' cried Nigel Griffiths, the deputy Leader of the House who resigned over the decision to replace our nuclear submarines. Well, don't we all, I thought. Sadly, most politicians are forgotten as soon as they go, as the obituary pages prove. I often think, ah yes, I remember him; isn't he long dead? The headline says something like 'Doughty fighter on Labour's left wing' or 'Loyalist Tory with hardline views', but through the fog of memory I recall that he was the bloke who never bought his round, or the one who used to stand too close and spray you when he talked.

Mr Griffiths continued. He wanted to be remembered not just generally but specifically – 'not so much for being the government's representative in the House, but the House's representative in government'. (Translation: 'I am on your side, unlike the rest of those time-serving lickspittles.')

He then segued smoothly from praise for the late Robin Cook, friend and mentor, to praise for the government from which both had resigned. The happy children in their new schools! The sick, healed in the brand-new infirmary! 'In my constituency thousands of citizens have been lifted from poverty and owe this government a great debt!'

This is standard resignation boilerplate. The implication is that the government is so wonderful, so perfect in every respect, that his bravery in leaving it is all the more astounding.

Having described the new Elysium that is south Edinburgh, he thanked 'this Prime Minister, and the funding provided by this Chancellor!' (Translation: 'I am demonstrating my fundamental loyalty, and hope to be reappointed by one or the other of you.')

'I have seen colleagues wrestle with their consciences, and lose their beliefs!' he added. (Translation: 'But I don't imagine for one moment that Margaret Beckett will get the top job, so I can afford to be rude about her.')

I do not know if all this subtext was decipherable in the Strangers' Gallery, where various anti-Trident celebrities such as Annie Lennox, Bianca Jagger and Vivienne Westwood were gathered. Mr Griffiths finished with his shiny new catchphrase: 'I go with a heavy heart but a clear conscience.' Once again, I yearned for the day when someone says, 'I go with a light heart but a laden conscience.'

But then the whole debate was conducted in code. After Margaret Beckett had opened for the government, William Hague appeared to praise her. He pointed out that she had been a long-standing member of CND and had even promised to remain a member if she ever became prime minister. Yet she had come to the conclusion that our nuclear deterrent should be retained, updated and replaced! It was a sly attack, delivered with artful panache.

So it was the kind of glad congratulation that no Labour minister wants, and Mrs Beckett looked, in P.G. Wodehouse's words, if not actually disgruntled, then very far from gruntled.

But all the Tories were at it. David Cameron told Mr Blair how heartily he agreed with him, and how vital it was that he ignored a large part of his own party. 'Because the Prime Minister has the support of the Conservative Party, we can work together in the national interest!' he declared.

Quite the last thing any Labour leader wants to hear, and for his part Mr Blair resembled the proud new owner of a

Porsche Boxster who finds himself stuck behind the Foreign Secretary's caravan on a single-carriageway stretch of the A303.

15.03.07

Gordon Brown was accused by Lord Turnbull, the former head of the civil service, of behaving like a bullying Stalin, intolerant and contemptuous of his colleagues, shortly before he presented his eleventh and final Budget. A few days before, the Prime Minister had taken part in a TV stunt for Red Nose Day in which he spoke to the comedian Catherine Tate in the manner of her best-known character.

The Chancellor isn't Stalin – he is New Labour's Robin Hood. He and his Gloomy Men sit under a tree. 'I say, Robin, isn't it our job to steal from the rich and give to the poor?'

'No, that would not be prudent. We shall steal from everybody and then give everybody something back, on a fiscally neutral basis.'

'Oh, that's no fun, Robin!' The Gloomy Men look even gloomier.

Lord Turnbull was wrong about him being like Stalin. Stalin didn't hold his rivals in contempt. He feared them, so that he had thousands of them shot, and then a few thousand more, just to be on the safe side. Gordon Brown simply ignores them. He is that most dangerous (and often most effective) type of politician – the one who knows he is right. Even Margaret Thatcher had some doubts.

The Stalin gags had begun early. David Cameron, at Prime Minister's Questions, said he didn't know why John

Reid was smiling. 'He'll soon be running a power station in Siberia.' A Tory backbencher asked whether Lord Turnbull was right, or wasn't the Prime Minister 'bovvered'?

Tony Blair, who is going to regret that catchphrase – though not as much as we already do – replied primly that he himself had not had to run the economy because he'd had someone who did a 'brilliant' job.

Mr Brown finally rose to cries of 'Uncle Joe!' from Tories and loud cheers from Labour. He said that the only chancellor before him who had presented eleven Budgets was Gladstone, 'and he combined the position of chancellor and prime minister, something no one should contemplate doing.'

'You will!' shouted a Tory.

Mr Brown then craftily deflected the Stalin jibe. 'May I thank, for all their hard work, and sometimes forthright advice, the civil servants – or should I say 'comrades' – who worked with me...'

Then, as ever, we were presented with a parade of Mr Brown's holographic statistics. These are all shiny and glittery. They seem to wobble and shimmer as you gaze at them, and if you try to look at them from the back, they disappear.

Investment higher! Productivity racing ahead! All of his figures are manipulated to within an inch of their lives.

At the end came his great coup – the announcement that from next year there would be 2p off the basic rate of income tax. (Next year? Won't we have a different chancellor then? Or is he going to combine the role of chancellor and prime minister after all?) Labour MPs, who had been underwhelmed so far, suddenly realized that this was his invitation to vote for him.

22.03.07

In March 2007, the Rev Ian Paisley and Gerry Adams announced
that the DUP and Sinn Féin would end their long-standing feud
and begin working together in a newly devolved government,
starting from May.

'NO!' cried a familiar booming voice. Douglas Hogg was
suggesting that it might be a good idea to change the parliamentary oath so Sinn Féin MPs might sit in the Commons.

'NO!' thundered the voice again. It was an evocative
moment – the Rev Ian Paisley was reprising his greatest and
best-loved hit. For us nostalgia fans (I first heard that mighty
roar on the streets of Belfast in 1968) it was like Pavarotti
singing 'Nessun Dorma' one more time, or John Mortimer
telling the anecdote that ends: 'Fax it up your honour.'
Repetition cannot dim its allure. It was also slightly
surprising. On the day that he had perhaps reached the end
of his life's march – from crazed, bigoted rabble-rouser, to
crazed, bigoted privy counsellor and probably next prime
minister of his homeland – he seemed to be fast asleep. The
old turtle was slumped on the bench, his body twisted and
immobile, his eyes shut.

Even as the Northern Ireland secretary, Peter Hain,
praised his 'courage and leadership', I thought he might have
marked his hour of triumph by dying on us. But then there
was an imperceptible stirring, as if he had suddenly realized
that after forty-three years the eggs might be hatching in the
sand.

Mr Hain was explaining why – after promising that if
there wasn't a new executive by Monday this week, the
assembly would be dissolved – he had changed his mind.
Some MPs seemed inexplicably cross about this, though any
parent will know the feeling: you threaten your child that if
that bedroom isn't tidy by twelve o'clock they won't go to

the cinema. Then at 11.59 they haul themselves up with a sigh and start tidying. So you change your mind.

Mr Hain was busily praising all those who had helped find the agreement – politicians, civil servants and of course the sainted Tony Blair ('he brought a forensic understanding and a fierce commitment'). It was getting like Oscar night, except everyone won an award.

Then the right honourable reverend doctor rose to praise the shopkeepers of Northern Ireland. They might be bombed but it was always business as usual and they never shut down.

As his first Commons statement since the historic non-handshake it seemed slightly banal (though I was reminded of the joke about the IRA man jailed for shoplifting – he lifted Woolworths by three feet).

Finally the hero of the day got his chance to speak. He was not a very cheery turtle. He seemed anxious to settle a few old scores. His party had never got any credit. After the Good Friday agreement there had been singing and hand-shaking – 'and kicking me!' Mo Mowlam even had him arrested.

As for the new era of peace and joy: 'I said to the leader of Sinn Féin, "This is not a love-in; it is a work-in!"' There would be hard work, difficulties, fights (probably literally, we reflected), 'tough talking and rough riding'.

In short, business as usual. Now we can only wait to see if there is anyone in Ulster who can out-fundamentalize the most turbulent priest since Thomas Becket.

28.3.07